IDIOT'S
GUIDES

AS EASY AS IT GET

Medicare

WITHDRAWN

by Tanya Feke, MD

ALPHA

A member of Penguin Group (USA) Inc.

To patients everywhere.
Because we all need an advocate.

ALPHA BOOKS

Published by Penguin Group (USA) Inc.

Penguin Group (USA) Inc., 375 Hudson Street, New York, New York 10014, USA • Penguin Group (Canada), 90 Eglinton Avenue East, Suite 700, Toronto, Ontario M4P 2Y3, Canada (a division of Pearson Penguin Canada Inc.) • Penguin Books Ltd., 80 Strand, London WC2R 0RL, England • Penguin Ireland, 25 St. Stephen's Green, Dublin 2, Ireland (a division of Penguin Books Ltd.) • Penguin Group (Australia), 250 Camberwell Road, Camberwell, Victoria 3124, Australia (a division of Pearson Australia Group Pty. Ltd.) • Penguin Books India Pvt. Ltd., 11 Community Centre, Panchsheel Park, New Delhi—110 017, India • Penguin Group (NZ), 67 Apollo Drive, Rosedale, North Shore, Auckland 1311, New Zealand (a division of Pearson New Zealand Ltd.) • Penguin Books (South Africa) (Pty.) Ltd., 24 Sturdee Avenue, Rosebank, Johannesburg 2196, South Africa • Penguin Books Ltd., Registered Offices: 80 Strand, London WC2R 0RL, England

International Standard Book Number: 978-1-61564-735-4
Library of Congress Catalog Card Number: 2014951303

17   16   15   8   7   6   5   4   3   2   1

Interpretation of the printing code: The rightmost number of the first series of numbers is the year of the book's printing; the rightmost number of the second series of numbers is the number of the book's printing. For example, a printing code of 15-1 shows that the first printing occurred in 2015.

Printed in the United States of America

Note: This publication contains the opinions and ideas of its author. It is intended to provide helpful and informative material on the subject matter covered. It is sold with the understanding that the author and publisher are not engaged in rendering professional services in the book. If the reader requires personal assistance or advice, a competent professional should be consulted. The author and publisher specifically disclaim any responsibility for any liability, loss, or risk, personal or otherwise, which is incurred as a consequence, directly or indirectly, of the use and application of any of the contents of this book.

Most Alpha books are available at special quantity discounts for bulk purchases for sales promotions, premiums, fundraising, or educational use. Special books, or book excerpts, can also be created to fit specific needs. For details, write: Special Markets, Alpha Books, 375 Hudson Street, New York, NY 10014.

Publisher: *Mike Sanders*
Associate Publisher: *Billy Fields*
Acquisitions Editor: *Janette Lynn*
Development Editor: *Ann Barton*
Cover Designer: *Laura Merriman*

Book Designer: *William Thomas*
Indexer: *Brad Herriman*
Layout: *Ayanna Lacey*
Proofreader: *Laura Caddell*

Contents

Part 3:   Breaking Down the Benefits 111

10   Medicare Part A 113

11   Medicare Part B... 127

Introduction

If you are ready to retire and know exactly how Medicare will take care of your health-care needs, good for you! You are in the minority. Odds are you need a little help understanding how Medicare works, and I am here to lend a hand.

I am a family physician by trade and have years of first-hand experience to guide the way. As a practicing doctor, early on I became frustrated by Medicare's complicated web of rules and regulations. Why were some tests I ordered being denied coverage by Medicare? Why were some of my patients paying more for the same services compared to other patients? How could I get my patients the medications they needed during gaps in Medicare coverage? If I was confused, I knew my patients were more so.

Talking with patients about their Medicare concerns only raised more issues. Some were angry that I, as their doctor, could not answer their specific questions about the program, when in truth health-care providers are given minimal training about Medicare. Sure, we may be trained on how to bill for our services, but beyond that, do we really learn how to maximize our patients' care and save them money under the program? All too often the sad truth is no. I wanted to fill that gap. I wanted to be more than a doctor to my patients; I wanted to be their advocate.

My curiosity brought me behind the scenes to work as a physician advisor consulting with hospitals nationwide about Medicare cases. The experience and specialized training was enlightening and set off more than a few light bulbs in my head. Now I had the full complement of tools to give my patients the insider information they needed. I have since returned to clinical practice.

Idiot's Guide: Medicare takes you behind the scenes to see not only how Medicare works in the grand scheme, but also how you can get the most out of the services it provides, all while keeping costs down. There are more than a few tips and tricks in these pages that may save you hundreds and even thousands of dollars every year.

In the United States, we are fortunate to have health-care options as we grow older, or even as we endure disability. Paying for private health plans can be costly, and the government has offered this federally funded program to assist you when you need it most. That does not mean that Medicare offers you everything, and by no means does it mean that Medicare is free. It still can put a significant dent in your wallet if you are on a fixed income.

Sadly, many people only start to think about Medicare once they're already late in doing so. You may miss out on critical enrollment windows and get caught paying expensive late penalties for years on end. You may even believe your current insurance coverage will be enough for you until you retire. Financially speaking, this is not always the case. In the end, misinformation can cost you considerably. Understanding your enrollment options can help to keep costs down as you get older and make the most of your savings to cover basic living expenses.

This leads us to think about your retirement years. How will you balance your life savings with your health-care needs? You never know what the future holds, and that is where Medicare comes in handy. Taking advantage of preventive screening services can help to catch diseases in their early stages, helping you to get treatments sooner rather than later. Those early treatments may improve your quality of life, if not extend your life. Chronic diseases can be expensive to manage, but working with a qualified team of health-care professionals can improve your odds for a healthier life. Medicare provides you many options for care.

Each of our experiences is different, medically and financially, and there are multiple strategies that can get you more for less. Medicare is one piece of that very important puzzle. Let us work together to give you the healthy retirement you deserve.

How This Book Is Organized

This book is broken down into five parts to make it easier for you to work through Medicare's many parts and pieces. Trust me, it will be far easier than navigating all those Medicare rules and regulations on your own!

Part 1, Welcome to Medicare, introduces you to the world of Medicare. A rundown of the historical elements of Medicare enables you to see where it started and how far Medicare has come. You will also learn the basic elements that make up Medicare from how much it costs to an overview of its coverage options. You can only build a puzzle if you have all the pieces.

Part 2, Enrolling for Medicare, shows you how to get started. Not everyone realizes your choices are limited when it comes to signing up for, or even cancelling, certain types of Medicare plans. Not signing up on time can literally cost you. With the wrong information, you could be caught paying late penalties as long as you have Medicare. This part unravels the confusing timelines and gives you strategies on when may be the best time for you to enroll in Medicare.

Part 3, Breaking Down the Benefits, shares with you the specific benefits that Medicare provides. As a physician, this is where I roll up my sleeves and get to work. I discuss not only what common tests are covered under the program but why and how they can impact your personal health. This part will guide you to make the best decisions for your health and your wallet.

Part 4, Living with Medicare, reviews issues you may experience with Medicare in everyday life. From receiving your Medicare card to reviewing billing statements and filing appeals, learn how to protect your rights as a Medicare beneficiary.

Part 5, Safeguarding Your Future, brings it all together. Medicare is not a static program, and changes may occur over time that will impact care you receive through the program and, perhaps more importantly, how much you pay for it. Anticipating changes in Medicare and how you can make your finances stretch into your retirement years are the focus of this part.

Extras

You will find sidebars throughout the book that will give you extra information to enhance your Medicare know-how. This is what you can expect.

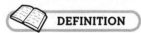

DEFINITION

With so many terms and abbreviations relating to Medicare, you need a quick and easy reference to learn what they all mean. Any terms found in these definition boxes or italicized in the body of the text will be listed in the glossary.

DID YOU KNOW?

Who doesn't love interesting factoids? Fun facts and statistics relating to a variety of topics covered in this book are shared with you to add color and perspective to your Medicare experience.

CAUTION

These thoughtful warnings go a long way to help you avoid costly missteps. You deserve to know when your medical or financial health may be at risk.

TIP

Advice to help you stay on track with good health is always welcome. These helpful tips show you how to make the most of nearly every aspect of Medicare.

ROUND TABLE

The best way to drive home a complicated concept is by example. This book introduces you to four characters; you may identify with one or more of them. We hold a round table discussion in each chapter to review their Medicare concerns. Their stories will show you how these Medicare concepts apply in real life scenarios.

Acknowledgments

Special thanks to Marilyn Allen, my literary agent, for believing in my skill set after meeting with me for mere minutes. I hope to work together with you on many projects in the future.

I need to specifically thank Jenny Valente, my dear friend who passed away from cancer before graduating high school. Her hope, encouragement, and inspiration led me to be the doctor I am today. You made a real difference in my life and because of you, I have made a difference in the lives of others.

I also want to thank my family and friends for standing by me as I pursue my passion for writing: my husband, Gil, for encouraging me to follow my dreams; my children, Gilbert and Charlotte, for always making me smile; my mom, Nina Brown, for telling me to shoot for the stars; my sister, Kim Algarin, for her spunky reassurance; my brother, Dennis Thomas, for keeping me on my toes; my best friend, Laurie Santos, for standing by me through the years; my other best friend, Loraine Coe, for being like a second mother to me; and last but not least, my late father, George Thomas, who gave me the strength to persevere. This is for you, daddy.

Trademarks

All terms mentioned in this book that are known to be or are suspected of being trademarks or service marks have been appropriately capitalized. Alpha Books and Penguin Group (USA) Inc. cannot attest to the accuracy of this information. Use of a term in this book should not be regarded as affecting the validity of any trademark or service mark.

Welcome to Medicare

Your health is your most important asset. While you can try to stay as healthy as possible by your lifestyle choices, there are certain medical circumstances that remain beyond your control. Thankfully, Uncle Sam has provided an option for health-care insurance to those who are aging or disabled.

Partnered together with the federal government, you may be able to access health care that half a century ago was not even an option. Health insurance can be expensive, and while Medicare is by no means free, it offers an affordable alternative to plans by private companies. Medicare offers a wide array of services. This part outlines what Medicare is, how much it costs, what it covers, and how it came to be.

History of Medicare

Summarizing Medicare is not an easy feat. The government program has evolved considerably over the last half-century, making it difficult to keep tabs on all the details. This chapter will look at how and why the program began and cover some of the major milestones in its development. Understanding where we have been and where we are going with Medicare will make it easier for you to get the most out of it.

Medicare in a Nutshell

I have found myself on all sides of the Medicare fence— looking in, looking out, and even sitting right on top of it. As a family member, I have cared for loved ones relying on Medicare for their health-care needs. As a consultant, I have advised hospitals sorting through the administrative regulations of Medicare. As a physician, I have held the hands of my patients as we worked together to get the care they needed. What I have learned best from these experiences is that most people, patients and health-care providers alike, are confused about what Medicare does and does not do.

In This Chapter

- The principles behind Medicare
- How Medicare differs from Medicaid
- Important advances in Medicare
- What to expect from Medicare today

Medicare has as many twists and turns as a corkscrew roller coaster. It can be overwhelming, even jarring, if you do not know how to secure yourself. The first step is understanding what Medicare is and why it came to be.

What It Is

Medicare is a federally funded social insurance program aimed at helping seniors and people with disabilities gain access to health care. The program was signed into law in 1965 and took effect in 1966.

The key objectives guiding Medicare legislation at that time were as follows:

- To provide health-care access to elderly people regardless of their health status, income, or race

- To offer insurance coverage without allowing governmental interference in the practice of medicine

- To pay doctors, hospitals, and health agencies for services rendered

DID YOU KNOW?

Medicare helped to end racial segregation in hospitals when it stated that reimbursements would only be granted to facilities that were integrated.

The program eventually added people younger than 65 years of age to its roster if they suffered from specific medical conditions or long-term disabilities.

The program is divided into four key parts, each labeled by a letter. Part A covers hospital care, Part B medical care, Part C supplemental care, and Part D medications. Medigap, which is not officially a part of Medicare, is a supplemental insurance plan that you can purchase from a private company to help pay for health-care costs that Medicare did not cover.

Medicare, overall, is health insurance offered through the government to aged and disabled Americans but functions similarly to a private insurance plan.

What It Isn't

Medicare is not a hand out. Many people misunderstand Medicare to be a freebie of sorts that allows people access to health care at no charge. However, this could not be further from the truth. As with most things, you get what you pay for.

Many people pay into the system for years in order to have access to Medicare services later in life. These taxes are paid into the Medicare Trust Fund. Once enrolled in Medicare, out-of-pocket expenses continue to increase as beneficiaries pay annual deductibles and monthly premiums on their chosen plans. Medicare may be a less expensive option for health insurance than some private insurance plans, but it is not cheap.

It is also far from an all-encompassing health-care program. There are many aspects of health care not addressed or covered within the benefits package. For example, vision and dental care are excluded, though problems in these areas are common in an aging population. As a Medicare *beneficiary*, you need to understand that there are many health-care services you may need for your specific medical problems that are not covered by Medicare.

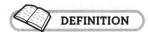

DEFINITION

A **beneficiary** is someone who is covered by an insurance policy, whether that be Medicare or a private insurance plan.

Why Do We Need It?

When the stock market crashed in 1929, the Great Depression took its toll on America. Families that had relied on the paychecks of hardworking sons and daughters struggled to survive amid a near 25 percent unemployment rate. With few insurance options available at the time, health-care access was dependent upon income. This left a large portion of the population unable to afford health care of any kind. With conditions like tuberculosis and malnutrition running rampant, the Great Depression raised awareness of the need for improved access to resources for the nation.

Something needed to be done. The degree of poverty was destroying the American way of life. The Social Security Act was enacted in 1935 to provide federal assistance to those in need. Though it provided funds to the states for maternal and child health services as well as general public health concerns, it stopped short of providing a national health insurance plan. Federally funded health care was controversial and would take decades to gain a majority consensus. Many government leaders, especially Republicans, were wary of increasing federal spending. Ultimately, Medicare would be created under an amendment to the Social Security Act in 1965.

Over the years, the economy has recovered but not without setbacks. The country is still feeling the effects of the recession that took place between late 2007 and mid-2009, when unemployment shot up and individuals and families had to decide how to best use their limited funds. With Medicare in effect, those over 65 years old and those with disabilities have a means to attain health care despite economic hardships. They do not have to struggle without health care as people did during the Great Depression.

The debate over Medicare runs long and deep. Some politicians favor enhancements of federally regulated programs while others prefer a more privatized system. Regardless of how you look at the issue, a health insurance strategy of some sort is needed to support American citizens with increasing health issues as they get older, and those with severe health issues that prevent them from gainful employment. Access to health care is needed when times get rough. At present, Medicare fits the bill.

Medicare vs. Medicaid

People often confuse the terms Medicare and Medicaid, for understandable reasons. They both start with "medic-," they both have a long *a* sound, and they both were enacted in 1965 as amendments to the Social Security Act. Beyond that, however, they are very different programs.

Medicare (medical care) offers health care for the elderly and the disabled. Participation in the program is not based on income or earnings. The program is managed by the federal government alone.

Medicaid (medical aid), on the other hand, is a federal and state-run program offered to anyone regardless of age or existing health conditions. Participation in the program is based on financial need with eligibility requirements set by each state and the District of Columbia. The United States territories of American Samoa, Guam, Puerto Rico, the Northern Mariana Islands, and the Virgin Islands are also included in the Medicaid program, though they receive a smaller percentage of federal funding. The program is intended to support those who do not have the means to pay for health insurance on their own. The federal government provides funds to the states to run their Medicaid programs, but the states are not required to accept these funds. In fact, any state can refuse to offer Medicaid. No state has deferred Medicaid offerings to date.

With the passage of the Patient Protection and Affordable Care Act of 2010, federal funding to Medicaid has changed. The act aims to expand Medicaid and offers increased funding to states that agree to its provisions. Not all states have chosen to be compliant with the new legislation, but this does not mean that they lose all federal funding. They may continue to receive federal funds for Medicaid at levels offered prior to the passage of the law.

Socialized Medicine

As the debate about national health insurance began in the 1940s, Americans found themselves entering a Cold War and wary of communist ideology. The prospect of a socialist program brought fear into the hearts of many. The term "socialized medicine" was in fact coined by the American Medical Association as a derogatory term in 1945 in opposition to President Truman's proposal for national health insurance. The fear tactic worked and the bill was not passed.

When the proposal for Medicare was made a key issue by virtue of John F. Kennedy's 1960 presidential campaign, there was an uproar between the political parties, with many Republicans adamantly opposed to the prospect of socialized medicine. Ronald Reagan, speaking in support of the standpoint of the American Medical Association (AMA) on the issue, stated "…if you don't [stop Medicare] and I don't do it, one of these days you and I are going to spend our sunset years telling our children and our children's children what it once was like in America when men were free." He expressed these concerns in a 1961 LP record, *Ronald Reagan Speaks Out Against Socialized Medicine for the AMA.*

Doctors, too, were fearful that implementing national health insurance would impact their ability to care for patients. It was thought that enacting Medicare would allow the government to dictate what physicians could and could not do from a medical perspective. The truth was that the government would offer coverage like any other private insurance plan and would cover or not cover certain services as per its policy. Physicians could choose whether or not to accept Medicare for payment.

DID YOU KNOW?

The World Health Organization ranked the world's best health systems in 2014 out of 190 countries. 13 of the top 20 countries participated in some form of universal health coverage. France ranked first and the United States thirty-seventh.

Other countries have taken the lead and have offered universal health coverage to varying degrees. The Soviet Union led the charge in 1937 and was followed by New Zealand and the United Kingdom in the 1930-1940s; Finland, Iceland, Norway, and Sweden in the 1950s; Canada, Denmark, Finland, and Japan in the 1960s; Australia, Italy, and Portugal in the 1970s; Greece, Israel, Netherlands, Spain, and Taiwan in the 1980s; and Switzerland in the 1990s. Austria, Belgium, France, Germany, and Luxembourg also have programs in place.

Medicare and Medicaid may be considered by some to be socialized medicine, but neither program is universal. There are eligibility requirements that must be met in order to access these programs as well as exclusions to participation.

Separate and Together

The Centers for Medicare and Medicaid Services (CMS), once called the Healthcare Finance Administration, is a single federal agency that manages both Medicare and Medicaid. Again, this can be confusing because the programs are separate entities, one federally run and the other regulated by the states with federal funds. However, someone who is on Medicare may also be on Medicaid if they meet eligibility criteria for both. In fact, seniors seeking long-term stays in nursing homes not relating to a recent hospitalization often need to apply for Medicaid due to financial constraints and the high cost of living in these facilities.

Major Moments in Medicare History

Back on the Medicare roller coaster, the evolution of the program has had its ups and downs. Many government leaders have left their mark on the program, some positively, others with failures. Understanding the evolutionary steps will offer perspective on the services available to you now and where Medicare may be heading in the future.

Key Players

A long line of presidents have had their hand in guiding Medicare's course. From the 1930s to the present, their influence has molded the program many of us rely on today.

The Social Security Act was enacted in 1935 under Franklin Delano Roosevelt (FDR). Health care coverage was not included as part of the act due to controversy about national coverage. Federal grants were given to states, however, to assist in public health measures.

Harry Truman succeeded FDR and proposed a national health insurance plan in 1945, but Congress stood firmly against it. Truman appealed Congress' decision in 1948 to no avail, though he did sign amendments to Social Security in 1950 that provided Old-Age Assistance to the elderly poor.

President Eisenhower also proposed a national health and welfare program that was ultimately rejected by Congress in 1954. In his term, he signed Social Security Disability Insurance into law.

President John F. Kennedy rallied for Medicare prior to his assassination in 1963. Medicare and Medicaid were passed into law under President Lyndon B. Johnson in the Social Security Amendments of 1965.

> **DID YOU KNOW?**
>
> President Harry S. Truman, the so-called "daddy of Medicare" according to then-President Lyndon B. Johnson, was the first person to enroll in Medicare.

Under President Richard Nixon, eligibility for Medicare expanded to cover people with end-stage kidney disease and those with long-term disabilities. People with disabilities could apply once they had received 24 months of Social Security Disability Insurance benefits. Federal monies were also used during his term to encourage the development of Health Maintenance Organizations (HMOs) to shift costs to private payers.

With Medicare's increasing price tag, President Jimmy Carter proposed a cost containment program for hospital stays but this failed to pass in Congress. President Ronald Reagan, who himself had voiced concerns about Medicare in the 1960s, encountered similar opposition when he enacted the Medicare Catastrophic Coverage Act of 1988. The law offered a prescription drug plan and improved inpatient coverage. While a well-intentioned program, the act was repealed by President George H.W. Bush the following year due to public outcry against the increased premiums and taxation.

Universal health-care coverage was once again the topic of great debate when President Bill Clinton proposed the Health Security Act in 1993. This too failed to be enacted.

The next major change to Medicare came when President George W. Bush passed the Medicare Prescription Drug, Improvement, and Modernization Act of 2003 (MMA) which implemented Medicare Part D.

President Obama expanded national health-care access with the Patient Protection and Affordable Care Act, commonly known as Obamacare, in 2010.

History in the Making

Medicare has had a rich history over the decades. Key changes to the program are highlighted in the following timeline, starting with the enactment of The Social Security Act in 1935.

The 1960s and 1970s

The Medicare program gets its start, establishing who should be covered and who should run the program.

1966   Medicare coverage begins on July 1. People aged 65 and older are automatically enrolled in Medicare Part A and given the option to sign up for Part B.

1972   Medicare is offered to people younger than 65 years old who have kidney failure and/or long-term disabilities, if they are on Social Security Disability Insurance (SSDI) for two years or more. Chiropractic services, physical therapy, and speech therapy are added to Medicare's list of covered benefits.

1977   The Healthcare Finance Administration is formed by the Department of Health, Education, and Welfare to manage Medicare.

The 1980s

The Medicare program focuses on cost cutting and improvements in standards of care.

1980   The Department of Health, Education, and Welfare is renamed the Department of Health and Human Services. The federal government begins oversight of Medigap plans. Home health services are expanded.

1982   The Tax Equity and Fiscal Responsibility Act (TEFRA) increases premiums for Part B and sets limits on hospital and nursing home payments. Medicare adds hospice care to its covered benefits. Federal employees begin to pay Medicare payroll taxes.

1983   Hospitals are paid fixed amounts based on the diseases they treat, diagnosis-related groups (DRGs), rather than what the hospital chooses to bill.

1984   Laboratory service fees are set. The Participating Physicians Program comes into effect.

1985   The Consolidated Omnibus Budget Reconciliation Act (COBRA) mandates Medicare coverage for state and local government employees.

1987   Medicare-enhanced quality standards for nursing homes are introduced. The Medicare and Medicaid Patient and Program Protection Act aims to prevent Medicare fraud and abuse.

1988   The Medicare Catastrophic Coverage Act (MCCA) is enacted. The Clinical Laboratory Improvement Amendments (CLIA) improves the quality of laboratory testing.

1989   MCCA is repealed. Limits are set on the amounts physicians can bill patients. Physicians can not refer Medicare beneficiaries to laboratory facilities if they have a financial stake in them.

The 1990s

Medicare expands its coverage options by working with private insurance companies and also enacts powerful legislation to protect health-care information.

1990   Medicare adds mammography and certain services at community mental health centers to its coverage. Medigap policy packages are standardized by the federal government.

1995   The Department of Health and Human Services separates from the Social Security Administration.

1996   The Health Insurance Administration Portability and Accountability Act (HIPAA) is established to protect patient information and improve Medicare efficiency.

1997   Medicare Part C (Medicare+Choice, later renamed Medicare Advantage) is developed. Payment systems are established for inpatient and outpatient services, including rehabilitation. The law also provides assistance to the qualifying poor to help pay for Medicare Part B premiums.

1999   Qualifying individuals with disabilities can return to work and maintain their Medicare eligibility under The Ticket to Work and Work Incentives Improvements Act (TWWIIA).

The Twenty-First Century and Beyond

Medicare undergoes the most significant changes since its inception, adding prescription drug coverage offerings and provisions under the Affordable Care Act.

2000   People with amyotrophic lateral sclerosis (ALS, commonly known as Lou Gehrig's disease) no longer have to wait 24 months before they became eligible for Medicare.

2001   The Healthcare Finance Administration becomes the Centers for Medicare and Medicaid Services.

2003   The Medicare Prescription Drug, Improvement, and Modernization Act (MMA) sets the groundwork for Medicare Part D to start in 2006. It also increases the cost of Medicare Part B premiums for those with higher incomes starting in 2007.

2005   Medicare adds "Welcome to Medicare" visits and increased preventive screening services, including diabetes testing.

2006   Medicare Part D benefits begin.

2010   The Patient Protection and Affordable Care Act, commonly referred to as Obamacare, is established.

2013   The "Two-Midnight Rule" sets timelines to define what qualifies a patient for an inpatient hospital stay.

Medicare Today

Although the Medicare program has come a long way, it still has much further to go. With an accelerating number of people eligible for Medicare every year, questions have been raised as to whether there is enough money to keep it going. The focus of Medicare today is to continue to offer quality health care while decreasing overall costs. Without intervention, projections estimate that Medicare will not have enough money to pay for hospital stays after 2030.

Baby Boomers

The conclusion of World War II in 1945 led to socioeconomic conditions in America that were highly conducive to increased birth rates. Rations were lifted. Soldiers came home. The G.I. Bill of Rights provided for low- or no-interest loans that fostered home ownership and pursuit of higher education. Economic growth was driven by consumer demand. During that period of celebration and prosperity from 1946 to 1964, many babies were born—an estimated 77 million of them! It is estimated that 20 percent of the United States population is attributable to the baby boomers.

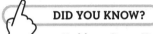

DID YOU KNOW?

Kathleen Casey-Kirschling became the first baby boomer to enroll in Medicare.

With modern medical technology, life expectancies are getting longer. CMS reports that men born in 1955 are expected to live to 83.8 years of age and women to 86.1 years of age. This is increased from life expectancies of 66.8 years and 73.8 years, respectively, when Medicare was first enacted in 1965. Living longer is fantastic for people as individuals but a challenge for a federal budget bursting at the seams.

More than 10,000 baby boomers turn 65 years old every day, and will continue to do so until 2030. With more and more Americans becoming eligible for Medicare, more and more dollars will be spent. Questions remain as to how Medicare will adapt to those changes with the rising number of participants.

Costs on the Rise

There has been tremendous growth in Medicare spending since its inception. In 1965, 19 million people were enrolled and it took $64 million to operate the program. Today, more than 50 million people are enrolled, costing the system more than $540 billion per year.

Increasing Medicare Costs Over Time

Year	Medicare Part A Deductible Per Hospital Stay	Medicare Part B Premium Per Month	Medicare Population in Millions
1966	$40	$3	19
1970	$52	$4	20.4
1975	$92	$6.70	24.9
1980	$180	$8.70	28.4
1985	$400	$15.50	31.1
1990	$592	$28.60	34.3
1995	$716	$46.10	37.6
2000	$776	$54.40	39.7
2005	$912	$78.20	42.3
2010	$1,100	$110.50	47.3

Less than 10 years from the enactment of Medicare, costs doubled although the Medicare population only increased by a third. In 20 years, costs increased 5-fold and 10-fold for Medicare Part B and Medicare Part A, respectively, though the number of Medicare beneficiaries only increased by two-thirds. As you can see, costs continue to rise, and the increases are at a disproportionate rate. For every additional Medicare beneficiary, costs increase by more than a simple one-to-one ratio. How will Medicare curtail the spending?

The Affordable Care Act

The Affordable Care Act (ACA), also referred to as Obamacare, has had significant impact on Medicare spending. While the media has focused predominantly on how ACA is increasing access to care with its Medicaid expansion, it does impact Medicare beneficiaries as well.

The ACA does not change eligibility criteria for those on Medicare. Therefore, it does not change who can apply for Medicare, but it changes how the care is paid for. Benefits have been added to include preventive screening tests and wellness visits. The Medicare Part D coverage gap, known as the donut hole, will gradually close under the legislation. These are all immediate benefits to patients.

Other effects of the law may be less palatable depending on how you look at it. The ACA increases Medicare premiums for those who earn higher incomes. This helps to reduce costs to the system, but individuals may feel they are paying more than their fair share.

The ACA also reduces federal spending on Medicare as a whole, decreasing payments to doctors, hospitals, and even to private insurance plans that contract with the government to offer Medicare Part C and Medigap plans. The cost cuts are estimated to be $716 trillion from 2013 to 2022 with the bulk taken from the following categories:

- $260 billion from hospital care

- $156 billion from Medicare Advantage

- $66 billion from home health services

- $39 billion from skilled nursing services

- $17 billion from hospice services

These reductions may make it less profitable for an insurance company to offer plans to beneficiaries. Concerns have been raised that some insurance companies will decrease options for beneficiaries or otherwise choose to discontinue participating in the Medicare Advantage and Medigap programs. Likewise, cost-cutting to physicians may result in some physicians not accepting Medicare for payment, which also limits options to patients.

There is controversy over whether the approach taken by the ACA is the best way to address health-care costs. It may be that no perfect solution exists. Regardless of what party takes the reigns of future administrations, there will almost certainly be more changes ahead on the Medicare roller coaster to address the evolving needs of the program.

The Least You Need to Know

- Medicare is a complicated, federally funded health insurance program.
- Medicare is distinct from Medicaid.
- Medicare evolved over time to include more benefits and services.
- The costs of Medicare are on the rise.
- The rising number of Medicare-eligible baby boomers is creating challenges for cost containment.

The Parts and Pieces of Medicare

Medicare, like the human body, aims to be a well-oiled machine. Understanding how the parts work is essential to keeping them in top form. This chapter addresses not only your medical needs but how Medicare works to keep you healthy.

Finding a Healthy Balance

To better understand how Medicare works, we first need to understand what health care is all about. To understand health care, we need a working definition of health. That is not as easy as it sounds, even coming from a doctor. What it means for you to be healthy will vary depending on your past experiences, your culture, and where you live, among other factors.

The World Health Organization defined health in 1948 as "a state of complete physical, mental, and social well-being, and not merely the absence of disease or infirmity." While this definition may sound appealing, 133 million Americans today live with at least one chronic medical condition which would exclude them from being called healthy. Does this make 45 percent of the American population unhealthy? We need to take a closer look.

In This Chapter

- What it means to be healthy
- Understanding the principles of health insurance
- How Medicare is broken down
- How Medicare works

DID YOU KNOW?

The World Health Organization (WHO) was founded April 7, 1948, as a specialized agency of the United Nations (UN), and World Health Day commemorates this occasion on April 7 of every year.

Physical Health

The first thing that comes to mind when many people think of health is the body. The physical nature of our existence is a key component to how we view ourselves and the world around us. Without a well-functioning body, we may feel poorly, weak, or even distressed.

Our organs need to perform certain tasks in order for us to survive. Our brain sends nerve signals, our heart pumps blood, our lungs circulate oxygen, our kidneys flush toxins, and our liver detoxifies. These are essential functions without which we could not live.

A person may have had their gallbladder removed or even their spleen and lead very functional and symptom-free lives. Some people live with one kidney, the sole kidney performing the job of two. An amputee may have lost a limb but participate in the Paralympics. These examples demonstrate the principle that you can be healthy without having all of your body parts.

DID YOU KNOW?

The American Medical Association officially defined obesity as a medical condition in 2014. Obesity is not a subjective finding. It is defined by the body mass index (BMI), a calculation based on your weight and height.

The key to physical health is to have the essential functions of the body in working order and to cure, reduce, or control to the best of our ability any conditions that could be a threat to those functions. Without the heart pumping effectively, the blood would not reach other essential organs to deliver oxygen and your life would be at risk. Strokes, heart attacks, or other organ damage could easily follow.

Diabetes remains one of the biggest threats to health in the United States. 25.6 million Americans over the age of 20 had diabetes in 2011, and the number is rising. If left uncontrolled, high blood sugars from diabetes can damage the heart and kidneys as well as the eyes and nerves, potentially leading to blindness, amputations, and even death. If sugars are controlled, these risks are considerably reduced though not necessarily eliminated. It will vary on a case by case basis depending on when a diagnosis was made.

TIP

Pain scales have been developed to help patients describe their pain to health-care providers. Pain scales may range from 1-10, one being the least and ten being the worst degree of pain. They may also be shown in picture form as a series of faces, the lowest level on the scale represented by a happy face and the highest level by one in marked distress.

While the essential organs are needed to maintain a standard of health, many other medical conditions exist that may not directly threaten harm to their functioning. For example, you may have chronic pain. Your physical symptoms may reduce your quality of life but do not risk injury to your organs. Does this mean you are healthy?

The absence of disease processes in the body would be an obvious definition for physical health but, for many people, this is simply not a possibility, whether by genetics or by circumstance. Being an optimist, I prefer not to think of the majority of the world as unhealthy when so many are working hard to take care of their bodies.

The perfect definition for physical health may be elusive. You can be considered healthy if your essential organs are working properly. You can be considered healthy if you do not have symptoms that cause distress or impair your quality of life. You can be considered healthy even if you have an illness as long as it is not life-threatening and you manage and control any symptoms or risks that could be caused by that disease.

A thoughtful health-care plan would need to support someone in treating disease, reducing risk to organ function, and reducing any physical symptoms in the body.

Mental Health

All too often, tragedy brings mental illness to the forefront of our collective consciousness. Whether it is the loss of a beloved talent due to suicide or the horror of a mass shooting, these events inevitably raise concerns about the state of our mental health resources.

The National Alliance on Mental Illness reports that one in four adults has some form of mental illness every year. According to the Anxiety and Depression Association of America, 40 million Americans have anxiety disorders, 14.8 million have major depressive disorder, and 3.3 million people have persistent depressive disorder. That is 18, 6.7, and 1.5 percent of the United States population, respectively. Other conditions to consider are schizophrenia and bipolar disorder.

Depression is an extremely debilitating disease all too common and frequently recurrent. The condition can result in physical symptoms including fatigue, headaches, digestive problems, muscle aches, and more. Those suffering from depression often withdraw from their social support networks. Early identification of depression is key to curtailing the disease process and improving the quality of life of its victim. With so many treatment options available from counseling to medications, it is a shame to see so many people suffering on the sidelines. Depression may not necessarily be cured but it can be managed.

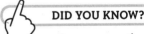

DID YOU KNOW?

In 2011, more than 39,000 people died as a result of suicides and 750,000 attempted to kill themselves.

Mental illness can be a risk not only to those suffering through it but also to society at large. It can trigger physical symptoms in addition to the anguish imposed on their emotional state. The ability for rational thought may be impaired. Delusions or psychotic patterns can develop, risking unsafe decisions for themselves and for those around them. Someone with mental illness could be physically fit but far from healthy.

A health-care plan would need to consider mental states as immediately pertaining to the health of the beneficiary and should take aims to treat conditions and lessen emotional suffering whenever possible.

Social Well-Being

A healthy body and a healthy mind are vital but we are social animals, too. Whether you consider yourself an introvert, an extrovert, or somewhere in the middle, social interactions add quality to life. Imagine being locked up in a room by yourself or stranded alone on a deserted island for months or years at a time. Strict isolation is often a slippery slope into some form of mental illness. Without social engagement, we are at risk for becoming unhealthy no matter how physically and mentally well we may be.

Situations that limit your social well-being place you at risk. Domestic violence or intimate partner violence affects one in four women and one in seven men in their lifetime. Abuse may be physical, psychological, or sexual, and not infrequently tied with economic coercion. Victims of domestic violence tend to develop mental illness with higher rates of depression and anxiety, as well as sleep disorders and headaches. Post-traumatic stress disorder is not uncommon.

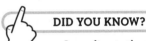

DID YOU KNOW?

According to the Centers for Disease Control and Prevention (CDC), domestic violence leads to more than 2 million injuries every year and as many as 1,300 deaths.

Stressors are all around us: some physical, others emotional; some avoidable, others not. Multiple studies have linked long-term stress to cardiac conditions, stroke, ulcers, depression, and even cancer. Understanding how to cope with daily stress can make a tremendous impact on your well-being.

Working excessive hours can decrease time spent in familial and social relationships, weakening personal ties. Limiting sleep can wear the body out, decreasing the necessary time for rejuvenation. Many people self-medicate with alcohol and other substances, from excess caffeine to illicit drugs, as a way to get through difficult times. Each of these lifestyle behaviors can stifle your physical and mental health.

We may not be able to make our bills disappear without winning the lottery but we can develop healthier approaches to managing our stress. Deep breathing exercises and meditation have proven effective in studies to reduce tension in the body while focusing the mind. Yoga, too, strengthens the mind-body connection. Daily activity, even walking 20 minutes for those who are able, can improve circulation and improve mood. There is so much we can do to put our lives in perspective if we slow down every now and then. We just have to choose to take the time.

Life is meant to be enjoyed, and too often we forget to do that. You may thrive in romantic relationships. You may flourish in family life. You may seek to engage with friends and acquaintances, whether in groups or one-on-one. You may have interests you wish to pursue and goals that drive your ambition. You must remember to make time to do the things you enjoy, the things that bring you happiness, even as you do the things you must do to make ends meet. In the end, life is about balance.

Bringing It Together

Health is a complicated and beautiful construct designed with physical, mental, and social building blocks. It takes effort to maintain lifestyles that promote health in all three domains but much reward comes from it. To those who achieve that goal, congratulations! The truth is, many of us will fall off the wagon some time or other. Who doesn't catch the occasional cold? Who never has unexpected life challenges thrown their way? We never know what is on the horizon. This is why we need a health-care system to fall back on when our health fails us, or better yet to keep us healthy so our health doesn't get the chance to fail us in the first place.

Principles of Health Insurance

Health insurance is meant to provide services that keep us healthy, but what does it include? More importantly, what should it include?

If it were up to the beneficiaries, every service under the sun would be included from the smallest piece of gauze to major surgery if it were needed. Think how wonderful it would be to have everything you could ever need at your disposal without the added cost. It would put health insurance companies out of business.

Companies that provide health insurance are looking to provide a service while making a profit. I wish it were a more altruistic affair, but this is capitalism at work. Before we get into Medicare specifically, let's take a closer look at general health-care plans provided by insurance companies.

Who Is Covered?

As a potential client, you can review care plans offered by the insurance company, but it is the insurer's decision whether or not to accept your application.

Until recently, an insurance company could deny you coverage or charge you more based on medical conditions you had before you signed up for their insurance plan (called pre-existing conditions). Certain medical conditions simply cost more to manage and will cost the insurance company more dollars in the long run. In theory, the insurer would prefer to have only healthy clients that pay monthly fees so they would not have to pay out anything for health care.

With passage of the Affordable Care Act, refusing coverage or charging higher rates based on pre-existing conditions is now against the law with the exception of certain grandfathered health plans. Grandfathered plans are plans that were in existence before the ACA came into effect. The plans are limited to individual plans, which are plans purchased by a person directly from the insurance company and not through their employer. As long as the plans do not decrease benefits or markedly increase costs, they can continue to deny coverage based on pre-existing conditions.

What Services Are Provided?

The specific services provided by insurers will be outlined in their insurance plans, but reading the fine print can often be difficult. Understanding that you are signing up for a plan that meets your needs is important. Understanding the nature of any medical conditions you have or those that run in your family will help you to make an educated decision.

Where Can I Receive Care?

Depending on the health plan you have chosen, your insurer may limit your coverage to a specified service area. Plans may be state driven, regional, or offer national coverage. Some even offer extended coverage in foreign countries. If you travel, you may need to take this into consideration when you select a plan.

How Long Will I Have Coverage?

Plans are usually offered on an annual basis, but timelines may vary depending on the plan you select. It is important to understand how long your coverage will last when you sign up and to know when or if you are able to make changes to your health plan. Some companies may charge penalties or increase the rate of the monthly fees if you change plans outside of a specified time period. Others may not allow you to change plans at all and you will continue to be responsible for monthly payments at the original rate. Understand what you are signing up for and write it on your calendar.

How Much Will It Cost?

Affordability will always be a concern. Beneficiaries get health insurance to save costs. When health care is needed, out-of-pocket expenses could be quite high, even bankrupting for some. With health insurance, those costs can be considerably reduced.

A beneficiary pays a fee, called a *premium*, to the insurance company so that the insurer can help pay for part or all of those services when they are needed. The more services covered in an insurance plan, the higher the premium. To offset the sometimes high costs of these premiums, beneficiaries may be given the opportunity to pay a *deductible*. A deductible is an amount that the beneficiary agrees to pay out-of-pocket before the insurance kicks in. Usually a higher deductible means a lower premium. Everyone's budgets and priorities are different. It is important to look to your expected expenses and calculate how much you will be able to reasonably afford.

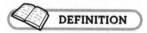 **DEFINITION**

> A **premium** is a fixed dollar amount paid on a schedule, usually monthly, to an insurer. This money compensates the insurer so the insurer can pay for health-care services when the need arises.
>
> A **deductible** is a set fee agreed upon when signing up for insurance coverage that you pay out-of-pocket before your insurance pays for services.

How Medicare Compares

Medicare functions similarly to private insurance plans, utilizing premiums and deductibles to pay for health-care services. It has multiple incoming sources of funds that it uses to operate the program, including:

- Monthly premiums paid by beneficiaries
- Fines paid into the system by health-care providers and hospitals that did not comply with Medicare's policies
- Late penalties paid by certain beneficiaries
- Taxes paid into the Medicare Trust Fund

DID YOU KNOW?

The Affordable Care Act initiated the Hospital Readmissions Reduction Program in 2013 to decrease payments to hospitals that have high rates of readmissions. When a patient is admitted to the hospital for the same medical problem within 30 days, it may suggest that the patient was discharged prematurely or without an adequate care plan. The program aims to financially incentivize hospitals to improve care to these patients so that subsequent admissions are not necessary in the short-term.

The specific health-care services that are covered by Medicare will be discussed in more detail as we move forward.

Meet the Crew

The time has come to tie together our goals for health with the details of our insurance plan, Medicare. Will we get what we need?

Life has offered each of us a unique set of experiences and circumstances. In that vein, we will all have different health-care needs. To offer up different scenarios and better understand how Medicare works, I have set up a round table discussion with a lovely set of characters to help us out. There are exceptions to most every rule, but hopefully you will find yourself in one of these characters. Let's meet the players.

Loraine

Loraine is a spit fire with a past medical history significant for high blood pressure. She is celebrating her sixty-fifth birthday this month and she is set to retire. For 40 years, she has worked in various roles ranging from a radiology assistant to an administrative secretary in a busy medical office. She is the happily married mother to three and proud grandparent to two. She is ready to sign up for Medicare.

Eileen

Eileen is a healthy 68-year-old homemaker who has been recently widowed. She raised three children and donates a great deal of time providing services to her community, especially the local soup kitchen. She did work for a period of time prior to the birth of her children, six years to be exact, but has not had formal employment since then. Her passion lies in her volunteerism.

Thomas

Thomas has had chronic health problems but makes the most of every day. He was diagnosed with diabetes in his thirties, and as a result he developed kidney disease. Unfortunately, his kidneys have struggled. He now requires dialysis and has been put on the waiting list for a kidney transplant. He is 48 years old, divorced, and continues to work. After 12 years on the job as a truck driver, he is considering applying for disability due to his kidney condition.

George

George is a 65-year-old Vietnam veteran. He lost his left leg from the knee down during his service and is receiving benefits from the Veteran's Administration as well as Social Security Disability Insurance. The woman he loved died during the war and he has never married, though he lives a close-knit family life supporting his nieces and nephews.

How to Follow Along

You will want to take note of the ages of each applicant, marital status, how long each person worked, and their medical conditions. Each of these factors will play a role in how Medicare will work for them. Don't worry; you will be reminded of their stories as we go along.

Round Table Summary

Name	Age	Marital Status	SSDI	Veteran
Loraine	65 years old	Married	No	No
Eileen	68 years old	Widowed	No	No
Thomas	48 years old	Divorced	Yes (ESRD)	No
George	65 years old	Single	Yes	Yes

A True Original

When Medicare was enacted in 1965, it was composed of two essential parts, Part A and Part B (collectively now referred to as Original Medicare). The federal government broke its health-care plan into two parts to decrease the burden of costs on the system. We will take a closer look at each of these now.

Medicare Part A

Medicare Part A focuses on care that is given in the hospital setting. Hospital costs, depending on the nature of the medical problem, can be quite high, especially if surgical procedures are involved. We are talking tens to hundreds of thousands of dollars in some cases. These high costs can be catastrophic to families. By offering coverage for the worst case scenario, an inpatient hospitalization, the government aids the elderly in avoiding personal bankruptcy.

As we age, we are at higher risk for developing medical conditions but hopefully that does not equate with going to the hospital. The bulk of care for seniors occurs outside of the hospital, referred to as the ambulatory or outpatient setting.

At its onset, Medicare made enrollment in Part A automatic for everyone over 65 years of age. The process has become somewhat more complicated now with some people being automatically enrolled and others having to actively apply for coverage. For those who apply outside of the initial enrollment period, late penalties will be charged for a set duration of time based on a calculation, typically lasting a number of years. These extra fees, in addition to taxes paid into the Medicare Trust Fund and monthly premiums for beneficiaries meeting certain criteria, help to pay for the Medicare program.

Medicare Part B

Medicare Part B focuses on care given in the outpatient setting. This encompasses the bulk of care that seniors receive. From doctor's visits to laboratory studies, X-rays, and ambulance rides, services are offered to seniors at a percentage of the cost. The typical rate paid by beneficiaries is 20 percent of each service provided. What the Part B plan does not include is prescription drug coverage, even though a majority of people over 65 years old rely on medications to treat their conditions.

Enrollment in Medicare Part B was not automatic and was offered to beneficiaries on a voluntary basis. This remains true today. It requires a monthly premium be paid into the system just like a private insurance company would charge. As with Part A, late fees could be applied if registration occurred outside of the enrollment window. Unlike Part A late fees, which expire after a certain period of time, Part B late fees are paid throughout Medicare enrollment.

Optional Medicare

Medicare expanded over time to include Part C and Part D services with legislation enacted in 1997 and 2003, respectively. A beneficiary may choose to opt in or out of either program. What do they have to offer that Part A and Part B do not?

Medicare Part C

Medicare Part C, also known as Medicare Advantage, is not run by the government directly. Private insurance companies have contracted with the government to develop extended care plans for you to choose from. Services not available to you in Original Medicare may now be available. The insurance company sets their own monthly premium rates and the government pays the insurance company a calculated rate for each person it covers.

Depending on the plan you choose, Part C plans may cover dental, vision, or hearing screenings that are not otherwise offered with Original Medicare. It could also support longer stays in nursing homes or provide access to nursing care in your home.

When you sign up for a Part C plan, you are no longer enrolled in Original Medicare (Parts A and B). Part C plans include all the services offered in Parts A and B and then some. They may also include a Part D plan as described below. Combination Medicare Advantage and Part D plans are known as *MAPD* plans.

DEFINITION

> **MAPD** stands for Medicare Advantage Prescription Drug plan, which is a Part C plan that includes Part D coverage.

Why would Part C be beneficial? It was thought that shifting care to the private sector could help decrease the mounting burden on the Medicare Trust Fund. Insurance companies could gain a market share of an aging population. Medicare beneficiaries get broader health-care coverage. It was a win-win-win, or so it seemed. Analyses have shown that the federal government has paid more toward Medicare Advantage plans in recent years than it would have paid to Original Medicare. Under the ACA, the government will decrease its spending toward Medicare Advantage plans, which could tip the scales back in its favor.

Medicare Part D

With the majority of seniors taking five or more medications, Medicare Part D was the long overdue prescription drug coverage plan that seniors needed. The glaring problem with Part D is a coverage gap referred to as the donut hole. Part D plans help to pay for medication coverage up to $2,850 before coverage drops off, leaving seniors to all but fend for themselves until they spend another $1,700. The cycle starts all over again the following year.

Granted, beneficiaries were not worse off than they would have been before Part D existed, but the sudden increase in out-of-pocket expenses after the coverage drops off can be jarring and raises ethical questions. The ACA will gradually close the donut hole but not fully until 2020.

In the meantime, this makes life difficult for Medicare beneficiaries. Someone who takes five medications may spend more or less depending on what prescription they need. Some medications may cost as little $10 per month while others can cost thousands. When the dollar amount of those drugs crosses the $2,850 threshold, the beneficiary enters the donut hole. Instead of paying small copayments each month for an average of $30-$150 for the five drugs, their monthly costs could increase by hundreds or thousands of dollars until they have spent $1,700 out of pocket. Few seniors can afford such a drastic swing in expenses.

Part D, like Part C, is run by private insurers contracted with the government to offer different care plans. No single plan offers all medications, though wouldn't that be a great idea?

It may be that you would prefer your expensive medications to be covered under your Part D plan. Alternatively, you may want to choose a plan that covers a wider range of possible medications. Everyone's needs will be different. Strategies to pick the best plan for you are discussed in Chapter 12.

Does Medicare Work?

If that isn't a loaded question, I do not know what is. Many seniors have had health-care services they would not have otherwise had in the absence of Medicare. Medicare, generally speaking, is also less expensive than the majority of private insurance plans. From this vantage point, Medicare has more pros than cons.

That said, it still does come at a cost. With more and more seniors approaching eligibility age every day, does it offer enough services to keep our nation healthy? Does it do enough to care for our physical, mental, and social well-being? Is it worth the dollars we as a nation put into it? For our sake, I sure hope so.

The Least You Need to Know

- Health relates to our physical, mental, and social well-being. A quality health plan will address all of these aspects in kind.
- Private insurance companies are for-profit entities that may not always have your best interest at heart. You need to look carefully at plans to select the one that best suits your financial situation.
- Medicare Part A is part of Original Medicare and covers costs for inpatient hospital stays.
- Medicare Part B is part of Original Medicare and covers costs for outpatient medical care.
- Medicare Part C, also known as Medicare Advantage, may be chosen to replace Original Medicare to provide broader coverage options, and may itself include a Part D plan.
- Medicare Part D covers costs for prescription drugs. Exactly which drugs covered depends on the particular plan.

Limitations of Medicare

Everyone is looking for a bargain and why shouldn't they? Health-care costs can quickly escalate, even with the advent of a single unexpected medical condition. Finding everything you could ever need in one insurance plan can be a daunting, if not impossible, task. While Medicare offers a financially viable option to many seniors and those on disability, there are still limitations on what it offers.

What Is Missing?

Many people look to see what a health plan provides, but it is equally important to analyze what it does not. Everyone's needs are different, so it is important to look at your own situation. Would these missing parts of Medicare matter to you? Our round table will fill you in.

Dental Coverage

Medicare does not cover preventive dental care or treatments, such as cleanings, X-rays, fillings, root canals, implants, or routine dental extractions. It certainly doesn't allow for cosmetic procedures, so put those thoughts of tooth whitening aside.

It does allow for dental services in very limited circumstances:

- Dental extractions that are required as part of another Medicare approved procedure

- Dental extractions that are needed to prepare the mouth and jaw for cancer treatments with radiation

- Dental procedures that require inpatient hospitalization

- Pre-operative examinations as clearance for kidney transplant or heart valve replacement surgeries (though treatment of any identified dental disease is excluded)

The exclusion of dental care has been in effect since Medicare first started in the 1960s with inpatient procedure coverage added in 1980. Since that time, strict criteria have been put in place as to what qualifies you to be an inpatient. It is all based on how long you are expected to stay in the hospital, this policy, called the "Two-Midnight Rule," will be discussed in Chapter 11.

Lack of routine dental services can be considered a fault in Medicare. There are known complications to gum and tooth disease. Heart disease and stroke have been associated with dental diseases such as gingivitis and periodontitis.

Dental disease is also highly correlated with chronic kidney disease. If you do not have your natural teeth, you are more likely to have kidney problems, which could lead to high blood pressure and subsequently heart disease. Also, a mother's periodontal disease has been found to increase the risk for pre-term delivery of her baby as much as five-fold. Babies born before 37 weeks of gestation are at higher risk for medical complications.

Today, 35 million Americans are lacking teeth—23 million having no teeth at all and 12 million with no teeth in one arch. Among seniors, 20.5 percent of Americans aged 65 years and older are missing teeth and 90 percent of them use dentures.

Dentures, or false teeth, can be a costly affair and an expense that recurs over time. Dentures that are well maintained can last five years or more. The cost of dentures is variable depending on the dentist, where you live in the country, and the material used to make the dentures. Upper or lower dentures may range from $500–$2,500, each with the added expense of the doctor's fees for making them that could add another $250–$1,000 to the final cost. Multiply that by two for a complete pair.

The National Association of Dental Plans (NADP) reports that only 60 percent of Americans had dental benefits in 2010. The sad truth is that few seniors carry dental insurance. Only 22 percent of those over 65 years old have private dental insurance.

The American Dental Association estimates that routine dental care—two cleanings with X-rays—would have cost $370 in 2011 where the NADP estimates a private dental plan would have cost $360 a year in premiums. It is a pretty even balance if those are the only services you need.

The big question remains whether or not dental insurance is worth the cost. It will depend on the plan you choose and the state of your oral health. If your teeth are in bad shape or you have many teeth missing, it may be a worthy investment. Many private dental plans limit how much they pay beyond routine care, often capping annual costs at $1,000–$1,500. This can be alarming when a root canal averages $400–$1,400 and a crown, depending on the materials used, can range from $500–$3,000.

Coverage for Hearing Impairments

Medicare does not cover the cost for screening hearing exams, fittings for hearing aids, or for hearing aids themselves. It will, however, offer coverage for diagnostic hearing and balance evaluations.

The term *diagnostic* means that a physician is ordering a test to investigate a specific symptom or concern. For example, George came in the office and mentioned that he has been having a difficult time hearing the television and he frequently leans in toward the doctor during the visit. Or maybe Eileen notes ongoing balance problems and the doctor finds scarring on both of her ear drums. The hearing test in these situations is not being ordered for preventive screening purposes based on age, but for diagnostic purposes based on physical and subjective findings.

The diagnostic hearing exam must be ordered by a Medicare approved provider and performed by a licensed audiologist. Regardless of the results of the testing, Medicare will not pay for treatment of a hearing deficit.

Hearing loss is prevalent; 30 to 40 percent of Americans over 65 years old report some sort of impairment. The number increases to nearly 50 percent for adults over 75 years old. Loss of hearing has effects on the psyche with increased depression and anxiety in those with the condition. Untreated hearing loss also raises a variety of safety concerns. Balance issues and poor hearing, especially when driving, dramatically increases the risk for accidents and injury to the individual and the public at large.

Hearing aid technologies continue to evolve but there is one thing they all share in common— they are expensive. A simple hearing aid may cost $1,500, and more sophisticated devices may cost as much as $5,000. Few seniors can afford these high out-of-pocket charges.

Vision Coverage

Medicare does not include routine eye exams under their benefits package, ultimately excluding coverage for eyeglasses or contact lenses.

It does allow annual examinations for beneficiaries who have specific medical conditions: diabetes, glaucoma, and age-related macular degeneration. These three conditions, in addition to cataracts (which are not covered), are the most prevalent age-related disorders that can lead to vision loss.

In order to be considered appropriate for glaucoma screening, a beneficiary must be considered at high risk. The risk factors that Medicare takes into consideration include the following:

- African American over 50 years old

- Diabetes

- Hispanic American over 65 years old

- Family history for glaucoma

Vision impairment is common, affecting 3.6 million people over the age of 40, with more than one million of these individuals meeting criteria for legal blindness. Americans between the ages of 65 and 74 and those older than 75 have vision loss at rates of 12.2 and 15.3 percent, respectively. By not providing routine screening examinations in an aging population, despite the fact that risk for vision loss continues to increase for every year that we age, Medicare's limitations to vision-related coverage put us all in an uncomfortable position. Many visually impaired individuals continue to drive without corrective lenses, increasing risks for public safety. Their potential for falls is also greatly heightened.

Services for the Blind

Certain services to the blind may be limited by Medicare. Seeing eye dogs, also referred to as service dogs, require extensive training to guide their users in a safe and effective manner. The training for these animals costs more than $10,000 in most cases. Given the high overall expense, Medicare does not offer this service to its beneficiaries.

There are many charitable organizations that do provide service dogs for free or at a low cost. This may or may not include veterinary care and feeding for the animal beyond the training period. The waiting lists to get a service dog can be as long as three years.

DID YOU KNOW?

There are 12 accredited schools in the United States that train service dogs. A dog's obedience training typically starts at 6 to 8 weeks of age and formal guide dog training is initiated at 14 to 16 months. This is then followed by a period when the blind person trains one-on-one with the dog, usually over several weeks. It is a labor intensive process.

Furthermore, white canes are also excluded from the covered benefits. These are the rigid canes or fold-out walking sticks that help the blind to sense the environment around them, from furniture in their path to the curb on the street. They are white to signify to the public that the person is blind. Though these canes are far more affordable than service dogs, averaging in the $10 to $30 range, Medicare's stance is that "a white cane for use by a blind person is more an identifying and self-help device rather than an item which makes a meaningful contribution in the treatment of an illness or injury."

Many would beg to differ. Service dogs and white canes do allow the blind increased independence and quality of life to more effectively engage in their communities. What could be a more "meaningful contribution" than that?

 TIP

The National Federation for the Blind offers free white canes through their program at nfb.org/free-cane-program.

Nursing Home Stays

As we get older, some of us may find it harder to live on our own. Many people need support that goes beyond a visiting nurse coming to their home a few days a week or even having a live-in home health aide when their faculties fail. Some may have family that steps in to help out, but others may not have that opportunity. Even then, sometimes the amount of care we require is intensive enough that family alone may not be sufficient to meet our needs. We may require intensive monitoring or full-time nursing care to assure our safety, basic necessities, and hygiene.

Dementia increases with age and often can lead to debilitating disease states. Alzheimer's disease alone affected more than 5.2 million people in 2014 and stood as the sixth leading cause for death in the nation.

Unless you have been recently hospitalized, Medicare will not cover the cost of a long-term nursing home stay. In fact, though Medicare may cover a skilled nursing facility after a hospitalization, and only if certain criteria are met, those days are still numbered and cannot be extended to long-term care. If you find yourself in need of a nursing home to live the rest of your days, you are sadly on your own financially and must pay out-of-pocket, or apply for Medicaid if you qualify.

Geographic Limitations

Medicare generally does not cover care provided outside of the United States and its territories including American Samoa, Guam, the Northern Mariana Islands, Puerto Rico, and the U.S. Virgin Islands. Some Medigap plans may extend your care to foreign countries.

When it comes to Medicare itself, few exceptions arise that will allow the program to pay for your care in a foreign country. You may find the details interesting:

Emergency situation in the United States. Though you are in the United States, if the closest available hospital for care is in a foreign country, Medicare will cover services.

Living closer to a foreign hospital. If the hospital closest to your home is in a foreign country, you may choose to use their facilities. This will affect those living near the borders with Canada and Mexico.

Travelling direct from Alaska to the contiguous United States or vice versa. Canadian care will be covered if the closest available hospital at the time of an emergency is in Canada.

Travelling on a cruise ship. Care will only be covered if the cruise ship is within six hours of a U.S. port or in U.S. territorial waters.

If you are a frequent traveler, you may need to consider purchasing a supplemental health-care plan in order to access emergency services as the need arises.

Other Exclusions

Medicare has excluded several common screening and preventive services from its menu. Without routine vision and hearing examinations, drivers may pose a serious risk to themselves and others. The Registry of Motor Vehicles does not require annual evaluations and people could slip through the cracks before any discrepancies are identified. This is a danger to public health.

DID YOU KNOW?

The Centers for Disease Control and Prevention (CDC) estimates that 500 people older than 65 years old are injured in car accidents and 15 are killed every day. It is noted that physical decline from aging due to conditions like vision impairment or cognitive decline may be contributing factors.

Other services not covered include acupuncture, cosmetic surgery, and many chiropractic therapies. Chiropractic services are limited to manipulations of the spine if the beneficiary has a condition called subluxation. Subluxation occurs when the bones in the spine are out of alignment.

Despite more common services being denied, the U.S. Department of Health and Human Services has lifted automatic denials for sex reassignment surgery stating the procedure may be medically necessary in some cases for those who do not identify with their born gender. This has fueled debate about how tax dollars should be spent. This does not mean that the government has agreed to pay for these surgeries but does allow individual cases to be presented for possible coverage.

Medicare Is Trying

All this talk about Medicare's shortcomings is in no way meant to belittle what it does cover. What it does cover is still very significant and far more than what many people would be able to access without the plan.

Partnering with Insurance Companies

It is not that Medicare is trying to turn its nose up at the people it is intended to support. The program would be more likely to consider offering more services if it were financially viable to do so. With the rising number of beneficiaries, hundreds of thousands every year, Medicare is at risk to run out of money before the baby boomers have had a chance to make use of its services.

Not Enough Federal Dollars

The costs of Medicare are staggering. Funds continue to come in to the Medicare Trust Fund from the taxpayer dollars of people of all ages, not just those over 65 years old. Premiums continue to be paid by beneficiaries over 65 years old and those with disabilities. Still, the aging population is increasing exponentially and the health-care expenditures are set to increase faster than dollars coming in. Add to that the cost of inflation and there is a real conundrum on our hands. The federal government needed to find other ways to decrease spending while trying to maintain the variety of services it already offered. It sought that balance by striking a deal with big business.

Working with the Private Sector

Private insurance companies were not going to jump on the Medicare roller coaster without some sort of financial incentive. As for-profit entities, they needed to make money while the government sought to save it. You have to spend money to make money.

To set quality standards, the government mandated that the private insurance companies participating in Medicare Advantage offer the same services available in Original Medicare. To do otherwise would be to jilt beneficiaries from their fair share.

What the government did allow was for the insurance companies to add additional services as they deemed fit. This allowed the insurers to set prices on different plans offered to the public. The companies could also set their own rules and regulations surrounding those additional services, for example requiring referrals. It could not make stipulations concerning Original Medicare benefits.

The federal government calculates a fixed fee for each Medicare Advantage enrollee and pays it monthly to the insurance company. You pay a premium to the insurance company. The insurance company, not the government, then becomes responsible to pay your health-care bills based on the contractual agreement. This relationship, so the government hopes, would cost less than paying out the health-care bills themselves. A similar relationship exists between Medicare and private insurers offering Part D plans.

Conflicts of Interest

Original Medicare has fixed fees for all who enroll. Because the final prices for Part C and Part D plans are set by private companies instead of the government, there is opportunity for a large range of price variability. One company may charge more for the same offerings than another, etc. Conflicts of interest can happen at many levels.

Any of the parties involved, from the insurance companies setting prices to marketers or vendors selling the products to hospitals, providers, and the pharmacies distributing the products, may have financial stakes depending on the relationships they have with one another. For example, an insurance agent may try to sell a Part D plan to a client but pushes one plan over another because he would get a greater commission or because he has a family member who owns stock in one of the companies. You can imagine a variety of scenarios where someone could manipulate the system for personal gain.

To prevent fraud, CMS hires claim processors to investigate irregular billing patterns and suspected cases of abuse. These processors then present suspicious cases to the Office of the Inspector General (OIG) for review.

 ROUND TABLE

Eileen decided a Medicare Advantage Plan would better suit her needs. She went to a local insurance agency to learn about her options. While she sat in the waiting room, she heard someone say that the daughter of one of the insurance agents had gotten promoted at a large health insurance company, Welcome Health (a fictitious company). When she sat down to review Medicare Advantage plans with the agent, he only offered her Welcome Health plans, even though the agency also sells plans from other companies. Eileen is concerned about possible conflicts of interest and decides to continue shopping at another agency.

In 2013, the Office of the Inspector General (OIG) expressed concerns over how these claim processors were selected. They found that two-thirds of the private companies had financial ties to these claim processors that were inconsistently reported or not reported at all. One example was a processor who worked for a company that also owned a Medicare Administrative Contractor (MAC), a private organization that manages Medicare cases for a certain jurisdiction. One could imagine that the claims processor could look the other way to allow the MAC to benefit financially without suspicious cases being referred to the OIG.

Recommendations were made to tighten policies surrounding conflicts of interest but CMS did not agree on all points. In the same year, CMS developed Fraud, Waste, and Abuse (FWA) Compliance Training for all people who work clinically or administratively with Medicare enrollees to provide Part C or Part D plans.

Fraud ultimately costs the beneficiary and the system more money, not only in higher premiums and copayments for enrollees but in secondary administrative costs needed to correct the problem. Controlling these abuses will be essential to containing Medicare costs in the long run and will protect your interests in Medicare's success. CMS has reinforced the following steps to try to reduce fraud, waste, and abuse in their mandated training:

Prevention. The goal is to prevent abuse by understanding existing regulations, verifying accuracy of information provided, and monitoring for suspicious activity.

Detection. Any suspicious activities are to be reported for fraud, waste, or abuse. Those reporting such activity are protected from retaliation.

Correction. Penalties may take the form of civil penalties, civil prosecution, criminal fines, imprisonment, loss of licensure, and exclusion from working with other federal programs.

To avoid conflicts of interest, CMS has also emphasized the need for seven key elements in their compliance training for people working with Part C and Part D plans.

1. Written policies, procedures, and standards of conduct

2. Compliance officer, compliance committee, and high level oversight

3. Effective training and education

4. Effective lines of communication

5. Well publicized disciplinary standards

6. Effective system for routine monitoring and identification of compliance risks

7. Procedures and system for prompt response to compliance issues

The conflicts of interest principles emphasize that multiple avenues of communication are required to report concerns about compliance. These lines of communication must be open between all entities working with an organization. The careful training offered by CMS will save money from being siphoned into the wrong pockets and hopefully will keep Medicare functioning as a well-oiled machine that will be there when you need it most.

The Least You Need to Know

- Medicare does not offer routine examinations for dental, hearing, or vision care.
- Medicare does not provide service dogs or white canes for the blind.
- Limited Medicare coverage is available to those who travel out of the country.
- Nursing home coverage is only offered to those who have been recently hospitalized.
- Private insurance companies have contracted with the federal government to offer Part C and Part D plans.
- CMS requires compliance training for all people and organizations providing Part C and Part D plans to beneficiaries in order to reduce the risk of fraud, waste, and abuse.

Costs of Medicare

Medicare is often referred to as an entitlement program because tax dollars are used to help pay for the government program. However, many people argue that it is not entitlement at all because each person pays into the system with taxes that they could otherwise use for their own health care down the road. Furthermore, Medicare beneficiaries pay a number of other fees and charges in order to access that health coverage. This chapter will carefully outline the different costs associated with Medicare.

Far from Free

Medicare is by no means free. There are many costs associated with the program, some transparent with others buried in fine print and regulations. Too many people do not investigate how much Medicare will impact their finances until they apply for the program or start using it. This could easily lead to paying more than you have to. Understanding where these costs lie can help you to better plan for your future.

In This Chapter

- How you will pay for Medicare
- How premiums, deductibles, copays, and coinsurance factor into your costs
- A breakdown of costs under each part of Medicare
- Calculating your contribution

Medicare Payroll Taxes

If you have worked in the United States, you have noticed that the pay you take home never equals what you earned. This is because taxes are taken out to pay toward your governing bodies and the public services they provide. Federal, state, and local income taxes are used to fund programs in their respective areas.

DID YOU KNOW?

Nine states—Alaska, Florida, Nevada, New Hampshire, South Dakota, Tennessee, Texas, Washington, and Wyoming—do not have broad-based individual state income tax.

Although you may or may not be subject to state taxes depending on where you live, federal taxes apply to everyone. Your federal tax rate depends on how much you earn. Generally speaking, the higher your earnings, the more you pay. To offset costs, many people will take advantage of tax credits, tax deductions, and tax breaks to reduce how much they have to contribute. Because tax laws change on a regular basis, it is important to familiarize yourself with any changes to the tax code before preparing your annual tax returns. It could be the difference between having to pay additional taxes or having the government refund some of the previously collected tax monies to you. If your tax situation confuses you, it may be helpful to consult with a tax professional or financial advisor.

DID YOU KNOW?

People who are employed by a company have taxes withheld from each paycheck. Those who are self-employed pay taxes to the Internal Revenue Service (IRS) on a quarterly basis on April 15, June 15, September 15, and January 15.

Though Medicare is a federally funded program, federal income taxes are not used to pay for it. A separate tax has been instituted known as the Federal Insurance Contributions Act tax or FICA. This tax is broken down into two key components, one for Social Security and the other for Medicare. Interestingly, Medicaid is not paid for with the FICA tax, even though like Medicare it is operated by CMS and also came into effect as an amendment to the Social Security Act.

The rate of FICA taxes may vary from year to year. For 2014, that rate was set at 12.4 percent of total earnings for Social Security and 2.9 percent for Medicare. If you are employed by a company, whether you are paid hourly wages or a fixed salary, your employer is responsible to pay half of these taxes, leaving you to only pay 6.2 percent and 1.45 percent of the individual FICA taxes. If you are self-employed, you are responsible to pay the full amount of each tax.

Half of those taxes, however, could be included as a business expense when you prepare your annual tax return.

There is a limit to the amount of tax dollars you will be required to pay into Social Security each year, but this is not the case for Medicare. In 2014, FICA taxes for Social Security were paid up to a salary of $117,000. This means that the maximum amount of these taxes anyone can pay is $7,254. For any dollars earned beyond $117,000, no Social Security taxes will be withheld. This number may change annually to adjust for inflation and the increasing dollars needed to fund the Social Security program.

Medicare taxes do not have a cap. You will pay a percentage of your total income for every dollar you earn. In fact, the more you make, the more you contribute, in some cases disproportionately more than other people.

 TIP

An employee will pay a 1.45 percent Medicare tax up to $200,000 of their earnings and then 2.35 percent after that. For example, if he earns $250,000 per year, he will pay 1.45 percent for the first $200,000 and 2.35 percent for the remaining $50,000.

The Affordable Care Act made changes to Medicare tax contributions based on your income starting in 2013. For individuals who earn more than $200,000, married couples who file separately earning more than $125,000 each, and married couples filing jointly earning more than $250,000, an additional 0.9 percent tax is added to every dollar earned over that threshold amount. This is referred to as the Additional Medicare Tax.

The tax regulations can get a bit complicated. Employers are required to withdraw the Additional Medicare Tax after $200,000 for all qualifying employees. While this approach is straightforward for single people, scenarios may arise for married couples that result in their paying too much or too little taxes.

For married couples filing separately, one member may earn more than $200,000, but their combined salaries do not exceed $250,000. They do not meet the threshold criteria to justify the Additional Medicare Tax. If too many taxes are withdrawn, you can apply for a tax credit the following year.

Likewise, if each member of the couple earned more than $125,000 and their combined income exceeds $250,000 (obviously), their employers may not have withheld enough taxes. As individuals, they did not meet the $200,000 criteria to signal to their employer that the applicable taxes needed to be withheld. The employer has no way to know what their employee's spouse is earning. Married couples who make more than $250,000 combined may elect to have more taxes taken out of their paychecks to reduce bulk payments upon completion of their tax returns.

The Additional Medicare Tax applies only to the employee; there is no sharing of the burden by the employer.

Monthly Premiums

Similar to private insurance plans, Medicare enrollees pay a fixed fee every month in order to continue their health-care benefits. This service charge is referred to as a premium. The cost of premiums may be set based on an individual's age and, in rare instances, pre-existing medical conditions. Passage of the Affordable Care Act has considerably restricted insurance discrimination based on your past medical history. Not paying these premiums would be the equivalent of cancelling your coverage.

Each part of Medicare—A, B, C, and D—as well as Medigap, has its own premium charge. These dollars are essential to help fund the program since tax dollars alone are insufficient to make ends meet, especially with the increasing number of baby boomers reaching Medicare eligibility age.

Copays and Coinsurance

Coinsurance and *copayments* can sometimes be difficult concepts to explain to beneficiaries. It is too often believed that paying a premium alone will pay for all of one's health-care costs. Nothing could be further from the truth.

While some services are free under Medicare (these will be discussed in later chapters), the majority of services require beneficiaries to contribute to the cost of the care provided. There are two approaches to managing these costs. In one case, the insurer, in this case Medicare, shares the costs with you as a percentage of the total charge. This is known as a coinsurance. For example, you may pay 20 percent of the cost for a medical expense and your insurance will pay the remaining 80 percent. Together, the service is paid in full and you, as a beneficiary, still benefit by paying a lesser percentage of the cost than you would have otherwise without the insurance plan in effect. Because coinsurance is a percentage of the total expense, the amount you pay will vary depending on the cost of the service.

Copayments, also referred to as copays, work in a similar way but apply a fixed fee to a service as opposed to a percentage. For example, you may be assigned a copay of $6 for a medication. If the medication costs $20 at the pharmacy, your insurer will pay the remaining $14. The copayment remains the same regardless of the total expense; if your medication was $150, you would still pay $6 and your insurance would pay $144.

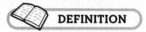 **DEFINITION**

A **copayment** is a fixed fee applied toward the payment of a service, while a **coinsurance** is a set percentage of the total cost paid toward a service.

There are no hard and fast rules about when an insurer will have you pay a coinsurance versus a copayment. Financial incentives must clearly exist in the background for the insurer to choose one form of payment over the other, while still providing you affordable access to health-care services. Medicare generally uses copayments for most medications and coinsurance for other health-care services.

Annual Deductibles

Deductibles help to reduce costs for both you and your insurer, at least when it comes to private insurance. A deductible is an amount that you agree to pay for your health-care services before your insurance kicks in. This could range from zero to thousands of dollars.

It may not sound like deductibles are in the best interest of the beneficiary, but they can provide benefits. Often, the cost of monthly premiums will be reduced if a beneficiary agrees to pay a higher deductible.

If you are healthy and do not frequently utilize health-care services, you may choose to pay a higher deductible. This could save considerable costs. Instead of paying high monthly fees, you will pay first from your deductible if you require preventive care or need emergency services. Since your healthy state makes it less likely that you will require medical care, the odds may be in your favor to spend less in this scenario. You still have the benefits of insurance should a catastrophic event occur.

Likewise, you could agree to pay higher premiums in order to lower your deductible. If you use health-care services more frequently, it may be less expensive in the long run to spread your costs out monthly as a premium instead of paying higher upfront costs from a deductible. A single hospitalization could result in significant out-of-pocket costs, an option that may not be financially viable for many seniors, or anyone for that matter.

In a perfect world, premiums would be low and deductibles nonexistent, but insurance companies would soon find themselves out of business. Plans without any deductible tend to be costly.

For Medicare, the benefit of a deductible is more one-sided. Because individual plan options do not exist when it comes to Original Medicare, the deductible is a fixed expense that you cannot negotiate. You get what you get. Medicare Part C and Part D plans, which are run by private insurers, however, do allow you to set priorities for how you would prefer your dollars spent.

Original Medicare

When Medicare was first enacted, all beneficiaries were on the same playing field. Regardless of how much money you made or had put into the system, you would be charged the same amount in premiums, copays, and coinsurance. This has evolved over time and beneficiaries need to be aware so that they can plan accordingly.

There is no negotiating with Original Medicare. Medicare Part A and Part B cover what they cover. No plan options exist from which you can pick and choose. For that reason, the costs for Original Medicare are straightforward and easy to project.

Medicare Part A

Most Americans do not have to pay a monthly premium for Part A because they or their spouse has paid more than 40 quarters (10 years) in Medicare-taxed employment. Medicare calculates these costs based on quarters as opposed to years, though years may be more instinctive for people to remember. If you have contributed fewer than 40 quarters, you have to pay a premium. Monthly premiums cost $234 for those who have worked 30 to 39 quarters (7.5 to 9.75 years), or as much as $426 for those who have worked fewer than 30 quarters (less than 7.25 years).

Rather than having a fixed annual deductible, Medicare Part A has deductibles that occur with each inpatient hospitalization or *skilled nursing facility* stay. Skilled nursing facilities may include convalescent homes, nursing homes, or rehabilitation centers if certain criteria are met.

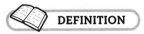 **DEFINITION**

> A **skilled nursing facility** (SNF) is a residential facility where an individual receives full-time care from trained professionals in audiology, nursing, occupational, physical therapy, and/or speech therapy.

For inpatient hospitalizations in 2014, the Part A deductible was $1,216 for each stay. This amount covers hospital expenses, excluding physician fees, up to 60 days. For hospital stays longer than this, Medicare charges $304 per day for days 61 to 90 and $608 for days 91 and over.

Medicare sets a limit on the number of days in the hospital they will pay for after you stay more than 90 days in a row. They cap this at 60 "lifetime reserve days." For example, if you stayed in the hospital for 100 days, you would have used 10 of your lifetime days (100 days in hospital – 90 days standard coverage = 10 lifetime reserve days used). You would have 50 days left (60 lifetime reserve days – 10 lifetime reserve days used = 50 lifetime reserve days remaining) to use if you needed to stay in the hospital for future extended stays. If you had another hospital stay lasting 100 days, your lifetime reserve days would then be reduced to 40, etc. After you have exhausted your 60 lifetime reserve days, Medicare no longer pays for the length of any stay beyond 90 days and the hospital will bill you directly.

If you are admitted to the hospital again within 30 days of your discharge and the admission is considered related to the same medical problem, you may not need to pay a second deductible. Your stay may be considered part of the same inpatient admission.

Admissions to skilled nursing facilities work similar to inpatient stays. Part A covers the first 20 days of your stay at no extra charge. For days 21–100, you will be charged $152 per day. After 100 days, you will be responsible for all costs.

Summary of Medicare Part A Costs in 2014

Type of Inpatient Stay	Number of Days in the Facility	Costs to You
Inpatient hospitalization	1–60	Up to $1,216
Inpatient hospitalization	61–90	$304 per day
Inpatient hospitalization	91+	$608 per day up to 60 days over your lifetime
Skilled nursing facility	0–20	Covered at no extra charge
Skilled nursing facility	21–100	$152 per day
Skilled nursing facility	101+	No coverage

Medicare Part B

Monthly premiums for Part B vary depending on your income, ranging from $104.90 for those earning less than $85,000 to $335.70 per month for those earning more than $214,000. Medicare will use your tax returns from two years prior to make the determination. This is because the last tax return that would be available to them would have been completed the year before and would have reflected taxes paid for the year before that.

The annual deductible for Part B in 2014 was $147 regardless of your income and remains unchanged for 2015. This deductible is projected to increase by $25 for new enrollees starting in 2018 with an additional $25 added to the deductible in 2020 and 2022, again for new enrollees only. Monthly premiums will also remain unchanged from 2014 to 2015.

Summary of Medicare Part B Costs in 2014

Beneficiary Income	Annual Deductible	Monthly Premium
Lowest income bracket (< $85,000)	$147	$104.90
Highest income bracket (> $214,000)	$147	$335.70

Optional Medicare

Because private insurance companies have contracted with the government to provide Medicare Part C and Part D plans, you will have a wide range of plans to choose from. Your final costs ultimately will depend on the plan you select, whether it is a basic or more extensive plan.

No one plan covers all medications or services. It is important to seek out a plan that offers services that best meet your needs, both medically and financially. Though similar plans may be offered by different insurance companies, each insurer may charge different rates. It is important to do your homework and shop around to get the most for your dollar.

TIP

You can choose to have Original Medicare (Parts A and B) or Medicare Advantage (Part C), but not both. Medicare Advantage plans include Part A, Part B, and can also include Part D plans among other offerings. A cost and plan comparison should be done to see which option better suits your needs.

There are no pre-set premium rates for Medicare Advantage plans, making it difficult to provide detailed information about costs without listing out rates from hundreds of insurance agencies across all states and some U.S. territories. You are encouraged to look into options in your state.

Medicare Part D plans, however, do have fundamental costs that we can talk about. The minimum monthly premium was set at $32.42 in 2014, though most people opted for more complex plans. While the final premium costs will be based on the plan you choose, additional fees may be tacked onto that premium depending on your income bracket. These additional fees do not apply if you earn less than $85,000 per year, but are as high as $69.30 per month if you as an individual earn more than $214,000. As with Medicare Part B premiums, these rates are projected to increase by 5 to 15 percent over the next 10 years, depending on your income bracket, if you earn more than $85,000 as an individual.

Buyer Beware

Deductibles, premiums, copays, and coinsurance are costs that many people anticipate they will pay when they sign up for an insurance plan. What isn't immediately transparent are the hidden fees. These are predominantly late fees for Parts A, B, and D. Understanding when you need to sign up for Medicare to avoid these late penalties can save you hundreds to thousands of dollars. This will be discussed in detail in Chapter 7.

What Will You Pay?

As you plan for the future or even for right now, understanding how much you are obligated to pay toward Medicare is essential to guiding your financial decisions.

ROUND TABLE

Loraine, Eileen, Thomas, and George all have different backgrounds and financial situations. You will see how their finances evolve as they maximize their Medicare benefits throughout the book.

Below is a summary of the basics of Medicare costs. The listed Part D costs outline the lowest possible projected costs you would pay with the most basic plan. Costs could be much higher depending on the plan you select.

Cost Estimates for Medicare in 2014

Medicare Part	Annual Deductible Costs	Annual Premium Costs	Total Annual Costs
Part A	Up to $1,216 per inpatient hospitalization if an admission is indicated	$0–$5,112	$0–$5,112
Part B	Up to $147	$1,112–$3,881	$1,259–$4,028
Part C	Variable by plan	Variable by plan	Variable by plan
Part D	$0–310	$389–$1,220 (lowest projected cost based on income)	$389–$1,530 (lowest projected cost based on income)

The Least You Need to Know

- Coinsurance, copayments, deductibles, and premiums are costs you must pay as part of Medicare.

- The Medicare payroll tax rate is 2.9 percent. Half of these taxes are paid by you and half by your employer. Self-employed individuals must pay the full amount.

- The Additional Medicare Tax charges an extra 0.9 percent tax to those who earn more than $200,000 as an individual or a combined $250,000 income as a married couple.

- Enrollment in Medicare Part A is free for Americans if they worked more than 40 quarters (10 years) in Medicare taxed employment.

- Medicare Part B and Part D plans may cost more based on your income.

- Medicare Advantage and Part D plans have variable rates and premiums based on the private companies that offer them.

- Original Medicare may cost as little as $1,259 to several thousand dollars a year.

PART 2

Enrolling for Medicare

If you thought signing up for Medicare would be easy, be prepared for the red tape. While some people are automatically enrolled in the program, many are not.

Initial enrollment periods, general enrollment periods, open enrollment periods, special enrollment periods, each one has a different timeline. The trick is that you can only sign up for certain parts of Medicare at certain times, and if you do not sign up at the right time, you could be on the hook for expensive late penalties.

Knowing which enrollment periods apply to you is key to getting a healthy start with Medicare. More importantly, understanding which parts of Medicare you should sign up for, and when to do it, will impact your future. This part will be your stopwatch.

Qualifying for Medicare

One of the keys to gaining access to health care in the United States is knowing when you are eligible. Private insurance policies are always available, but they can be expensive. Too often the costs are not feasible for individuals and families. For this reason, many people opt out of health care. In 2010, 49 million people were without health insurance according to the 2011 Current Population Survey conducted by the U.S. government.

The reality is that a single health crisis can break the bank, costing hundreds to thousands of dollars in some cases. This is all the more reason why people need to educate themselves about their options to protect their health and longevity, both medically and financially. The Affordable Care Act has proffered health-care opportunities to families with limited resources, but Medicare remains a key tenant for those who qualify.

In This Chapter

- Meeting criteria for Medicare by age
- When taxes count and when they don't
- Medical conditions that qualify for Medicare
- The long road for disabilities
- What to do when you are denied Medicare

When Age Is Not Just a Number

No one likes to think of themselves as getting older but it's one of those facts of life that cannot be denied. As we age, our bodies change. Our hearts are more likely to slow down and our arteries tend to get stiffer, losing some of their elasticity. This can increase the risk of high blood pressure and heart disease. However, many of these things can also happen in younger people who are predisposed to these conditions based on their genetics or whose lifestyles may be unhealthy.

Other medical issues that may worsen with age include the following:

- Bone thinning

- Constipation

- Dry mouth

- Muscle weakness

- Hearing loss

- Memory changes

- Receding gums

- Skin fragility with thinning and increased bruising

- Urinary problems (enlarged prostates in men, incontinence in women who have given birth to children or have had hysterectomies, etc.)

- Vision changes (cataracts, macular degeneration, etc.)

Many of these changes are associated with medications used to treat a number of medical conditions, and many others are triggered by nutritional deficiencies caused by not eating the proper balance of fiber, protein, or vitamins. That said, the majority of these changes are a consequence of wear and tear on our bodies over time. Our bodies do not rejuvenate as well as they did when our cells were younger, making us more prone to disease and illness. Research continues to explore ways to slow the aging process. Alas, we do not have the answer just yet.

 TIP

While you may always remain young at heart, your age can provide you benefits. Not only does your age gain you life experience but it also offers you opportunities to save. You may become eligible for many services, most importantly Medicare. Make the most of it.

This does not mean you have to be a victim to age. The best way to minimize these changes is to life a healthy lifestyle with regular activity, a healthy balanced diet, and engagement in social activities to keep the mind sharp. How you take care of your body will decide how well it feels and for how long. You may not be able to stop the aging process but there are things you can do to slow it down.

Hitting Age 65

There comes a time when you will be considered a senior citizen and that unwanted "e" word, elderly, sneaks its way into the dialogue. There are different definitions for what it means to be a senior citizen. Colloquially, a senior citizen may refer to someone who is retired. I know many people who have worked into their 70s and they would love that definition! Long live their youth! Does this also mean you never become a senior citizen if you never worked in a paying job? What about all those stay-at-home parents out there who have the best and hardest job in the world?

Clearly, that definition is insufficient because it cannot be standardized for the purposes of offering government support. Worldwide, it becomes a bigger conundrum. With different life expectancies in developing versus modernized countries, how can we set an acceptable social definition for old age?

The United Nations has designated old age as anyone living more than 60 years. The World Health Organization has set their old age definition at 50 years for those in Africa. As of this publication, the United States government recognizes the magic number to be 65. The possibility of extending the Medicare eligibility age to 67 years old remains a hot topic and that will be discussed in a later chapter.

Age is more than chronology. Functionality plays a major role. In our country, the odds of having reduced functionality after age 65 are considered higher, and federally funded support services are deemed appropriate. Up until age 65, gainful employment is likely for most adults, statistically speaking. With gainful employment, in theory, comes the ability to pay for health care. To this end, Americans 65 years and older are deemed eligible for Medicare.

Enrollment Prior to 65

It is possible for those younger than 65 to gain access to Medicare. Their eligibility is based on medical conditions or disabilities that are expected to have long-term consequences.

Similar to the aging principles discussed above, specific medical problems and disabilities can limit your functionality, deeming it a challenge to earn wages or finance your own health care. Conditions recognized for Medicare eligibility include end-stage renal disease and amyotrophic lateral sclerosis, among others. Eligibility for Social Security Disability or Railroad Retirement Board benefits may also entitle you to Medicare.

Medicare Tax Dollars

It is a common misunderstanding that you have to pay Medicare payroll taxes in order to be eligible for the program. Generally speaking, anyone over 65 years old who is a United States citizen or permanent legal resident is eligible for Medicare, no matter what. Whether or not you paid Medicare payroll taxes will determine how much you pay for the program, not your eligibility. For those who worked more than 40 quarters in a Medicare-taxed job, Medicare Part A is free. Those who worked a lesser amount or not at all will pay a monthly premium. This will be addressed in detail in Chapter 10.

 TIP

To be eligible for Medicare by age 65, you must first be either a United States citizen or a legal resident of the country for five consecutive years. Legal residency must be established and actively ongoing before you can sign up for Part B.

Noncitizens who have paid sufficient Social Security taxes or who have participated in the U.S. military may be eligible for Social Security benefits as well. If they are disabled, they can then become eligible for Medicare after 25 months of receiving SSDI benefits.

Those who meet Medicare criteria based on underlying medical conditions or disabilities may need to meet additional requirements. Forty quarters of employment are required to achieve eligibility based on end-stage renal disease.

Qualifying Under a Spouse

Apparently, who we marry makes a difference to the federal government. If your spouse meets Medicare eligibility requirements, you may too. It depends on whether you are currently married, widowed, or divorced and whether or not you remain single or remarried.

If you are 65 years old and have not worked 40 quarters of Medicare-taxed employment, you could still get Medicare Part A for free if your spouse worked the mandatory amount of time, assuming you have been married to that person for at least one year. Your spouse must be at least 62 years old for this to apply.

You are also eligible if you remain single after divorce or become widowed. Once you remarry, if your former spouse is alive, you can no longer benefit from that spouse's record. If your former spouse is deceased and you remarried after you were 60 years of age, you could still be eligible for benefits based on your former spouse's record.

Widowed status for Medicare purposes only counts if you were married for at least nine months and divorced status only if you were married for 10 years or longer.

Remarriages can be tricky for Medicare purposes. If your second marriage dissolves for any reason, be it divorce or death, you may then be eligible to use either spouse's record to meet eligibility requirements.

Different rules may apply for those in domestic partnerships or same-sex marriages. The Defense of Marriage Act (DOMA) will be discussed in Chapter 6.

Qualifying Under Disability

When Medicare was enacted in 1965, the program was limited to senior citizens. In 1972, Medicare underwent the first of a series of expansions to cover people with certain diseases and long-term disabilities, regardless of their age. While many of us are likely to develop health problems as we get older, people at any age may be at risk for medical problems based on genetics or plain old bad luck. It seems morally fitting to address the needs of those with physical and mental handicaps who would otherwise have difficulty accessing health-care coverage.

If you have a long-term disability, you may qualify for Social Security Disability Insurance (SSDI) benefits. When you do, this may also make you eligible for Medicare, even if you're under age 65. Likewise, if you qualify for Railroad Retirement Board (RRB) benefits, a separate social security system specific to American railroad employees and their families, you may also meet Medicare's criteria for coverage.

Kidney Disease

Kidney disease is all too common in our country. The United States Census Bureau estimates that 1 in 10 Americans has some degree of kidney impairment. For some people, the kidneys only have temporary deficiencies that recover to normal, or at least functioning, levels. For others the kidneys continue to struggle and even fail, unable to properly filter the blood and flush toxins out of the body. This condition could be life threatening.

When kidney failure cannot be reversed, it is called end-stage renal disease (ESRD). People with ESRD are often started on dialysis or put on the National Organ Transplant Waiting List. In 2011 alone, 113,136 Americans were treated for ESRD. In August 2014, more than 100,000 were on the waiting list for a kidney transplant.

Medicare recognizes ESRD to be a severe disease warranting coverage regardless of someone's age. In order to be eligible for Medicare coverage, as an ESRD patient you must also meet two other criteria:

1. You must satisfy eligibility requirements for SSDI or RRB benefits.

2. You, your spouse, or your guardian (if you are a dependent) must have paid Medicare taxes into the system for at least 40 quarters as your *employment duration*.

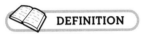 **DEFINITION**

Medicare defines **employment duration** based on quarters worked rather than years. There are three months in a quarter and four quarters in one year.

If you have ESRD, these conditions qualify you for Medicare. There is no need to go through an application process and multiple waiting periods that those with certain other disabilities are subject to. You can apply for Medicare immediately and receive the health care that you need. Benefits begin three months after you begin dialysis treatment.

ALS

In 2000, Congress passed legislation to add Amyotrophic Lateral Sclerosis (ALS) to Medicare's list of covered medical conditions. ALS is less common than ESRD but the disease is rapidly progressive and life threatening. Commonly referred to as Lou Gehrig's Disease, ALS is a devastating neurologic condition that attacks nerves in the brain and spine. As the nerves break down and degenerate, muscles in the body weaken, ultimately resulting in paralysis and an inability to breathe. There is no cure for the condition though studies are underway.

The ALS Association reports that on average 30,000 United States citizens have ALS at any given time and 5,600 new diagnoses are made every year. Similar to ESRD, if you are suffering from ALS you would qualify for Medicare coverage when you demonstrate eligibility for SSDI or RRB benefits, without the application process and multiple waiting periods that those with certain other disabilities must undergo.

Other Disabilities

Kidney disease and ALS are specifically mentioned in the Medicare legislation, but that does not mean that other disabilities are not given fair consideration. Disability can happen for a number of other reasons, both physical and mental. The government requires that a series of steps be taken to demonstrate the extent of a disability before it will consider appropriateness for Medicare coverage. If you have other qualifying disabilities, in addition to demonstrating eligibility for SSDI or RRB benefits, you must wait for the actual approval of your application and subsequent waiting period before you can apply for Medicare.

Applying for Disability Benefits

The first step requires completion of an application for SSDI. It is a cumbersome process that requires you to complete paperwork explaining and justifying your functional limitations. In addition, you must be evaluated by a physician. Your doctor needs to document the nature of your condition, report physical examination findings, and provide an expectation of how long your disability will last. An anticipated illness duration of more than 12 months is necessary to meet eligibility criteria.

Your application must then be forwarded to the Social Security Administration (SSA) for approval. Unfortunately, the SSA process can be very slow, taking anywhere from three to six months to respond yes or no to an application. SSA's Compassionate Allowances Program lists 225 medical conditions that may hasten consideration of a case. The conditions on this list tend to be more aggressive and often have poor prognoses. Examples of conditions on this list include acute leukemia, early-onset Alzheimer's disease, malignant multiple sclerosis, and pancreatic cancer. The complete list can be found at ssa.gov/compassionateallowances/conditions.htm.

 DID YOU KNOW?

Sixty-five percent of initial SSDI applications are denied by the Social Security administration. This often requires applicants to appeal their cases to the courts.

Once your application is approved, SSDI benefits do not begin immediately. There is a five-month waiting period before they take effect. During this time, you remain ineligible for Medicare. In the meantime, it is important to have other health insurance coverage if possible to make sure you have access to the care you need.

Next comes a second waiting period. Medicare eligibility is not granted until you have received SSDI benefits for at least 25 months (24-month waiting period with an application for Medicare in the twenty-fifth month). Lobbyists are actively trying to decrease or discontinue this second Medicare waiting period, stating that it is leaving people in need without access to health care for years at a time.

If SSDI is discontinued for any reason, your Medicare eligibility is also lost. You may become eligible for Medicare in the future if you meet disability criteria and again undertake the application process. Having gone through the SSA process once does not necessarily mean that your second application will be processed at a faster rate. Once eligibility age is reached, regardless of disability status, you qualify for Medicare.

The application process for RRB disability benefits is a little more streamlined. Necessary forms and documents regarding your medical condition, including medical examination, are submitted as with SSDI. The expectation of a disability lasting longer than 12 months remains. Within 100 days, a decision will be made regarding your application. If approved, there is no five-month waiting period before you receive those benefits, but the 25-month waiting period remains before you will be eligible for Medicare, unless you have ESRD or ALS as discussed previously.

Returning to Work with Disabilities

You may want to return to work even if you have a disability. This would suggest that your disability is not severe enough to warrant continuation of your SSDI benefits. Without ongoing SSDI benefits, you lose your eligibility for Medicare. How do you proceed?

The government does not want to discourage people from seeking gainful employment. In fact, it wants to do the exact opposite. It aims to encourage people to become independent so that they can rely less on cash benefit programs from the government over time. For this reason, the Ticket to Work and Work Incentives Improvements Act (TWWIIA) was enacted in 1999.

Tickets are awarded to qualifying SSDI beneficiaries who apply to the program between the ages of 18 and 64 years of age. These tickets allow them to access training services that may allow them to reenter the work force. The tickets are essentially used as vouchers to purchase training.

The Social Security Administration establishes approved employment networks (ENs) that will provide training and work to those requesting entry into the Ticket to Work program. These ENs may include vocational rehabilitation programs and other employment support services. These can range from state to local agencies as well as for-profit and non-profit agencies, including colleges and universities.

As an enrollee, you work together with an EN to set an individual work plan that will provide the skills that will most assist your return to work in light of your disability. You may work with one EN at a time but may transition to another EN as needed to garner additional skills and resources. An individual EN is not required to provide every type of service.

 ROUND TABLE

Thomas is struggling with a decision. After sustaining an injury from a motor vehicle accident several years ago, he has undergone repeated surgeries and suffers from tremors in his arms and legs, chronic pain, and difficulty walking. He wants to return to work, but he is uncertain if his condition will allow him to be successful. He is afraid to lose his SSDI and Medicare benefits. As long as he applies and is accepted into the Ticket to Work program offered through Social Security, he can continue his benefits while he explores his options.

If you just jumped into training and started working, you would lose eligibility to SSDI and therefore Medicare. If after you began employment you realized that your disability proved to be too limiting to sustain meaningful work, you would be stuck between a rock and a hard place. It would take another application for SSDI with the waiting periods of 5 months for SSDI benefits and another 24 months for Medicare before your benefits are restored to their previous level. The Ticket to Work program allows you to continue to receive benefits while you establish and test your skills.

The Ticket to Work program is divided into two phases. The first of these is the trial work period (TWP), which spans nine months; these months do not need to be consecutive. You may be eligible for a second trial work period if you work less than nine months over a five year period. During your TWP, you continue to receive SSDI benefits and Medicare. At the end of the period, it will be determined if you have achieved substantial gainful activity (SGA). If your gross income is more than the designated dollar amount set for SGA, your benefits will be discontinued.

If you are found to still have a disability after your TWP, you may then enter the second phase of the program known as the extended period of eligibility (EPE). The EPE extends your SSDI benefits an additional 36 months and your Medicare eligibility for 93 months. For months when you earn more than the SGA amount, you will not receive SSDI benefits; for those you don't, you will receive a benefit check. There are few exceptions to the rule.

The first Tickets to Work were provided to beneficiaries in February 2002 across 13 states and the program was extended in January 2003 to all states in addition to the U.S. territories of American Samoa, Guam, Northern Marianas, Puerto Rico, and U.S. Virgin Islands. It has provided a tremendous resource to disabled individuals to encourage them toward a road of financial independence.

Does Age Matter?

Medicare offers coverage for approved disabilities regardless of age but some limitations apply. Once you meet Medicare eligibility based on age, you may have additional options, including access to Medigap plans. If you had been penalized with Medicare late fees, those late fees could be discontinued once you reach 65 years old. These issues will be addressed in more detail in subsequent chapters.

Meeting Plan Requirements

The good news is that there are no plan requirements for Original Medicare outside of the eligibility requirements listed previously. The optional components of Medicare—Part C and Part D—as well as supplemental Medigap insurance, however, have more leeway to set requirements since they are run by private companies.

Pre-existing conditions is a cringe-worthy phrase that makes you shift in your chair for the ethical issues surrounding it. For private insurance, this is capitalism at work. If you have a pre-existing medical condition, you will spend more health-care dollars and cost the company more than someone without those conditions. Insurance companies in the past could charge you more in fees to make up for anticipated lost profits. In some cases, insurers would even refuse to cover someone if they thought their health-care expenses would be too high for their company goals. This, unfortunately, decreased affordable health-care access to those who needed it most.

The Affordable Care Act (ACA) turned that all around, stating that an insurance company could not deny coverage to people for pre-existing conditions nor could they increase costs to beneficiaries for that reason. This took effect in 2010 for children and subsequently for adults as of January 1, 2014.

Still, there are always exceptions—so called "grandfathered plans." Plans that were in existence prior to passage of the law on March 23, 2010, could continue as they had pre-Obamacare as long as they did not make considerable changes to what they covered. Such changes would signify the creation of a new plan that would then have to meet ACA standards.

 TIP

If you have a grandfathered plan, you may need to change your health-care plan in 2015 to one that meets the rules and regulations set by the Affordable Care Act. Consult your insurance agent to see if you fall into this category to avoid missing enrollment periods that could otherwise result in late fees.

If you are enrolled in a grandfathered plan, you could still be denied coverage or charged more for pre-existing conditions. The government mandates that these plans lose their grandfathered status in 2015, meaning that the insurance companies will have to add coverage for those conditions or otherwise discontinue the plan altogether.

Applying for optional components of Medicare or Medigap may cost you more money if done outside designated enrollment periods.

What to Do If You Don't Qualify

Not everyone will qualify for Medicare and that could leave some in a costly bind. As we discussed, private insurance can be expensive. When the chips are down, what other options do you have to make ends meet? Once you turn 65, you will become eligible as long as you meet residency requirements. Here are some tips to get you through until that time.

Hopping onto Your Spouse's Coverage

If you are married and do not qualify for Medicare benefits, your best option may be to make the most out of your spouse's coverage. That is, if they have some and it's under a private insurance plan. If they are on Medicare, you are out of luck.

Insurance plans usually have an open enrollment period when a beneficiary is allowed to make changes to their coverage, including adding spouses or dependents to their plan. This is when you can get in on the action, no questions asked.

If you want to sign up for insurance outside of that open enrollment period, you need to justify why to the insurance company. For example, if you just lost your job and subsequently your health insurance, this would be considered a life-changing event that most insurers would allow for immediate sign-up. However, if you had other insurance and wanted to change to your spouse's coverage for a better deal, that would not be enough to qualify you for coverage outside of open enrollment, at least for most companies. Some insurers may allow you to sign up but at higher rates. Essentially, there needs to be some "qualifying life event" that takes place to warrant adding you to your spouse's health insurance outside of the open enrollment period and at the same cost.

Extending Employee Benefits with COBRA

Thanks to the Consolidated Omnibus Budget Reconciliation Act (COBRA) of 1986, you may be eligible for health insurance through your employer when you leave that job. If you worked for a company that employed more than 20 full-time equivalent employees, COBRA mandates that an employer provide insurance coverage to those who left their position for qualifying reasons. The coverage offered must be the same as that offered to you while you were actively employed. This coverage extends to the former employee, their spouse, and their dependents for a limited amount of time.

You have 60 days to decide whether or not to sign up for COBRA coverage. This is known as an election period. If you initially decline COBRA benefits for you and your family, you can always change your mind and sign up for coverage as long as you do so within this election period. Coverage under COBRA may extend as long as 36 months.

 **CAUTION**

A company must employ the equivalent of 20 full-time employees to be mandated to offer COBRA coverage. Part-time employees will count toward that number based on their percentage of full-time employment. For smaller companies, this distinction is significant. Take the example of a company that employs 28 people with some of them being part-time. This could be 10 full-time employees plus 18 half-time employees (equal to 9 full-time employees). This would equate to 19 full-time employees. This company would not have to offer you COBRA coverage, but a company that employed those 18 employees at three-quarters employment would cross that threshold of 20 full-time equivalent employees. Know your rights.

Insurance offered by your employer is usually cheaper than insurance you could purchase on your own because your employer has negotiated a group rate with the insurance company. Also, as part of your employment contract, your employer may also pay a percentage of the cost toward your health-care expenses when you are actively working.

When you stop working, your employer is required to offer you COBRA insurance benefits at the group rate, but they do not have to contribute the dollar amount they had paid on your behalf when you were actively working. For this reason, the costs of COBRA insurance are often considerably higher than what you paid when you were on the job. Still, the expenses are lower than they would otherwise be if you were paying for that same insurance plan on your own without a group rate.

Medicare eligibility affects the timeline for COBRA benefits. Different scenarios that could qualify you or disqualify you from COBRA benefits will be discussed in Chapter 14.

Participating in the Health-Care Exchange

People who had not previously been able to afford health insurance may now have options based on health-care exchanges developed by the Affordable Care Act. These health-care programs are run by participating states who accept subsidies from the federal government.

The ultimate goal of the ACA is to improve access to care for all Americans. In fact, Americans who did not have health coverage by March 31, 2014 are subjected to a monthly fine. Businesses with more than 100 full-time equivalent employees were able to offer these exchange plans to their workers for health-care coverage after November 2014 and those with less than 25 full-time equivalent employees may even get tax breaks for offering health-care coverage.

The ACA does not come free. In order to generate funds for the program, the government will increase taxes on small businesses, in particular those earning more than $250,000 per year and those employing more than 50 full-time equivalent employees, if they do not offer health insurance to their employees by January 1, 2016. Insurance companies also face increased taxation. Budget cuts to other government programs in addition to raising Medicare Part A premiums also assist in funding the ACA.

Using Your Retiree Health Benefits

Employers may offer retiree health benefits, though this trend is on the decline. Larger companies, usually those employing 200 full-time equivalent employees or more, are more likely to contribute to plans than smaller companies. In 1988, 66 percent of these larger companies offered the benefit, but the number decreased to 29 percent in 2013, according to the Henry J. Kaiser Family Foundation.

Retiree health plans fall into two categories, those offering benefits before 65 years old and those after. Pre-65 plans often include the same level of coverage benefits as active employees, whereas those tailored to retirees older than 65 years of age tend to be supplements to Medicare. On average, pre-65 retiree health plans cost employers twice as much as supplemental plans.

Employer-health plans may even negotiate with private insurance companies offering Medicare Advantage and Medicare Part D plans to group rates for reduced premiums. The number of Medicare Advantage group plans increased from 1.7 million in 2008 to 2.5 million in 2013. Health reimbursement accounts may also be used to fund retiree benefits. In this case, funds are set aside for the employee to use for nongroup based coverage.

How are these plans funded? It depends. Premium costs may be completely covered by the employer, shared between the employee and the retiree, or directed in full to the retiree. It depends on the contractual agreements made. Make sure you understand where your plan falls if you will be relying on a retiree plan now or in the future.

More and more employers are tightening restrictions on their retiree benefit plans, e.g., increasing eligibility requirements or capping how much they will pay, and some have stopped offering them altogether. In this time of health-care reform, they may be too expensive for some employers to maintain into your retirement years.

Benefitting from Your Union Dues

Depending on your job, you may have had opportunity to join a labor union. Unions are organizations that represent employees in different industries, examples being the American Federation of Teachers and the United Mine Workers of America. Using collective bargaining, unions aim to improve wages and benefits for their members and also provide resources to them during times of labor disputes. Benefits sometimes include pensions that pay a fixed income to members upon retirement. These services come at the expense of union dues.

Health benefits have been negotiated between unions and employers for decades. According to the American Federation of Labor and Congress of Industrial Organizations (AFL–CIO), 85 percent of union members nationwide have health care access compared to only 54 percent of nonunion workers. The insurance plans negotiated by unions tend to be less expensive, averaging 9 percent less for individuals and 15 percent less for families. If you have the opportunity to join a union, you may be able to spend less toward health-care costs.

This may be changing with passage of the Affordable Care Act, however. Because smaller employers do not have to offer coverage to part-time workers under the new regulations, a concerning trend has been seen where worker hours are being reduced. By working fewer hours, these union workers not only lose wages but also their important health-care benefits.

Employers may no longer be incentivized to offer employer-sponsored health plans if they can have their workers enroll in plans offered through ACA's health-care exchanges for less money. It will be interesting to see what happens once contract negotiations expire.

The Least You Need to Know

- You qualify for Medicare only if you have U.S. citizenship or can supply proof of continuous legal residency of at least five years.
- To be eligible for Medicare, you must be age 65 or older, or you must meet certain disability criteria.
- People with certain medical conditions or disabilities have a waiting period of at least 25 months before being eligible for Medicare.
- You can return to work with a disability and keep your Medicare benefits if you participate in the Ticket to Work program.
- You may qualify for free Medicare Part A if your spouse or former spouse contributed 40 quarters in Medicare-taxed employment.
- You cannot be disqualified for coverage based on pre-existing conditions.
- If you do not qualify for Medicare, you may consider ACA's health-care exchanges, COBRA, retiree health plans, and union-negotiated health benefits as alternatives.

How to Enroll

In order to use Medicare, you must be enrolled in the program. For some, this happens automatically, but others who are eligible need to take action and sign up. You cannot get the health care you are entitled to if you don't take the necessary steps.

Automatic Enrollment

If you meet the right criteria, you will automatically be enrolled in Medicare without taking any additional action on your own. It's important to understand what those criteria are so you know whether or not you need to act.

Retiring with Social Security

Automatic enrollment in Medicare is dependent upon enrollment in Social Security. The majority of Americans will rely on Social Security benefits as the full complement or a supplement to their income when they retire. How much income you earn depends on when you were born.

In This Chapter

- When you are automatically enrolled in Medicare
- When you have to apply for Medicare on your own
- How to apply for Medicare benefits
- How Medicare relates to your other health insurance
- Special considerations that may affect how you enroll for Medicare

Social Security's Definition of Retirement Age

Year of Birth	Retirement Age
1937 and prior	65 years old
1938–1942	65 years old + 2 months added for every year in series
1943–1954	66 years old
1955–1959	66 years old + 2 months added for every year in series
1960 and later	67 years old

You will receive the full retirement benefit from Social Security if you stop working at the designated retirement age. If you begin to collect Social Security at a younger age, the youngest eligible age being 62 years old, you will only receive a percentage of the benefit and that lower value will continue long-term. Whether or not to make this sacrifice is a decision each person must make based on their financial needs.

Even if you are eligible for Social Security, you do not automatically receive SSI benefits. You need to contact your local Social Security office to decide at what age you want to begin to receive payments. For most retired people, you can elect for benefits starting at 62 years old, though payments will be lower unless you wait until you reach Social Security's recommended retirement age as listed in the above table. If you are widowed or disabled, you may be able to collect benefits earlier.

TIP

You can calculate your expected Social Security benefits based on your birthday and expected retirement age at ssa.gov/oact/quickcalc/. Know that this is only an estimate. Social Security cannot give you official numbers until you apply.

People who work beyond the designated retirement age are able to earn additional dollars as delayed retirement credits. For every year beyond the full retirement age, you can earn a percentage increase to your Social Security benefits. These benefits add up year after year but stop accruing when you turn 70 years old, meaning you keep the delayed retirement credits that you have earned but you won't earn more after that time. That being the case, there is no benefit to working beyond 70 years old with regard to Social Security.

Social Security's Delayed Retirement Credits

Year of Birth	Percentage Increase in Benefits per Year
1933–1934	5.5%
1935–1936	6.0%
1937–1938	6.5%
1939–1940	7.0%
1941–1942	7.5%
1943 or later	8.0%

When you choose to retire will not only impact how much money you will receive from Social Security but will also determine whether or not you need to apply for Medicare.

Benefits of Social Security

If you actively receive Social Security benefits when you are 65 years old, whether it is for the purposes of retirement or disability, you will be automatically enrolled in Part A and Part B. If you are younger than 65 years old but meet Medicare eligibility for disability after receiving 24 months of SSDI or RRB benefits, you will also be automatically enrolled in your twenty-fifth month of disability.

Any premiums that are due to Medicare will be automatically deducted from your Social Security or RRB checks.

This means you won't have to apply for health care and you do not need to worry about late fees, which can add up to a costly amount. Because Medicare costs are deducted from your Social Security or RRB checks, you won't even get bills from Medicare in the mail.

 TIP

If you live in Puerto Rico or another U.S. territory and are actively receiving Social Security benefits when you turn 65 years old, you will automatically be enrolled in Part A but not Part B.

With every convenience comes a caveat. In this case, you are automatically enrolled in Part B. If you do not want Part B coverage, you will need to take action. If you do not express to Medicare that you want to discontinue your participation in Part B before your coverage begins, you will be responsible to pay those premiums.

As discussed in Chapter 16, instructions are written on the back side of your Medicare card on how to proceed. If you decide to opt-out of Part B after your coverage begins, you need to submit a formal request to Social Security. After SSA receives your request, your coverage will stop on the first day of the following month, e.g., if SSA receives your request on July 11, your coverage will end on August 1. You will be responsible to pay for all premiums up to that time, whether or not you made use of any Part B services.

Medicare gives you a window of time to address your Part B needs. You will receive your Medicare card in the mail three months before your sixty-fifth birthday or three months before your twenty-fifth month of disability benefits. Your Medicare coverage will not take effect until the first day of the month you turn 65, the exception being if your birthday actually lands on the first of the month then your benefits would begin on the first day of the month prior to your birthday. Altogether, this leaves you with two to three months to cancel your Part B coverage before you would be responsible for paying premiums.

 CAUTION

Keep an eye out for your Medicare card if you are eligible for automatic enrollment. If you do not receive your card two to three months prior to your sixty-fifth birthday or by your twenty-fifth month of disability benefits, it could be lost and could affect your window of opportunity to opt-out of Part B, if this is your preference. Contact the Social Security Administration to notify them and make sure your card is on its way.

You are also automatically enrolled for Parts A and B the first month you are eligible for disability benefits by way of SSDI or RRB benefits if you have ALS.

Even though enrollment for Part A and Part B is automatic for those on Social Security or RRB, enrollment in Part D still requires an application. Applying late for Medicare Part D could result in penalties as discussed in Chapter 12.

Not For Everyone

Many people continue working beyond age 65 in order to take home their full Social Security benefits. Looking at the previous charts, you do the math. With baby boomers born between 1946 and 1964, the majority of people approaching Medicare eligibility age will need to work past age 65 to make the most of Social Security.

 TIP

If you have end-stage renal disease, you are eligible for Part A and B but are not automatically enrolled in Medicare.

With people working longer, fewer will be on Social Security when they reach Medicare eligibility age. This means that most Americans will not be automatically enrolled in the program and will need to apply for Medicare. Be aware that Social Security will not send you a reminder notice to let you know your Initial Enrollment Period is approaching. If you do not sign up on time for Medicare, it could cost you, literally. Fines associated with late applications are detailed in Chapter 7.

Applying for Medicare

What are your options to apply for Medicare? You do not apply through CMS as you might expect but through the Social Security Administration. You can apply in one of three ways:

In person. You can schedule an appointment at your local Social Security office. Search for local offices online at secure.ssa.gov/ICON/main.jsp.

By telephone. You can contact the SSA at 1–800–772–1213. A TTY number for the hearing impaired is also available at 1–800–325–0778. Both numbers are toll-free.

Online. This option takes 10 to 30 minutes to complete depending on the complexity of your situation. You can apply at socialsecurity.gov/medicare/apply.html.

You can choose which option is most convenient for you; all are equally effective.

What Information You Need

You will need information on hand to complete your application depending on whether you are applying for Medicare alone or for Medicare with Social Security benefits. Here is what you will need:

Bank information. This includes domestic or international bank accounts with bank names, bank codes, routing numbers, and transit numbers for purposes of direct deposit.

Birth information. This includes your birth date, your birth name, where you were born, and your Permanent Resident Card number if you are not a U.S. citizen.

Dependent information. This includes the names and birth dates of your unmarried children younger than 18 years old, your children aged 18 to 19 years old who are in secondary school, or your children who were disabled before they turned 22 years old.

Employment and self-employment history for the past three years. This includes the business name, dates of employment, and net income if self-employed.

Health insurance information. This includes current employer-sponsored health insurance, dates of coverage, and dates of employment associated with coverage. This would also include Medicaid account numbers and effective dates of coverage, if applicable.

Marital status. This includes the names, birth dates, and social security numbers of your current and any former spouses, if applicable. Former spouses need only be included if you were married for 10 years or more, or if you were widowed after being married for at least 9 months. The dates and locations of marriage are also taken into consideration.

U.S. military history. This includes the branch of the military, your position, and dates of service.

With this information at your disposal, your Medicare application should be easily completed. Social Security will process your application, and coverage will begin according to the enrollment period you used to sign up. See Chapters 7 and 8 to review the details about each type of enrollment period.

Using MyMedicare.gov

Once you are approved for Medicare coverage, you will be given access to your own personal account at MyMedicare.gov. You will receive a welcome letter by mail or email that will review how to register at the site.

The website carries a wealth of information where you can access the status of your Medicare application, review claims and statements, keep track of your medications, and see what preventive screening services you are eligible for. There are video tutorials to guide you through how to use the site to your best advantage. Your computer does need Adobe Flash player and JavaScript installed on it in order for the videos to work properly. The website provides links to download these programs as necessary.

DID YOU KNOW?

The CDC reports that 78 percent of outpatient physician practices used some variant of an electronic health record (EHR) in 2013. The number continues to increase as CMS establishes new reimbursement criteria that will require use of an EHR.

MyMedicare.gov is optional for you but could be a helpful tool to keep track of the ins and outs of your benefits. The website is secure and also allows you to select your own password.

Initial Enrollment Questionnaire

When you are first enrolled, Medicare will not know the details of any other health coverage you have. It could be you have supplemental insurance or you still have a health plan through your employer or your spouse. Medicare will process claims differently depending on the scenario. In some cases, Medicare should be billed first; in others, it should be billed second. Chapter 14 will tackle those situations in more detail.

In order to set the stage for proper claims processing, you will be required to complete an Initial Enrollment Questionnaire (IEQ) when you are first eligible for coverage. This questionnaire can be found on MyMedicare.gov, but for those who choose not to use the website, there remains an option to call in your information at 1–855–798–2627. The questionnaire will be available to you 90 days before and up to 180 days after your coverage begins.

Medicare Secondary Claim Development Questionnaire

There is a second questionnaire that you may or may not need to complete depending on your coverage and the nature of your treatment or injury. You will receive this form, the Medicare Secondary Claim Development Questionnaire, each time a claim is submitted and Medicare is considered appropriate to pay after another insurance provider. In this case, the Medicare Secondary Payer (MSP) provisions apply.

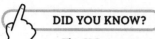

DID YOU KNOW?

The U.S. government enacted the Black Lung Benefits Act of 1973 to provide Worker's Compensation benefits to coal mine workers who developed disability from pneumoconiosis, also known as black lung disease.

You may be asked to complete this form if you have health insurance based on either your own or your spouse's employment, if you are entitled to Black Lung benefits, if you submit a Worker's Compensation case, if you sustain an injury in the setting of no-fault automobile insurance, or if you suffer an injury where another insurer is liable for damages. The sooner you complete this form, the faster the claim can be processed.

Keeping Track of Your Insurance Coverage

Medicare will keep tabs on your health-care coverage through their Benefits Coordination and Recovery Center (BCRC). You need to be proactive in making changes to your account as needed, for example if you change employers or employer-sponsored health insurance. Otherwise, there could be errors made in processing your bills.

The BCRC gathers information from your IEQ, your health-care providers, your other health plans, and your employer. However, you still need to be actively involved. Medicare clearly states that you are responsible to make notifications on your account to assure accuracy.

Applying Under Special Circumstances

As with many government-run programs, things are not always simple and clear cut with Medicare. When applying for Medicare there are certain scenarios that need clarification.

Citizens Living Abroad

If you are a U.S. citizen who lives outside of the country, you will still be automatically enrolled in Part A if you receive Social Security or RRB benefits. However, you must understand that not everyone who lives overseas will be able to collect Social Security. If you are planning to live overseas when you turn 65, you need to know whether or not you will be eligible for automatic enrollment. Otherwise you could be subject to late sign-up fees.

The United States government considers you to be living outside of the country after 30 consecutive days. In order to receive benefits when you are outside of the country, you must meet certain criteria, and these will depend on the country where you are living and whether you have citizenship or residency there. Of course, this assumes you are still eligible for Social Security benefits in the first place.

Countries Where You May Receive U.S. Social Security Benefits Without Restrictions

If You Are a Citizen of the Country	If You Are a Resident of the Country
Austria	Australia
Belgium	Austria
Canada	Belgium
Chile	Canada
Czech Republic	Chile
Finland	Czech Republic
France	Denmark
Germany	Finland
Greece	France
Ireland	Germany
Israel	Greece
Italy	Ireland

If You Are a Citizen of the Country	If You Are a Resident of the Country
Japan	Italy
Luxembourg	Japan
Netherlands	Luxembourg
Norway	Netherlands
Poland	Norway
Portugal	Poland
South Korea	Portugal
Spain	South Korea
Sweden	Spain
Switzerland	Sweden
United Kingdom	Switzerland
	United Kingdom

Benefits may be available in other countries as well but usually with restrictions. If you plan to live for an extended period of time in a country not listed here, visit the Social Security website at (ssa.gov) for details. If you do not qualify for Social Security payments, you will need to enroll in Medicare yourself.

The U.S. government will not provide Social Security benefits if you live in Cuba or North Korea. If you are a U.S. citizen, these payments will be made available to you retroactively if you later move to an approved country, but noncitizen legal residents of the U.S. will lose those dollars altogether.

Even if you actively receive Social Security benefits when you turn 65 years old, if you are living abroad, you will need to apply for Part B. Interestingly, if you are not eligible for Social Security, you cannot enroll in Part B until you return to the United States. In the latter case, you will not need to pay late fees when you sign up for Part B. Otherwise, the usual Part A (if you were not automatically enrolled) and Part B late penalties will be charged if you sign-up after the initial enrollment period. If you have qualifying health insurance or you volunteer in the foreign country, you may still be eligible for sign-up during a Special Enrollment Period without having to pay those penalties.

TIP

You may contact your U.S. Embassy or consulate if you have questions about Medicare enrollment while you live in a foreign country.

If you live outside of the country, you cannot enroll in a Medicare Advantage, Part D, or Medigap plan. These plans require that you live in the United States. You can apply for Part C and Part D when you return to the country. You have two months after returning to the United States to enroll, after which you may need to pay a late fee for Part D coverage.

ROUND TABLE

Eileen decided to take the trip of a lifetime when she retired. She travelled across Europe for nine months, and oops, she missed her Initial Enrollment Period for Medicare. Because she was not on Social Security benefits at the time, she was not automatically enrolled in Original Medicare though she was eligible for free Part A. Now she can apply for Part A and Part B but will have to pay penalties on her Part B premiums for as long as she has Medicare.

Medigap plan access, however, will vary. Once you apply for Part B, you trigger an Open Enrollment Period for Medigap that lasts six months. If you apply after that time, you may have to pay a higher cost for a plan.

You may recall from Chapter 3 that with rare exception, Medicare will not cover health-care services given in a foreign country. Why would someone want to pay for Medicare if they could not use it? If you are planning to return to the United States for any length of time, it could potentially save you money to pay monthly premiums at a lower cost than to pay considerably higher monthly premiums after you return because of late penalties. You will have to make the financial decision that works best for you.

Domestic Partnerships

The Defense of Marriage Act (DOMA) of 1996 caused a great deal of controversy in the United States when it allowed states to refuse to acknowledge same-sex marriages. A consequence of the law was that homosexual couples who lived in states that did not recognize their marriages as valid were therefore not eligible for federal programs based on married status, not able to file joint income taxes, and certainly not able to meet Medicare eligibility based on their spouse's history.

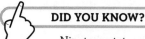

DID YOU KNOW?

Nineteen states and the District of Columbia had legalized same-sex marriages by September of 2014.

DOMA was deemed unconstitutional in 2013, affecting how same-sex couples were viewed when it came to these federal programs. However, it did not change the fact that individual states could set their own restrictions. Because not all states recognize same-sex marriages, it will depend where you live or applied for benefits if you will be eligible for certain Medicare benefits.

If a same-sex couple lives in a state that recognizes their marriage, they now have more rights and entitlements to Medicare that can save them money.

- Whereas the federal government had previously recognized only single income tax returns, your joint income can now be used to define how much you pay for Part B premiums or Part D-IRMAA.

- Now that these marriages are legally recognized, you can become eligible for Medicare based on your spouse's employment record.

- You are now eligible to use a Special Enrollment Period if you receive health benefits through your spouse's employer. In fact, Part A and Part B late fees that had been charged to you because this coverage had not been recognized in the past may be reversed.

If you do not live in a state that recognizes same-sex marriages, you may be out of luck. As of the time of this publication, these federal benefits may not be applied in a state that does not recognize your spousal relationship.

There is one exception, however. If you applied for Medicare benefits when you lived in a state that recognized your marriage but then you moved to a state that does not, your benefits may still apply. If you waited to apply for Medicare until after you moved, you would not be eligible for those federal protections.

Those Who Are Incarcerated

The penal system, not Medicare, pays for health-care services when you are incarcerated. This does not mean that you should not apply or continue your Medicare benefits. You may need these services upon being released from jail or prison. If you delay coverage, you could be subject to late penalties and fees that would significantly increase your premium rates and health-care costs in the future.

Eligibility remains the same as for any other U.S. citizen or legal resident. You will be automatically enrolled in Original Medicare if you are receiving Social Security benefits when you turn 65 years old. However, again, there is an exception. It depends on the length of your incarceration. After 30 days, Social Security will suspend your benefits, and you may need to enroll through the formal application process.

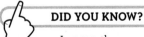

DID YOU KNOW?

In 2013, there were more than 246,000 people incarcerated over the age of 50.

If you are already receiving Medicare benefits when you are incarcerated, you are still responsible to pay those premiums. Since most people get Part A for free, this is rarely the problem. The challenge comes with Part B premiums. Unless you are set up for automatic deductions from your bank account, it can be difficult to pay for Medicare, especially if you never receive those premium statements. Most people who are incarcerated do not change their billing address with Medicare. This means their bills are being sent to an incorrect address, and after three bills have been sent without payment, Medicare will discontinue your coverage.

This can result in significant gaps in coverage once you are released. You will not be eligible to reapply for Medicare until the next General Enrollment Period that runs from January to March. Your coverage will not begin until July 1 of that year.

You need an advocate. A family member, loved one, or even a hired representative can assist you in checking your mail and making timely payments. This could save you considerable cost down the road.

The Least You Need to Know

- You may be automatically enrolled in Part A and Part B if you are receiving Social Security when you turn 65 years old.
- Your Social Security benefits may be withheld if you are living in certain foreign countries or if you are incarcerated, affecting whether or not you will be automatically enrolled in Medicare.
- If you do not apply for Medicare during appropriate enrollment periods, you will be charged costly penalties.
- If you are in a same-sex marriage, you have more entitlements to Medicare since the Defense of Marriage Act was ruled unconstitutional.

Initial Enrollment Periods

Knowing your Medicare eligibility requirements is only half the challenge. Understanding when to sign up for Medicare and how it will impact your wallet makes all the difference. This chapter will discuss the Initial Enrollment Period and the General Enrollment Period.

Initial Enrollment

This is it! If you do not fall in the automatically-enrolled category as discussed in Chapter 6, then this is your one and only chance, your Initial Enrollment Period (IEP). With rare exception, you become eligible for Medicare only once. The decisions you make here will have a lasting impact on how much you spend on your health care down the road.

When You Turn Sixty-Five

Nothing says happy birthday like becoming a senior citizen! Maybe your sweet sixteen comes close. These are all defining moments in our lives, and although you may cringe at the numbers, you should be proud of every single digit. You have a life of unique experiences behind you and more to come.

In This Chapter

* When to take advantage of the Initial Enrollment Period
* Understanding the cost and duration of late penalties
* Calculating the cost of late penalties
* Budgeting for the future

Now that you are eligible for Medicare, hopefully those experiences will be healthier ones at that. At the very least, experiences that are well cared for.

 TIP

> If you are approaching Medicare eligibility age, set a reminder for yourself on when to enroll. There are many apps available for free or for purchase that can be used on your smartphone to set alarms and reminders months and even years in advance. You can even set an alarm on your computer. Do not fall victim to deadlines. Protect yourself and your wallet.

Your IEP begins three months before the month you turn 65 years old and extends for three months beyond that. When you include the month of your birth, this is a seven month window to apply for Medicare if you are not otherwise automatically enrolled.

The age-based IEP applies whether you are living in the United States, living in a foreign country, or in the event that you are incarcerated.

You will not be forewarned about your eligibility date by the Social Security Administration or CMS, which can make it easy for you to miss signing up at the right time. You need to find a clever way to remind yourself.

Why is this so important? Because if you miss this one time deadline, you may be exposed to late penalties in the future. You are eligible to apply for Part A, Part B, Part D, Medicare Advantage plans, and Medigap policies during this IEP.

ESRD

End-stage renal disease qualifies you for Medicare if you demonstrate eligibility for SSDI or RRB benefits and you or your spouse has worked an adequate amount of time in Medicare-taxed employment. This is true regardless of age.

Your window for sign-up is a bit shorter for ESRD than with an age-based IEP. Once you are eligible for Medicare by ESRD, your IEP starts that month and extends three months beyond that for a grand total of four months. Unlike with other disabilities, there is not a 24-month waiting period after meeting SSDI or RRB criteria before you are eligible for Medicare coverage.

No IEP for You

Generally speaking, if you are automatically enrolled in Medicare, you do not have an IEP for Parts A and B. The following conditions fall into that category:

- **ALS.** You are automatically enrolled once you meet SSDI eligibility.

- **Disabilities on SSDI or RRB benefits.** You are automatically enrolled the 25th month of receiving SSDI or RRB benefits.

- **Ongoing Social Security benefits.** You are automatically enrolled if you are receiving benefits when you turn 65.

You will, however, have a limited period of time in which you can apply for Medicare Advantage and Part D plans. Once you are automatically enrolled in Parts A and B, you have three months to make decisions about these optional plans.

If you do not fall into these categories, it is important to verify the dates of your IEP so you can meet enrollment requirements for Parts A and B.

Late Enrollees to Part B

Some people choose to participate in Part A but elect to enroll in Part B after their eligibility date. They may add Part B coverage during the General Enrollment Period that will be discussed in Chapter 8. In this scenario, they are given a new IEP to sign up for Medicare Advantage and Part D plans between April 1 and June 30.

Medicare Payroll Taxes

The amount of time you have paid taxes toward Medicare will impact your coverage options in the future. Taking a careful look at your employment history, or that of your spouse, will decide how much you pay out-of-pocket for years to come.

How Long, Not How Much Paid

Here is where Medicare balances things out. You do not get better Medicare coverage if you put more tax dollars into the system, but you have to put at least the same minimum number of calendar quarters.

For fairness, Medicare taxes are taken out of your paycheck based on a percentage of your income. This does not mean you get better Medicare coverage simply because you put in more dollars. That would be like saying someone who had a higher paying job deserves better health care than someone who did not have the same opportunities in life. Everyone is offered the same options under Original Medicare.

CAUTION

Be careful with any work performed "under the table." This refers to wages that are paid to you without being reported to the federal government. As a result, no taxes are paid. It is illegal for the employer to offer this to you, and it is illegal for you to accept these wages and not report them on your income taxes. Not only are you putting yourself in a position to be investigated by the IRS, but any work you have performed is not counted toward your Medicare eligibility.

Medicare bases eligibility on the number of quarters worked, with three months equaling one quarter. Anyone who works more than 40 quarters (10 years) is eligible to receive Part A for free. The 40 quarters requirement is based on full-time employment, so if you only work part-time you likely need to work for more calendar quarters in order to meet the requirement. From Medicare's perspective, anyone who has not worked the equivalent of 40 full-time quarters has not contributed their fair share and will be required to pay a premium. Someone who worked between 30–39 quarters will pay $234 per month based on 2014 standards. Someone who worked less than 30 quarters will pay $426 per month.

Prior to 2013, spouses in same-sex marriages were unable to use their spouse's employment history to get free Part A. This changed when the Defense of Marriage Act was ruled unconstitutional in 2013. Now you and your spouse will be recognized for Medicare eligibility if you live in a state that recognizes same-sex marriages.

Delay Retirement to Save on Medicare?

You may want to take a very close look at your employment history. Free Medicare Part A can save you anywhere from $2,808 to $5,112 per year depending on how long you or your spouse contributed to Medicare payroll taxes. You can be eligible for free Part A based on your spouse's record if you are 65 years old and your spouse is at least 62 years old and has contributed the necessary 40 quarters in Medicare payroll taxes.

DID YOU KNOW?

> Based on current life expectancies, the average Medicare beneficiary turning 65 years old today will live into their mid-80s. If they receive Part A coverage for free, they would save more than $28,000 over their lifetime compared to a beneficiary who worked less than 30 quarters, and more than $23,000 compared to someone who worked between 30 and 39 quarters in Medicare-taxed employment.

If you are close to earning 30 quarters, it may be worth your time to work longer to at least move to a lower premium bracket. Moving from less than 30 quarters to between 30 and 39 quarters would save you $2,304 per year. Likewise, if you are close to crossing into the 40-quarter bracket, you could save $2,808 per year based on 2014 premium rates. It doesn't take long before you are saving tens of thousands of dollars.

Everyone's situation is different. Taking into consideration your life expectancy, your skill set, and your savings, you can make the choice that best meets your needs.

Penalties for Late Sign Up

The government has a surefire way to add dollars to the Medicare Trust Fund, and it is through your wallet. We have already talked about taxes and premiums, but what I refer to here are the hidden fees.

Of course, the government will say it is not hiding the fact that it charges late penalties. The information is available on its Medicare.gov website. However, people generally do not look at the website or for any information about Medicare until they are actively applying. By then, it may well be too late.

The Social Security Administration will not send you a notice to tell you when you are due to enroll in Medicare. For all intents and purposes, those fees are hidden to you. It is up to you to do your research and prevent those added costs.

Medicare Part A

If you sign up late for Part A, you may be charged a penalty equal to 10 percent of your premium. For those working 30 to 39 quarters, this will amount to an extra $23.40 per month for a monthly total of $257.40 in 2014. Those working less than 30 quarters will be charged an extra $42.60 per month for a monthly total of $468.60.

Costs can add up quickly. If you worked 30 to 39 Medicare-qualifying quarters, you will pay $280.80 more per year due to the late penalty alone. Those working less than 30 quarters will pay out an extra $511.20 annually.

TIP

For most enrollees, Part A will be free. Any percentage of zero is zero. Therefore, the late penalty does not apply.

The penalty duration is twice the number of years you were delinquent in signing up for Medicare. That is to say, if you applied for Medicare when you turned 68 years old, like Eileen, you would be three years overdue based on your eligibility by age. Medicare would charge you the penalty for six years (2 × 3 years) before discontinuing it.

It is important to note that Medicare only counts a full 12-month period toward its calculations. If you were two years and 11 months overdue to apply for Medicare, you would only be charged a late penalty for being two years past your enrollment deadline. You would use the end of the IEP to calculate how many months you were overdue, not your birthday or other designated eligibility date.

Medicare Part B

The Part B penalty has far more consequences for your long-term finances. This is because the penalty lasts for the life of your Medicare coverage, with rare exception.

Medicare will charge you an extra 10 percent for each year you were eligible for the program but did not sign up. Similar to the Part A penalty, only full 12 month intervals count toward the calculated amount.

Keep in mind that Medicare does not take into consideration the reason for your delayed enrollment. It does not matter whether you elected to discontinue your automatic enrollment or you plain old forgot about the deadline. The late penalties will apply in either case.

TIP

If you missed your Initial Enrollment Period by 11 months or less, you will not incur any Part A or Part B penalties. Penalties only come into play after a full 12 months.

Eileen, who had not signed up for three years despite being eligible for Medicare, would be charged 30 percent more on her monthly Part B premiums. Let us take a closer look at how much this could cost her in the long-run.

If she were in Medicare's lowest income bracket, the usual expected Part B monthly premium would be $104.90. Ten percent of this would be $10.49, and she would be required to pay this three-fold based on her eligibility date, adding up to an extra $31.47 per month. Her new monthly premium would total $136.37, costing her an extra $377.64 per year due to the penalty alone.

If Eileen were in the highest income bracket, her baseline $335.70 monthly premium would be increased by $100.71 (30 percent of $335.70) to a grand total of $436.41. Over one year, she would pay an extra $1,208.52.

Now take into consideration that these penalties go on for as long as you have Medicare. The longer you go without Medicare, the more impacting these penalties can be on your finances. When you consider that some seniors work to age 70 to maximize their Social Security earnings, they may be at high risk for adding 50 percent to their Part B premiums if they hold out on applying for Medicare until then.

Parts A and B late penalties may be waived if one of two criteria is met:

- You were charged late penalties because your same-sex marriage was not recognized by the government even though you would have qualified for a Special Enrollment Period based on your spouse's health insurance coverage. Your penalties may be reduced regardless of when you were married or even where you live. This is a consequence of the ruling that DOMA is unconstitutional.

- You develop end-stage kidney disease after age 65. How unfortunate that it takes a health-care crisis to save you money!

Understanding the penalties associated with Original Medicare will allow you to better prepare for the future.

Medicare Advantage

Medicare Advantage plans are run by private insurers. The premium amounts are determined not by the federal government but by each individual company. There are no late penalties associated with sign-up though your window of opportunity for sign-up will be limited to your IEP and Open Enrollment Periods as discussed in Chapter 8.

Medicare Part D

Medicare Part D may be optional, but its late fees are not. You may be charged 1 percent more for every month of missed eligibility after your IEP. Note this penalty is calculated in months, not years, as with the Parts A and B penalties. A full month must have passed before it would count toward the calculation for your late fee.

In addition, your other health coverage options come into consideration. For any consecutive 63-day period that you do not have creditable prescription drug coverage, you will be charged the penalty. Creditable prescription drug coverage means you have an insurance plan in place that will cover the costs of your medications, and that plan is at least as good as what Medicare can offer you. If you have a creditable plan in place, late penalties will not be charged. If you lose your creditable coverage and do not apply for Part D within 63 days, you will be assessed a penalty regardless of when you lost that coverage.

Because premium costs for Part D plans can differ depending on the insurance company and even where you live, the government standardizes how much these late fees can cost by calculating them based on a preset number, the *national base beneficiary premium (NBBP)*. In 2014, the NBBP was $32.42. Since the NBBP can change every year, your penalty amount will also be adjusted on an annual basis.

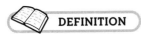 **DEFINITION**

> The **national base beneficiary premium** is a value set each year by the government for Part D plans. It designates the lowest dollar amount that may be established for a monthly premium that year.

The Part D penalty is rounded up to the nearest $0.10 and lasts as long as you have Medicare. Let's take Eileen again as an example. She applied for benefits three years past her eligibility date, and to keep it simple, we will estimate that time period as being exactly 36 months in duration. This means she would be charged 36 percent of the $32.42 NBBP ($0.36 \times 32.42$), resulting in $11.70 being added to her premium every month. Regardless of the specific Part D plan she chooses and how much it costs, this amount will be added to that premium every month.

If you sustained a Part D penalty before you turned 65, e.g., you became eligible based on disability, the penalty will be waived after you turn 65 years old.

Medigap Policies

Medigap policies, despite their name, are not an official part of the Medicare program. However, there is a designated period when you can first sign up for these supplemental plans. Once you sign up for Part B, your Medigap Open Enrollment Period begins and extends for six months. Medigap policies purchased outside of this window may potentially be more costly, but this is not considered to be a late penalty per se. Medigap policies are discussed in detail in Chapter 13.

Should I Enroll When I Turn 65?

You have a big decision to make when you become eligible for Medicare. Should you sign up and when? What benefits are there for waiting, if any? What is the most effective way to save money? You need to develop a strategy to make the most of it. You need to consider not only how much it will cost but whether you are making choices that will best suit your health-care needs.

When You Have Other Health Insurance or Benefits

If you have access to another health insurance plan, whether it is through your own employer, your spouse's employer, or even through a retirement plan, you have to ask yourself several questions before you decide whether or not to opt-in or opt-out of Part B coverage:

- Can you afford to pay premiums for both your employer-sponsored health plan and Medicare?

- Does your employer-sponsored health plan or retirement plan offer coverage that is not offered by Medicare?

- How long will you have access to your employer-sponsored health plan? What will you do when you are no longer eligible for those benefits?

- Are your retirement benefits guaranteed or can they be altered or even taken away in the future?

Specific concerns relating to employer-sponsored health plans are addressed in Chapter 14, union and retirement benefits are addressed in Chapter 5, and federal employees as well as other special groups are covered in Chapter 9.

In any case, since Part A coverage is free for most beneficiaries, it is encouraged that you take advantage of the program.

When You Are a Veteran

The exact cost of health-care offerings through the Veterans Administration will depend on whether you have a service- or non–service-related medical condition. Coverage is generally less expensive compared to other health-care insurance plans and requires copayments for prescription drugs, outpatient services, inpatient stays, and extended care stays. Services must be provided at facilities specifically run and managed by the VA.

However, benefits may not be guaranteed for all veterans in the future, according to the U.S. Department of Veterans Affairs website. Veterans are divided into different priority groups and lower priority groups may be dropped from coverage depending on availability of funds. This may be a major factor in considering whether or not to seek alternate health-care coverage. Veteran health benefits are addressed in detail in Chapter 9.

Pull Out the Calculator

Understand your options. It may be in your best interest to crunch some numbers. The following worksheet may be helpful to review how much you would be expected to pay in different scenarios. Using your (or your spouse's) employment record as well as income-based tables available on Medicare.gov, you can estimate your Parts A and B costs when you become eligible for Medicare.

Worksheet Comparing Health-Care Costs Before Late Penalties

Insurance Option	Monthly Premium	Annual Cost (Premium × 12)
Medicare Part A		
Medicare Part B		
Employer-sponsored health plan		
Retiree Benefits		
Union Benefits		

You must then decide if the costs are feasible for your situation. Based on your current income, can you afford both Original Medicare and your employer-sponsored health insurance? Can you afford both Original Medicare and retiree benefits? And so on. Look at each scenario closely, if it applies to you.

You also need to look to what those costs will be in the future if late penalties are applied. If your health-care choices are affordable now, will they be affordable later?

Have you already retired? If not, how much will your income increase, stay the same, or decrease? How will this affect how much you can afford to pay for health-care coverage on a monthly basis?

You have to look at the big picture.

The calculations get more complicated when it comes to late penalties but the following worksheets may help you on your way:

Calculating Medicare Part A Late Penalties

Row	Calculation	Your Calculation
A	Part A Premium Without Penalty (PWP)	
B	Part A Late Penalty: 10% of Premium = (PWP × 0.10)	
C	New Total Monthly Premium: (Row A) + (Row B)	

Row	Calculation	Your Calculation
D	Annual Total Cost: (Row C) × (12 months)	

Keep in mind that these higher Part A annual costs will only last twice the number of years you missed your eligibility period.

Calculating Medicare Part B Late Penalties

Row	Calculation	Your Calculation
A	Part B Premium Without Penalty (PWP)	
B	Part B Late Penalty: 10% of Premium = (PWP × 0.10)	
C	# of Years You Missed Eligibility	
D	Part B Late Penalty: (Row B) × (Row C)	
E	New Monthly Premium: (Row A) + (Row D)	
F	Annual Cost: (Row E) × (12 months)	

As you recall, these elevated Part B costs continue for the duration of Medicare with rare exceptions. You can add these adjusted Parts A and B numbers to the following worksheet to see how added penalties would impact your health-care coverage options in the future.

Worksheet Comparing Health-Care Costs After Late Penalties

Insurance Option	Monthly Premium	Annual Cost (Premium × 12)
Medicare Part A with Late Penalties		
Medicare Part B with Late Penalties		
Employer-sponsored health plan		
Retiree Benefits		
Union Benefits		

86   **Part 2:** Enrolling for Medicare

Compare the costs between these different worksheets to make an informed decision about what health-care options you can best afford.

> **ROUND TABLE**
>
> Eileen's three year delayed enrollment leaves her in an unfortunate position. On the one hand, although she did not work 40 quarters of Medicare-taxed employment herself, her former spouse, from whom she is now widowed, did. As a result, her Part A premiums are free.
>
> On the other hand, she will pay 30 percent in late Part B fees over the life of her Medicare coverage. She is in the lowest income bracket for the Part B premium. Once her late penalties are calculated, she must pay $136.37 per month.
>
> Since she does not have other health-care options through an employer or other benefits, she chooses to stick with this Medicare option. She will have to adjust her budget to cover these health-care costs.

Know Your Budget

It is difficult to make an educated decision about how much to spend on health-care if you do not have a reliable budget in mind. Chapter 20 outlines different strategies to help you assess your financial situation and offers advice on how to maximize your savings while getting the best care.

The Least You Need to Know

- Initial Enrollment Periods vary in length depending on whether you became eligible for Medicare based on age or disability.
- If you are automatically enrolled in Medicare, you do not have an IEP.
- It is how long you pay Medicare payroll taxes, not how much you contribute, that will determine if and how much you pay for Part A.
- Part A late penalties are in effect for a limited time, whereas Part B and Part D penalties are long-standing.
- There are rare situations where Parts A and B late penalties will be waived.
- VA health-care access may not be guaranteed for certain veterans in the future.
- You have to consider your health-care needs and your financial resources when deciding whether to opt-in or -out of Part B.

Other Enrollment Periods

Navigating Medicare's schedules can be tricky. Not only does each Medicare Part have its own unique set of rules, but each scheduling window has a different name. General enrollment periods, open enrollment periods, special enrollment periods—who can keep them straight? You will be able to, after you review what this chapter has to say.

General Enrollment

You would think your General Enrollment Period (GEP) would apply to all Parts of Medicare. The word "general" implies quite a wide range of options. However, this is not the case. It depends on your A, B, C, and Ds.

If you missed your opportunity to enroll in Part A or Part B during your Initial Enrollment Period, you can take advantage of the General Enrollment Period that occurs every year from January 1 to March 31. Unless you meet Special Enrollment eligibility, this is your only chance to sign up during the year. Your coverage will begin on July 1.

In This Chapter

- How to cope if you miss your Initial Enrollment Period
- Managing General Enrollment Periods and Original Medicare
- Making the most of Open Enrollment Periods for Medicare Advantage and Part D plans
- Qualifying for Special Enrollment Periods

Applying for Part B during the GEP also opens another enrollment window. This is a Special Enrollment Period (SEP) where you can elect drug coverage. You may add a Part D plan from April 1 to June 30. Alternatively, you can choose a Medicare Advantage Plan that includes drug coverage. What you cannot do is elect a straight-up Medicare Advantage Plan that does not include prescription benefits. You will have to wait for the Open Enrollment Period to pick such a plan, if you so choose.

Open Enrollment

Open Enrollment Periods (OEP) generally apply to Medicare Advantage and Part D prescription drug plans, though any choices you make during this time may also affect whether or not you continue or discontinue your Original Medicare coverage.

For clarification, you cannot have Original Medicare and a Medicare Advantage Plan at the same time. Medicare Advantage Plans already include the services offered by Original Medicare within their individual plans. It would not make sense to have you pay for both.

The Open Enrollment Period occurs once a year from October 15 through December 7. Your new coverage will begin on January 1.

What You Can Do During the OEP

You need to understand what you can and cannot do during the annual OEP. During the OEP for Medicare Advantage you can …

- Change your Medicare Advantage Plan with drug coverage to another Medicare Advantage Plan with drug coverage.

- Change your Medicare Advantage Plan without drug coverage to another Medicare Advantage Plan without drug coverage.

- Change your Medicare Advantage Plan without drug coverage to another Medicare Advantage Plan that includes drug coverage.

- Change your Medicare Advantage Plan with drug coverage to a Medicare Advantage Plan that excludes drug coverage.

- Change from a Medicare Advantage Plan without drug coverage to Original Medicare.

- Change from a Medicare Advantage Plan with drug coverage to Original Medicare with additional purchase of a Part D plan.

During the OEP Part D prescription drug plans you can ...

- Sign up for Part D coverage.

- Change your Part D plan to another Part D plan.

- Discontinue your Part D plan.

- Change from a Medicare Advantage Plan with drug coverage to Original Medicare with additional purchase of a Part D plan.

During the OEP for Original Medicare you can ...

- Change from Original Medicare to a Medicare Advantage Plan.

- Change from a Medicare Advantage Plan to Original Medicare.

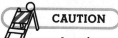 **CAUTION**

In order to participate in Medicare Part D, you must be enrolled in Parts A and B. Since many Medicare Advantage Plans also include prescription coverage, you do not need to purchase a Part D plan in addition to Medicare Advantage. For this reason, if you sign up for a Part D plan, your Medicare Advantage Plan will be discontinued in favor of Original Medicare.

During the OEP for Original Medicare you cannot ...

- Sign up for Part B, even if you were already receiving Part A benefits. This requires use of the General Enrollment Period.

- Sign up for Original Medicare if you were not previously enrolled in a Medicare Advantage Plan. This must be done during the General Enrollment Period.

You will not generate late penalties for not having been enrolled in Original Medicare if you had been on a Medicare Advantage Plan. This is because you were still within the Medicare system.

Annual Notice of Change to Your Plans

In order to make the most of your Open Enrollment Period, you need to look into what your current plan options do and do not cover. Each year your plan is obligated to send you a notice that reports any changes to their care plan. You need to take a close look to see if this plan will still be effective for you or if you need to consider changing plans altogether.

Access to health-care providers. Are there changes to which doctors and health-care providers you can access in the plan? Are your preferred providers covered by this plan? Are your options limited to certain hospital networks? Will this affect your ability to access care when you need it?

Breadth of the plan. Have your health-care needs increased since you first signed up for the plan? Are the services offered in this plan adequate to meet your current medical situation? Will you need extended coverage?

Overall costs. Will the cost of the plan increase for the coming year? Specifically, look to the cost of premiums, deductibles, copays, and coinsurance. How do these costs compare to the prior year? Is the increased price tag within your budget?

Prescription drug coverage. Do you require prescription drugs? If so, does your current plan cover medication costs? Are all your current medications covered by this plan? If you have underlying medical problems, are they well-controlled on your current regimen or does your health-care provider anticipate frequent medication adjustments in the future?

 ROUND TABLE

> Eileen signed up late for Medicare. Because she missed her IEP, she will need to sign up for Original Medicare during the annual General Enrollment Period from January to March. She could then enroll in prescription drug coverage via a Part D or MAPD plan during a Special Enrollment Period from April to June. If she wants to change to a Medicare Advantage Plan without drug coverage, Eileen will then need to wait until the Open Enrollment Period that occurs from October to December. Three enrollment periods in one year. Whew!

Everyone will have unique circumstances that will guide his or her decisions, whether those circumstances are physical, emotional, or financial. You cannot use someone else's experience with a health plan to decide whether or not it is right for you. You are the only you. Take the time to make an educated decision.

Comparing Plans

Once you have decided whether or not your current plan is feasible for you in the coming year, you will want to make sure you have the best deal. Medicare Advantage and Part D plans, being run by private insurance companies, will have varied costs associated with them. Shopping around will be worth the time invested.

You need not make any decisions on your own. There are tools and people to guide you on the way. After all, you will be caught for another year before you are able to make any change to your plan. This leaves you on the hook for the premiums you agreed to during the OEP. If you need help, get it!

Medicare offers a useful tool on its website to compare different plans. The tool is available at medicare.gov/find-a-plan. Since Medicare Advantage and Part D plans are purchased locally, you will be asked to provide your zip code to enter the site. You will then be asked what Medicare coverage you currently have, information about any financial programs you are enrolled in, and the names of any prescription drugs you currently use. This information will be used to help identify local plans that are best suited for you.

Whether or not you include prescription drugs in your search is up to you. Including them could potentially limit your search listings. Less expensive plans that cover different medication options may be excluded. If your medications were to be changed by your health-care provider for any reason, whether by choice or by medical need, one of these other plans could be more financially viable for you.

After entering your history, you are brought to a screen where you can compare your options. This is especially helpful as it lines up the plans in simple rows and columns so you can easily compare costs and coverage benefits. You will be able to look at estimated annual drug costs, monthly premiums, deductibles, copays, coinsurance, out-of-pocket spending limits, choice of doctors, whether there is additional coverage during the donut hole, restrictions on drugs, and estimated annual health and drug costs.

An added benefit of this online tool is the labeling of each plan with a Star Rating. Medicare assesses each plan using specific quality measures, 36 criteria for health plans and 15 for drug plans. MAPD plans must meet all criteria to be ranked at the highest level. Ratings range from 1 to 5, with 5 being the best of the plans. Five-star ratings are so special that they earn their own Special Enrollment Period as you will see in the following pages.

Armed with this information, you can make a more informed decision. You can also discuss your options with your local insurance agent, but be forewarned that he could be biased. Your pharmacist may be able to provide valuable information based on your prescription drug plans. Speaking with your doctor to discuss your current health status may help you to estimate how much coverage you will need in any given year. That said, your health-care provider is not a fortune teller, and unexpected illnesses all too commonly occur.

Medicare Advantage Disenrollment Period

If Medicare Advantage turns out to not be such an advantage for you, you can opt out, but your window of opportunity to disenroll is limited.

This Medicare Advantage Disenrollment Period (MADP, not to be confused with MAPD!) occurs from January 1 to February 14 every year, with your new plan starting the month after you apply, either on February 1 or March 1.

During this time, you can …

- Change from a Medicare Advantage Plan, with or without drug coverage, to Original Medicare.

- Change from a Medicare Advantage Plan, with or without drug coverage, to Original Medicare with additional purchase of a Part D plan.

During this time, you cannot …

- Change from Original Medicare to a Medicare Advantage Plan.

- Change your existing Part D plan to another Part D plan.

- Change your existing Medicare Advantage Plan to another Medicare Advantage Plan.

If you wish to make any of these additional changes, you will need to wait until the annual Open Enrollment Period.

Special Enrollment

Your Special Enrollment Period (SEP) is an opportunity to sign-up for Medicare if certain criteria are met. Applicable scenarios include ongoing health insurance from you or your spouse's employer, changes in where you live, changes made by private insurers to your Medicare Advantage or Part D plans, Medicare processing errors, and specific changes in your financial situation, among others. Think of SEPs as being "special" because they are rare, often one-time-only scenarios.

When Your Employment Ends

The most common SEP relates to employer-sponsored health insurance. You have eight months from the time your health coverage ends or your employment ends, whichever comes first, to apply for Medicare without having to pay late penalties. If these employment changes occur during your IEP, you will follow the rules of the IEP, not the SEP.

Multiple factors must be considered when looking at your appropriateness for this SEP. First and foremost, you must meet Medicare eligibility criteria by age or disability. You or your spouse must also have been actively employed during this eight-month window. This raises an important issue. Even if you are covered by health insurance, you may not be granted an SEP in the following circumstances:

- COBRA insurance

- Retiree benefits

Since you are not actively working when you receive COBRA or retiree benefits, you will not qualify for an SEP. This does not mean that you cannot have COBRA and Medicare, or retiree benefits and Medicare, at the same time. Of course you can. You may be subject to penalties, however, depending on whether you signed up for Medicare when you became eligible or afterwards. The details of how retiree and COBRA benefits coordinate with Medicare are discussed in Chapters 5 and 14.

DID YOU KNOW?

The U.S. Census Bureau's Survey of Income and Program Participation (SIPP) reported that more than 1.7 million people over 65 years old were covered by an employer-sponsored health plan in 2010.

Working hard is not enough to guarantee you an SEP. The company you work for counts in the grand scheme. One size does not fit all, according to The Tax Equity and Fiscal Responsibility Act (TEFRA), which was enacted in 1982. TEFRA set into effect legislation that specifies how large a company should be for their employer-sponsored health insurance to allow you exemption from the IEP.

If you work for a company that employs fewer than 20 full-time employees or the equivalent, you will not qualify for an SEP, even if your company offers employer-sponsored health plans. If you do not enroll in Medicare when you are first eligible, you will be subject to late penalties. This is one of those rare cases in life where bigger really is better.

ROUND TABLE

Loraine and Thomas had a decision to make. Both had employer-sponsored health plans and both were now eligible for Medicare. Should they opt-in for Medicare now or defer Medicare in favor of their employer-sponsored insurance?

Loraine worked for a company that employed the equivalent of 18 full-time employees, while Thomas worked for a company that employed 30. Because Loraine's employer does not meet the threshold to qualify her for an SEP, if she does not sign up for Medicare now she will be subjected to late penalties when she does enroll in Medicare. Thomas, however, could choose to delay enrolling for Medicare without paying late penalties because he does qualify for an SEP based on the size of the company he works for.

If you have employer-sponsored health coverage based on your spouse's work history, your SEP eligibility could be impacted if you are in a same-sex marriage depending on where you live or where you first apply for Medicare benefits. Chapter 6 reviews same-sex marriages in more detail.

It is essential to know whether or not you can use an SEP to your advantage. Deferring the cost of Part B premiums while you pay for employer-sponsored coverage may save you considerable dollars. Few people want to pay double premiums. It can be harmful to the wallet while it is happening, even if it saves money in the long-run once you consider the impact of late penalties.

Too many people falsely assume that they have an SEP based on existing health coverage when in fact they do not qualify. This could result in costly late penalties that may last years, potentially as long as you're enrolled in Medicare.

The government does not really care that you may have actually saved them money by delaying your use of the program. Think about it. You have not even used their resources! For them, though, it is an opportunity to collect dollars when dollars are desperately needed. Know where you stand and protect your financial stakes.

When You Move

Your Medicare options may change if you move to another address. This may affect your eligibility for Original Medicare or your access to Medicare Advantage and Part D plans.

You move from one U.S. address to another U.S. address. Because Medicare Advantage and Part D plans are based on local service areas, you may no longer have access to your prior plans once you move. If by chance you move within the same service area, it is also possible that your specific location may have more plans available to choose from. Your SEP to change your Medicare Advantage and Part D plans in either situation is two months from the time you move.

DID YOU KNOW?

CMS reports that 313,914,040 nursing home beds were available in 2012. Depending on the state, 75.8 to 92.1 percent of those beds were occupied by people over 65 years old that year. The numbers decreased to 28.6 to 58.4 percent for those over age 85, and to 4.1 to 13.2 percent for those over age 95.

You live in or recently moved out of a skilled nursing facility or nursing home. You are granted an SEP to change your Medicare Advantage and Part D plans as long as you live in the facility and for two months after you leave. You can even change from a Medicare Advantage Plan to Original Medicare during this time.

You return to the United States after living in a foreign country. You are offered a two-month grace period to sign up for a Medicare Advantage or Part D plan.

You are released from jail or prison. You are granted a two-month SEP immediately upon your release from incarceration to apply for a Medicare Advantage or Part D plan.

For all of these scenarios, you will have to wait for the General Enrollment Period to apply for Parts A and B if you had missed your Initial Enrollment Period.

When Your Insurance Changes

Sometimes it is not your choice to change your Medicare coverage. A private insurance company essentially does the job for you. Here are some scenarios that could happen to you.

Medicare and the private insurance plan do not renew their contract agreement. You are given an SEP to change your Medicare Advantage or Part D coverage from October 15 to February 28/29.

A private insurer changes your Medicare Advantage or Part D plan so that the drug plan is no longer creditable. You have a three-month SEP after you lose or are notified of loss of coverage to change to a Medicare Advantage or Part D plan.

A private insurer cancels your Medicare Advantage or Part D plan. Your SEP opportunity to find a replacement plan begins one month before and extends one month after the plan ends.

 **CAUTION**

Your Medicare Advantage Plan may be discontinued for a variety of reasons. If you do not use your Special Enrollment Period to sign up for a new Medicare Advantage Plan, you will automatically be transitioned to Original Medicare. You will not be able to apply for another Medicare Advantage Plan until the next Open Enrollment Period.

Alternatively, there may be times when you, not the insurance company, are the one who makes a change. You have the opportunity to sign up for drug coverage that is creditable and less expensive than a MAPD or Part D plan. In this case, you may disenroll from these plans at any time. This commonly happens for those with military benefits, either via TRICARE or VA coverage.

You may even have an opportunity to sign up for an employer or union based plan. You may cancel your Medicare Advantage or Part D plans but timing will vary based on your plan requirements.

When You Have Financial Hardship

Medicare acknowledges financial hardships by allowing wider windows of time to adjust your coverage options.

Your eligibility for Medicaid can affect your Medicare coverage. Once you are eligible for Medicaid, you have free rein to sign up or discontinue Medicare Advantage or Part D plans at any time. If you lose eligibility for Medicaid, you are limited to a three-month SEP to change these plans.

Medicare Advantage or Part D plans can be changed once a year if you participate in a State Pharmaceutical Assistance Program (SPAP). Again, a three-month SEP follows loss of eligibility for any reason.

The Extra Help program can save you dollars if you meet certain income requirements. Similar to Medicaid, you can change your Medicare Advantage and Part D plans at any time, but your SEP is set for the following January 1 through March 31 to change these plans should you ever lose eligibility.

If you become eligible and participate in a Program of All-inclusive Care for the Elderly (PACE) plan, you can discontinue Medicare Advantage or Part D coverage at any time. You have a three month SEP to sign back up for coverage when or if you disenroll.

Details of programs available to those on a limited income are outlined in Chapter 19.

When You Are Misinformed

If the government learns that you were not properly informed about your plan options, you will receive an official notice from Medicare in the mail. This could occur if you were told a drug plan was creditable when it was not, or you were not informed you would be losing creditable drug coverage. You have two months after receiving this notice to make changes to your Medicare Advantage or Part D plan.

When You Want a Five-Star Plan

Five-Star Medicare plans, Medicare Advantage, and Part D plans alike, are considered of high value not only based on the quality of their benefit coverage but also based on their customer service as surveyed by beneficiaries and health-care providers.

To offer the best care options to its beneficiaries, Medicare allows an SEP for anyone who wants to sign up for one of these Five-Star plans. You can change from a non–Five-Star Medicare Advantage or Part D plan to a Five-Star plan or change from one Five-Star plan to another.

The SEP begins on the December 8 before the plan earned its Five-Star status and extends to November 30 each year. Though this SEP lasts the majority of the year, you can only opt to use the SEP once annually. Use it wisely. You will otherwise be subject to the premiums of that Five-Star plan until you can change your plans during the following Open Enrollment Period or the MADP.

Enrollment Period Overview

With so many enrollment periods to keep track of, Medicare can become quite confusing. The following outline simplifies the complicated calendar.

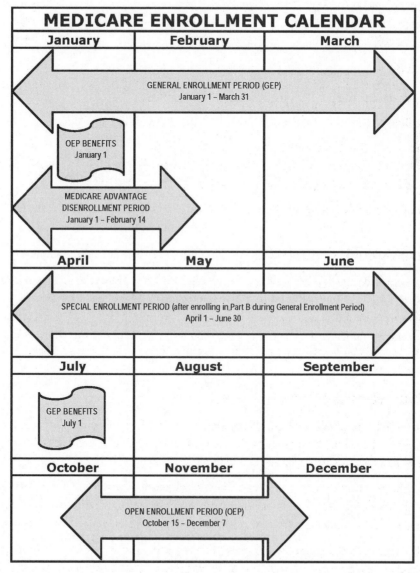

If you want to apply for Original Medicare, you can apply during the following periods:

- Initial Enrollment Period
- General Enrollment Period for Parts A and B (January 1–March 31)

- Medicare Advantage Disenrollment Period if you cancel your Medicare Advantage or MAPD plan (January 1–February 14)

- Open Enrollment Period if you are switching from a Medicare Advantage Plan (October 15–December 7)

- Special Enrollment Periods

If you want to apply for a Medicare Advantage Plan, you should look to these timelines:

- Initial Enrollment Period

- Open Enrollment Period (October 15–December 7)

- Special Enrollment Period if you are changing to a Five Star Medicare Advantage Plan (December 8–November 30)

If you want to apply for a Part D plan, your options include these periods:

- Initial Enrollment Period

- Open Enrollment Period (October 15–December 7)

- Special Enrollment Period if you signed up for Part B during the General Enrollment Period (April 1–June 30)

- Special Enrollment Period if you are changing to a Five Star Part D plan (December 8–November 30)

It may still seem a bit daunting to you, but hopefully you now have a resource in hand to easily sort out when to do what with Medicare.

The Least You Need to Know

- If you miss your Initial Enrollment Period, you can sign up for Original Medicare during the annual General Enrollment period.

- Open Enrollment Periods allow you to change your Medicare Advantage and Part D plans.

- You can compare different Medicare Advantage and Part D plans on the medicare.gov website.

- If you deferred Medicare coverage while you continued your employer-sponsored health plan, you will only qualify for a Special Enrollment Period if the company you work for is sufficiently large.

- A number of Special Enrollment Periods exist for financial hardships.

Special Groups

Medicare is complicated, but when you take into consideration its many exceptions, the program takes on a whole new level of intricacy. This chapter summarizes information about special groups and where exceptions to Medicare coverage apply.

While the information here may not be all inclusive, it will cover many common questions beneficiaries have about the program. Please note that retiree benefits, same-sex marriages, and union benefits are addressed in Chapters 5, 6, and 14, respectively.

Health-Related Circumstances

Your health may be the deciding factor for how well, and even if, Medicare will work for you. This section offers some reminders as well as new information regarding how your physical and mental well-being affects your Medicare coverage. Armed with this information, you will be better prepared to receive the care you deserve.

In This Chapter

- How Medicare works based on your health condition
- Taxation for government employees and small businesses
- Military benefits and Medicare coverage
- Medicare regulations affect hospital employees

Disabilities

Eligibility requirements for people with disabilities are outlined in Chapter 5. Disabilities are unfortunate unto themselves, but knowing it may take years before you achieve eligibility for health-care benefits is a dismal prospect. What can you do in the meantime?

Depending on whether you apply for SSDI or RRB benefits, you may wait anywhere from 28 to 33 months before Medicare eligibility kicks in. Not only does it take time to apply and get approved for disability benefits, but waiting periods follow before those health-care benefits kick in. What resources do you have to access health care in the years you are left waiting?

- If you are disabled, you are unlikely capable of work. Without working, you are not able to access employer-sponsored health plans, unless you can get coverage through your spouse.

- If you are leaving your current place of employment due to your incapacity, you may elect for COBRA coverage. COBRA coverage can extend as long as 36 months but could be quite costly.

- You may apply for insurance through the ACA health exchange program at healthcare.gov.

- You may apply for Medicaid if you meet qualifying criteria.

If your disability improves and you lose your disability status through SSDI or RRB, you also lose your Medicare eligibility until you meet Medicare eligibility criteria either by age or by subsequent disability. Even if your former disability recurs, you will need to go through the requisite waiting periods a second time.

This should not make you fearful to reenter the work force, or at least try. You can do a trial run of work if you sign up for the Ticket to Work program offered through the Social Security Administration. Until you establish your ability to work at an acceptable level, you will still retain your Medicare eligibility as long as you participate.

You do not have to worry about late penalties for Original Medicare because your SSDI and RRB benefits will qualify you for automatic enrollment. However, you may still be liable for Part D penalties.

Specific Medical Problems

Amyotrophic lateral sclerosis and end-stage renal disease allow you to bypass the waiting periods required for other disabling medical conditions, as discussed in Chapter 5. For ALS, you become eligible for Medicare when you demonstrate eligibility and apply for SSDI or RRB benefits. You will be automatically enrolled in Original Medicare.

However, ESRD works a little differently. Disability status alone does not qualify you for the program. You must also have earned adequate Medicare-tax employment credits. Enrollment is not automatic, and you could be faced with late penalties. Also benefits do not necessarily kick in immediately. It depends on the status of your health condition.

New to dialysis. You must participate in a self-training program before your third month of dialysis. Medicare coverage begins on the first day of the first month of the training program. For example, if you started dialysis on September 4, you would have needed to start your self-training program by June. If you started the program on June 4, your benefits would kick in on June 1.

Already on dialysis. If you are already in dialysis, you do not need training. Benefits kick in on the first day of the fourth month you receive dialysis. For example, if you start treatment on March 3, your benefits would kick in on June 1.

Kidney transplant. Benefits kick in the month you are admitted to a hospital for pre-operative evaluation or for transplant. The transplant must occur within two months.

Medicare coverage based on ESRD can be retroactive up to one year but will be lost after 36 months if your kidney function remains in an acceptable range after a kidney transplant. This leaves you on the hook to pay for any immunosuppressive medications required to prevent your body from rejecting your transplanted kidney. You will need to seek another means of health-care coverage to cover these costs unless one of the following occurs: 1) you turn 65 years old, 2) your kidneys fail again, or 3) you develop another disability, in which case you regain Medicare eligibility.

If you develop ESRD after you turn 65 years old, you may be able to waive any late penalties you had incurred for Parts A, B, or D. You must re-enroll in Medicare through your Social Security office. Your unfortunate condition gives you a fresh start on the Medicare slate.

Black Lung Program

Coal miners are exposed to hazards every day ranging from dangerous conditions to coal dust exposure. Long-term exposure to coal dust increases the risk for pneumoconiosis, also known as black lung disease. The condition is irreversible, causes the lungs to stiffen, and increases risk for pulmonary infections and even death.

DID YOU KNOW?

More than 75,000 coal miners have died from black lung disease since 1969, and the number may be increasing. The number of diagnosed cases more than doubled from the 1990s to 2000s with rates jumping from 4 to 9 percent for workers exposed to coal dust for more than 25 years.

After much needed lobbying by the United Mine Workers of America, the government enacted the Black Lung Benefits Act of 1973 to address the high-risk conditions and health needs of this group. The resulting Black Lung Program allows for diagnostic screening and health care benefits to manage the condition for those with confirmed disability. Benefits extend to include medical treatment but stop short of paying for skilled care in a nursing home. A monthly stipend may also be provided to the coal worker or to his beneficiaries in the event of his death. These funds are not taxed.

If you qualify for the Black Lung Program, you should still apply for Social Security Disability Insurance benefits. However, your payments will be decreased by the amount that is paid to you by the Black Lung Program. It is important to have SSDI in place so that you can become eligible for Medicare by disability criteria.

The program generally works in parallel, not in concert, with Medicare. If a medical condition or treatment relates to the underlying lung disease, the U.S. Department of Labor (DOL) and the Black Lung Program will be responsible to pay your health-care expenses. Medicare may be billed secondarily for services if the Black Lung Program does not cover the charges in full, but there is no guarantee Medicare will cover them. Medicare will require the denial letter from the DOL to make a determination.

Medicare should not be billed first-line when there are any diagnostic codes related to black lung disease listed for a particular treatment or service. Medicare will deny payment. Medicare may be billed secondarily as noted above.

However, if you develop a medical issue not related to your black lung disease, for example, you have a fracture that requires surgery, Medicare may pay and can be billed first.

Because the Black Lung Program is not all-inclusive of your health-care needs, you are encouraged to also apply for Medicare coverage when you become eligible by disability or age, whichever comes first.

Government Employees

Working for the government allows you to give back to the community, but it can also mean dealing with lots of confusing rules and regulations. From taxes to retirement benefits, it is important to know how Medicare will work for you when you need it.

State and Local Employees

When you work for your state or local government, you may or may not have provisions for Medicare coverage built into your job description. Much of this depends on when you were hired.

If you were hired before March 31, 1986, you are not guaranteed Medicare rights through your employer, meaning they do not have to pay Medicare taxes. As you may recall from Chapter 4, most jobs split the cost of Medicare taxes between you and them. If you contribute to FICA taxes, you may have to pay the full share.

DID YOU KNOW?

As of 2014, there were 23 million public employees in the United States.

Certain employees hired after March 31, 1986, will also not have Medicare taxes paid by their employers. These include but are not limited to:

- Election workers who earn less than a designated amount each year

- Inmates performing work performed in a facility where they reside

- Medical residents who work less than full-time

- Nonresident aliens with certain work visas

- Patients performing work in a facility where they reside

- Students performing work at an educational facility where they are enrolled

- Temporary emergency employees

DID YOU KNOW?

Medicare-qualified government employment means that Medicare taxes, but not Social Security taxes, have been paid for by the employer.

Your employer must pay Medicare taxes for you if you were hired after March 31, 2014, or if your position meets Section 218 criteria. Section 218 allows agreements to be made between the government and your employer so that Social Security and Medicare taxes will be paid for by your employer just like any private sector job.

Federal Employees

Federal employee health benefits (FEHB) are available to eligible employees both during and after active employment. You are given access to discounted health insurance through the program but may only access these benefits in retirement if you had been enrolled in the FEHB program for the five years preceding your retirement and were also eligible for retirement annuities.

A variety of health plans are made available through private insurance companies. There is an Open Season period annually that allows for changes in your plan selection as needed. Premium rates remain the same during active employment and in retirement, i.e., you do not get a discount as you get older.

The decision on whether to participate in Medicare is an individual one. There may be several factors to consider before you make a decision:

Dependents. Medicare does not extend coverage to dependents, but FEHB benefits will allow coverage for your dependents up to 26 years old.

Drug coverage. Drug coverage will be comparable between FEHB and Medicare Part D benefits. FEHB would meet creditable standards to avoid Part D penalties if you ever needed to go that way. However, there are financial assistance programs available for those enrolled in Part D plans that are not available for those opting to use FEHB benefits for prescriptions.

Services covered by FEHB but not by Medicare. Medicare does not offer routine physicals, dental care, vision screenings, or emergent care outside of the United States, whereas FEHB may cover these services.

Services covered by Medicare but not by FEHB. FEHB may not cover home health services or durable medical equipment, though Medicare may offer these benefits.

Provider access. FEHB plans are generally HMO based, meaning the network of providers to choose from is more limited, whereas Medicare may offer payment to a broader range of health-care providers. That said, Medicare Advantage Plans may be similarly limited as FEHB plans.

Your window to apply for Medicare will depend on when you retire. You are granted a Special Enrollment Period to apply if you work past 65 years old or if you continue to receive FEHB health benefits through your spouse who is actively working. You have a one-time opportunity to change your FEHB plan starting 30 days before you reach Medicare eligibility. Otherwise, you must wait until the annual Open Season period (the lingo for their Open Enrollment Period) for your FEHB plan to make adjustments.

If you elect to have both FEHB and Medicare, after you turn 65 years old Medicare will pay first and your FEHB benefits will pay second, unless you continue to work after 65 years old in which case your FEHB benefits pay first and Medicare second.

Military Service

The United States is the land of the free and home of the brave thanks to those who have served in the military, past and present. Your willingness to give of your time and stand for the rights of all Americans entitles you to certain health-care benefits.

TRICARE

Tricare, formerly known as the Civilian Health and Medical Program of the Uniformed Services (CHAMPUS), is a health-care plan offered by the U.S. military to eligible members of the military and their families. Benefits are offered to members of the Army, Navy, Marine Corps, Air Force, Coast Guard, Public Health Service, and the National Oceanic and Atmospheric Administration and the program is managed under the Defense Health Agency.

Eligibility for Tricare is open to active duty service members; uniformed service retirees, their spouses, and unmarried children; Medal of Honor (MOH) recipients and their families; unmarried widows of service members and their unmarried children of service members; children under the custody of a service member; certain victims of abuse relating to a service member; members, spouses, and children of North Atlantic Treaty Organization (NATO) and "Partners for Peace" (PFP) representatives; and former spouses of active, retired, or former military members meeting certain requirements.

Tricare got its name from its three basic care plans—Standard, Extra, and Prime. Different deductibles, coinsurance, and enrollment fees apply depending on which of these specific plans is chosen. Prior to 2001, Tricare coverage extended up to age 65, at which time all health-care coverage was shifted to Medicare. Tricare for Life was instituted in 2001 to extend Tricare coverage after you reach Medicare age. However, this requires that you still apply for Medicare.

 ROUND TABLE

George is a 65-year-old veteran and amputee who receives both Tricare and Medicare benefits, the latter based on his underlying disability. He was unfortunately hospitalized for an inflamed gallbladder and required surgery. Medicare was billed first, and Part A services covered his hospital expenses after charging a $1,216 deductible for that benefit period. Tricare, which pays second, covered the cost of the deductible.

If you are eligible for free Part A, you must sign up for Part B to maintain your Tricare eligibility. The only exception to this Part B requirement is if you participate in Tricare Reserve Select plans that are available to National Guard and Reserve members, or Tricare Retired Reserve that is available for Retired Reserve members.

If you are not eligible for free Part A, you must present your "Notice of Disapproved Claim" from Medicare to your uniformed services office to prove that you cannot receive free Part A before you can be approved for continued Tricare coverage. You will then be given a new card for the future.

When you sign up for Medicare depends on whether or not you remain active in the military. If you are an active service member, you may choose to delay applying for Part B until your Special Enrollment Period comes around. This period starts when your active duty status ends and extends for eight months. If you do not enroll within your Special Enrollment Period, you will be liable for Medicare's late penalties for Parts A, B, and D. You are not eligible for a Special Enrollment Period if you develop ESRD. In this case, you must apply when you are eligible by ESRD criteria or you will incur penalties for Part B when you finally do apply.

Tricare is second in line to make health-care payments on your behalf. Medicare gets billed first and Tricare second. This means that Tricare can help to pay off your Medicare deductibles and coinsurance. If Medicare approves coverage, Medicare will pay its share and Tricare will pay the rest. If Medicare denies coverage for any reason, so will Tricare.

It is important to note that if health care is provided by a provider that does not accept Medicare, Medicare will not pay any dollars toward your expenses and Tricare will only contribute the amount it would have paid if Medicare had offered coverage, usually a 20 percent coinsurance. It is in your best interest to seek health-care providers that accept Medicare for payment to keep your costs down.

VA Benefits

The Veterans Health Administration (VHA), a division of the United States Department of Veterans Affairs (VA), may extend health-care benefits to those who have served our nation. Specifically, benefits are offered to those who completed active military service and were not dishonorably discharged.

Veterans are divided into one of eight priority groups. Factors that determine placement into a specific priority group include disability status, income levels, Medal of Honor recipients, Prisoner of War, Purple Heart medal, VA pension benefits, and Medicaid eligibility. VHA benefits are not guaranteed and could change at any time depending on budgeting by the Department of Defense. Veterans in lower priority groups may be at higher risk for losing benefits.

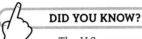

DID YOU KNOW?

The U.S. government spent $134.3 billion on health benefits for veterans between 2001 and 2013, and is expected to spend an additional $7.6 billion and $8.0 billion in 2014 and 2015, respectively.

Health care is offered at VA facilities, but that may be changing. In 2014, an internal investigation unveiled a scandal, finding that more than 57,000 veterans were forced to wait more than 90 days to receive care. Deficiencies in the program and long wait times have led to changes within the system to improve access to care.

Not only were increased funds allocated to hire more health-care professionals, the Patient Centered Community Care (PC3) program was also instituted in 2013 to allow veterans to access providers not affiliated with the VA. Initially, this included referrals to specialists, mental health care, emergency care, and newborn care. After the scandal broke, a legislative decision was made to include primary care services within the program.

If a veteran cannot schedule an appointment within 30 days at a VA approved facility, or if the veteran lives more than 40 miles away from a VA center, he may seek referral through the PC3 program. Veterans must be able to schedule an appointment within five days and attend an actual appointment within 30 days. Once they are seen and evaluated, the non-VA provider must return medical records to the VA within 14 or 30 days for outpatient or inpatient care, respectively. Contracts are currently in place with two insurance networks, Health Net and TriWest, and providers that work with these insurance companies may sign contracts to provide PC3 care.

You would think that working in the military leads to increased health benefits. Tricare benefits and VA benefits do not necessarily go hand in hand, however, even though some veterans may be eligible for both.

If you want to use Tricare benefits for care, Medicare must first be billed. Because the VA cannot bill Medicare for services, any care received at a VA facility will be considered as if it were completed by a provider that opted out of Medicare. As discussed in the previous section, this means that Tricare can only pay the amount that it would have paid if Medicare had accepted payment, ultimately covering only about 20 percent of your costs. This leaves you on the hook for 80 percent of the bill. It could be more financially viable to not use the VA if you have Tricare for Life and instead go to a provider that accepts Medicare.

DID YOU KNOW?

Physicians employed by the VA do not need to purchase malpractice insurance, but those participating in the PC3 program do.

You must decide whether or not to sign up for Medicare if you have VHA benefits. Though you may receive quality care at VA facilities, there is no guarantee of benefits for the long haul, and you will be faced with late penalties if you enroll after you were initially eligible for Medicare. If you require care outside of the VA system and that care is not accessible within the PC3 program, you will be charged the full amount of any services provided, whereas Original Medicare could have covered the majority of expenses. It seems to be in your best interest to sign up for Medicare, both Parts A and B, when you are eligible to assure health coverage for your future.

That being said, prescription drug coverage through the VA is quite good and may even be better than many Medicare Part D plans. You are unlikely to require a Part D plan, but if you did enroll in one at a future date, you would not incur a late penalty because VA benefits are creditable.

Self-Employment and Small Business Owners

Where you work and who you work for can mean the difference between paying less or more for Medicare. Know where you can cut costs and where those costs can hurt you.

If You're Self-Employed

If you're self-employed you may have the best boss in the world, but your taxes can be tricky. While those who are employed by an organization share the cost of their FICA taxes with their employers, you will have to pay the full amount, 2.9 percent of your earnings for Medicare and 12.4 percent for Social Security. You may be able to deduct half of those taxes on your federal income tax return.

You may have other tax breaks as well. As of 2010, you can deduct health-care premiums on your taxes if you are the sole proprietor or business partner of your business, member of a limited liability company, or shareholder who owns at least 2 percent stock in a company. This means you can deduct the premiums for Parts A through D, which could be a considerable dollar amount. The one caveat is that you cannot use this deduction if you are eligible for employer-sponsored health care by another employer or your spouse.

If You're a Small Business Owner

Small business owners can offer employer-sponsored health plans to their employees through the ACA health exchange if they employ 100 or fewer full-time employees, though until 2016 states may limit participation to businesses with up to 50 employees. These plans are offered through the Small Business Health Options Program (SHOP). Starting in 2017, SHOP plans will be available to businesses employing more than 100 employees. Small business owners are only required to offer these plans to employees working full-time. Employers of more than 50 full-time employees will be fined if they do not provide appropriate coverage options for their workers.

If an employee becomes eligible for Medicare while they are on a SHOP plan, whether or not they need to enroll in Medicare right away will depend on the nature of their eligibility. Medicare always pays first for disability, and if you do not have Part B coverage, you could be left to pay the bulk of your bills, even with a SHOP plan in place. Other SHOP plans may pay first or second to Medicare, depending on the plan. When your SHOP plan pays second, Medicare is always a good idea.

Working for a small business owner could mean you are at risk for paying late penalties for Original Medicare if you are not careful. If your boss employs fewer than 20 full-time employees, you do not qualify for a Special Enrollment Period based on any employer-sponsored health insurance you may have, whether a SHOP or another plan. Applying after your Initial Enrollment Period for Medicare could result in late penalties.

Indian Health Service

The Indian Health Service (IHS) is a program under the Department of Health and Human Services that provides health care access and employment opportunities for American and Alaskan Indians. Those eligible for services include not only Indians from federally recognized tribes, but also Canadian and Mexican Indians recognized as part of the American Indian community, and non-Indian women pregnant with an Indian child through the course of her pregnancy and up to six weeks post-partum.

Health care is provided through hospitals run by IHS or by tribal facilities. IHS facilities must treat all Indians recognized by the program, whereas tribal facilities may limit care to members of their own tribe. Care can extend outside of IHS-regulated facilities to contract health services (CHS), which have signed agreements with IHS. There are geographic limitations put on these CHS services so that moving out of a given service area may make it difficult to access care.

 DID YOU KNOW?

The United States recognizes 566 tribes across 35 states, and offers benefits to them through the Indian Health Service.

To reduce costs to the program, the Medicare Prescription Drug, Improvement, and Modernization Act of 2003 required that federally recognized Indians be granted Medicare-like rates for hospital stays if the hospital in question participated in the Medicare program. This is the case even if the IHS member had not yet reached Medicare eligibility by age or disability.

If you are a federally recognized Indian, you are still encouraged to get Medicare. Access to IHS does not prevent Medicare from charging you late penalties for sign up. You may also apply for Medicaid or a health-care program through the ACA health exchange, for which there are no enrollment periods—you can sign up at any time.

It is important to have an alternative health-care plan in place to cover services that may not otherwise be offered to you. Especially when you travel or move from IHS-serviced territories, you may be left without viable health-care options.

The Least You Need to Know

- You lose Medicare benefits 36 months after a successful kidney transplant, unless you are eligible for Medicare by other criteria.

- Employment in certain state or local government positions after March 31, 1986, or jobs under Section 218 of Social Security, require that your employer pay Medicare taxes.

- If you are self-employed, you may be able to deduct your Medicare premiums from your federal income taxes.

- To maintain Tricare eligibility after age 65, you need to enroll in Part B if you receive Part A at no cost.

- The VA cannot bill Medicare.

- Medicare has made significant cuts to hospital reimbursements that may correlate with hospital layoffs.

- It is usually in your best interest to enroll in Medicare when you become eligible, regardless of your particular circumstances, to avoid late penalties.

Breaking Down the Benefits

The best way to develop a solid understanding of any topic is to dismantle it and rebuild it from the pieces. Let us break down what services Medicare covers across each of its Parts.

Each component of Medicare offers different services: Part A hospital coverage, Part B outpatient coverage, Part C extended hospital and outpatient coverage, and Part D prescription drug coverage. Medigap, which is not officially a part of Medicare, provides supplemental coverage to help you pay off any costs that Medicare has left behind.

Only when you know what each component offers can you understand what Parts you should enroll in. Everyone's situation will be different. This part will arm you with valuable information to make the best decision for your needs.

CHAPTER 10

Medicare Part A

Medicare Part A is the heart and soul of Medicare. Hospital stays can cost a great deal of money, and avoiding catastrophic expenses for the elderly was one the primary reasons Medicare came into existence. Part A is often referred to as hospital insurance, but it is much more than that. Understanding what it covers, when it provides coverage, and how it works can help save you a lot of money.

The Medicare/Hospital Relationship

Medicare has a long-standing relationship with hospitals. With the majority of hospitalizations involving the elderly, Medicare payments are essential to keeping hospitals financially viable. Care that is provided to hospital inpatients is covered under Part A.

Medical Necessity

Hospital care implies that you are urgently sick, that there is an acute medical need. *Medical necessity* is an important concept to understand because without medical necessity, Medicare is not going to pay.

In This Chapter

* The importance of medical necessity
* The difference between inpatient and observation status
* Understanding your Part A benefit periods
* Qualifying for skilled nursing care
* The requirements for hospice coverage
* Calculating your costs with Part A coverage

What is medically necessary may differ depending on who you ask. Your doctor may have certain experiences and training that guide him to order certain tests and treatments. Medical training, as discussed in Chapter 15, is quite extensive and builds the foundation for patient care. Medical learning, however, is a life-long process. With ongoing research and studies, the way health-care providers practice medicine changes constantly, always with the goal to improve care quality.

However, it may take years before a specific medical test or procedure becomes a *standard of care* in a given medical field. Tests and procedures that are new may raise questions for insurers, Medicare included, about whether they are truly more effective compared to other available diagnostic and treatment methods. New medications, tests, and treatments generally tend to cost more as well.

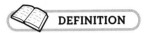 **DEFINITION**

> **Standard of care** is a legal term used to define care, which is provided in a given medical situation that meets the general consensus of appropriateness by medical professionals in that field. There may be more than one standard of care for the same medical condition. For example, there may be different ways to approach cancer treatment.

Insurers may be hesitant to pay for newer services and technologies until they have established their worth in the field. Are there risks for complications from the procedure? How does it compare to existing procedures? How many patients would benefit from the new procedure as compared to existing procedures? These are all questions that have to be taken into consideration.

It may take time before health-care providers incorporate newer diagnostic methods into their practice routine, but sometimes they hop on board quickly if there is strong data to support their use. Medicare tends to favor services that meet standard of care guidelines as well as services that are cost-effective.

Medicare may define medical necessity differently than your health-care provider. One specialty's standard of care may not need Medicare's guidelines for medical necessity. The problem is that Medicare is not always transparent about what services it considers to be medically necessary.

Complicating matters further, there are not always formal guidelines available that outline standards of care. Certain organizations will list guidelines for care but that does not mean all health-care providers in that field are members of that organization or that they will follow those guidelines. If a malpractice lawsuit comes into play, for example, it falls on the plaintiff to prove what would be considered the standard of care for that specialty in that particular medical situation. Even community standards may come into play.

What does this mean for you? It could mean complications, at least financially. Medicare does not want to pay for expensive care if other less expensive options are available that could meet the standard of care. If your health-care provider insists on a test or service that Medicare does not consider medically necessary, where does that leave you?

Medical necessity as a concept touches on the whole of Medicare, not just Part A. Be prepared to face the issue as we run through each of Medicare's benefits.

Hospital Costs

Hopefully, you only go to the hospital when it is medically necessary to do so. Unfortunately, some people use emergency rooms as if they are primary care offices. Of those who went to the emergency room in 2010 but were not ultimately admitted to the hospital, 79.7 percent of adults acknowledged they accessed care there because they did not have access to other health-care resources. Only 66.6 percent actually thought they had an urgent medical need.

DID YOU KNOW?

During 2012, 19.5 percent of all Americans over age 18 visited an emergency room at least once. This number increased to 22.2 percent when only people over 65 years old were taken into account.

Hospital care costs considerably more than care offered in an outpatient setting, such as a doctor's office. More expensive tests may be pursued than in an outpatient setting, but the urgent need for those tests allows hospitals to charge more than would be charged for those same services performed in another setting.

A 2013 study funded by the National Institutes of Health used data from The Medical Expenditure Panel Survey to investigate emergency room costs across more than 8,300 emergency room visits from 2006 to 2008. Ten common conditions were reviewed to compare costs: back problems, headache, intestinal infections, kidney stones, sprains, pregnancy, upper respiratory infections, urinary tract infections, wounds to the extremities, and other injuries. These conditions generally comprise 32 percent of all outpatient emergency room visits. The average cost for the emergency room visit was $1,233, but cost variability was rampant. For example, a urinary tract infection could cost as little as $50 to as much as $73,000! These out-of-pocket charges depended on the patient's insurance plan or lack thereof. It is important to note that none of the emergency room visits in this study led to a hospital admission.

Now consider how high the costs would be if you actually stayed overnight in the hospital! More services, more care, more charges—costs increase exponentially. Understanding how Medicare pays for your health care is essential, because even when you go to the hospital, Medicare Part A may not pay for your services. Part A will only cover those services if they are considered medically necessary.

The Two-Midnight Rule

In order for Part A to come into play, your health-care provider needs to first admit you to the hospital as an inpatient. If tests are performed on you in the emergency room, even if you stay in the hospital overnight to have them completed, that alone does not mean that you are considered an inpatient. You may be defined as being under observation. In this case, your health-care provider has not yet decided whether or not your medical needs qualify you for an inpatient admission. He may be waiting for more information or testing in order to make this decision.

> **DID YOU KNOW?**
>
> When you are under observation, Medicare Part B, not Part A, covers your care. There is a significant cost difference on what you will be required to pay out of pocket. With Medicare Part A, you pay a fixed hospital deductible for all the care you receive, whereas with Part B you may have to pay as much as 20 percent of all costs.

Your health-care provider's decision to admit you as an inpatient may signify that your hospital care is medically necessary. Medicare may not always agree. If Medicare deems that it is more appropriate for you to remain under observation, Medicare will not pay for any inpatient care. This puts the burden on your provider to make the proper designation according to Medicare guidelines. Otherwise, the hospital will not get paid.

On October 1, 2013, Medicare put into effect a new provision that is referred to as the two-midnight rule. With these regulations, not only are medical necessity criteria required for Part A coverage, but an additional timeline requirement was added. Medicare will not consider a beneficiary's case appropriate for inpatient status unless the hospital stay is expected to span at least two midnights.

When you consider that there are life-saving surgeries that may not require you to stay more than two midnights in the hospital, you have to wonder if this rule really makes sense, other than to save money for the Medicare Trust Fund. What if you were admitted at 12:01 A.M.? You will have to go through a whole extra day to meet criteria compared to if you were admitted at 11:59 P.M.

For example, the average stay for a ruptured appendix is less than two days. Clearly, the hospital stay is medically necessary because you could die without the surgery, but without a sufficiently long hospital stay, Medicare may not pay under Part A.

However, even if you stay in the hospital more than two midnights, do not assume that you will automatically be considered an inpatient. Medicare still needs to decide if the stay is medically necessary on each given day. For example, you may be considered appropriate for observation status on day one and day two, but if you stay in the hospital a third day, Medicare will look at what care you are receiving on that day to see if it meets medical necessity criteria for inpatient status. Each day is its own entity in Medicare's eyes.

You also need to know that there is a time limit on how long you can be placed under observation. Medicare will usually pay for observation care for two days, under certain circumstances up to three days. Any further days under observation will not be covered by Medicare, not even Part B.

TIP

Ask if you are admitted to the hospital as an inpatient or if you have been placed under observation. Ask your health-care provider how long they think you will be expected to stay in the hospital and if they can document that on your chart. Just the documentation that your stay is expected to span more than two midnights could save you thousands of dollars.

This does not mean all is left to chance as far as the timeline of your hospital stay. Medicare may still consider a case appropriate for inpatient status even if your hospital stay does not span two midnights. It requires that your health-care provider document on your chart that they expect your hospital stay to cross two midnights. This signifies to Medicare that your provider considers your stay to be medically necessary at that time. If your condition responds to treatment faster than anticipated, Medicare may still consider the case appropriate for inpatient status if it also meets medical necessity criteria by their standards. Coverage by Part A in this case is not guaranteed, but your odds are much improved.

What may be difficult to grasp is that you receive the exact same care and services whether you are placed under observation or admitted as an inpatient. In the end, how much you pay for that same level of care may be based merely on your timeline and how well your provider documented his concerns.

The American Hospital Association has brought a lawsuit against the U.S. government regarding this legislation, but it may take years before any changes are made.

The Three-Day Inpatient Requirement

There are other timelines to consider. If you are admitted as an inpatient, returning home may not be a safe or medically appropriate course of action. You may need additional care after you leave the hospital. That care may require that you be supervised by trained staff at a skilled nursing facility (SNF) or rehabilitation center.

To qualify as a skilled nursing facility (SNF), trained professionals must be available at the site to provide you care. These professionals may include doctors, physician assistants, advanced nurse practitioners, audiologists, nurses, occupational therapists, physical therapists, and speech-language therapists. For you to qualify as needing a SNF, you must require skilled care from one of these professionals at least five days weekly.

Medicare Part A may cover your stay in a SNF or rehabilitation center if you meet certain criteria. Specifically, you must have been admitted as an inpatient for three consecutive days. The day you are transferred from the hospital to the new facility does not count toward this three-day requirement. This means that you have to actually be in the hospital for four days as an inpatient.

 DID YOU KNOW?

Hospitals are not allowed to go back in time and change your admission status on previous days from observation to inpatient or vice versa. This means that even if the hospital believes it made an error in assigning your case, it cannot make reparations. Medicare only recognizes the original order for billing purposes.

This is where the two-midnight rule starts to get a bit ugly. Hospitals may place you under observation during your first two days if there is a question about whether or not Medicare will pay for inpatient care. This may mean you have to stay even longer to qualify for a SNF or rehabilitation stay, even if the medical necessity is clear. You may need to rely on other sources of insurance coverage. Certain Medicare Advantage plans may offer you additional coverage that Original Medicare does not.

Hospitals would prefer that you not be placed under observation. They stand to make a larger profit if they are paid by Part A rather than Part B. This is because many seniors are unable to afford their costly share of the charges, resulting in many bills going unpaid. Hospitals ultimately take a financial loss. This may explain to some extent the variability of hospital charges reported earlier in this chapter. Some hospitals may charge higher bills across the board in an attempt to recover dollars they may have lost based on these Medicare regulations.

The two-midnight rule may save money for the Medicare Trust Fund, but it makes hospital care more expensive for both patients and the facilities that provide their care.

Services Covered by Part A

Labeling Part A as hospital insurance can be somewhat misleading. Regardless, this is the phrasing used on your Medicare card. Know that Medicare may pay for some of your hospital expenses but not all of them. It can also provide care for you beyond the hospital at other facilities like nursing facilities and sometimes even your own home. The cost of services will vary depending on where you receive the care.

Inpatient Care

Part A covers costs toward your inpatient hospital stays. These expenses include a variety of services such as anesthesia, laboratory studies, medications, mental health care, nursing care, occupational therapy, physical therapy, social services, speech therapy, surgical procedures, X-rays, and other imaging studies. Medical supplies, such as bandages, catheters, intravenous lines, etc., are part of this coverage benefit as well. Room and board is also included as part of your stay. Unless your care medically necessitates a private room, such as would be the case with highly infectious diseases like tuberculosis, Medicare will cover the cost of a shared room only. Note the previous list is not all-inclusive.

Physician services, though they are an integral part of your hospital stay, are not paid for by Part A. They are covered under Part B.

Inpatient services that are not covered by Part A include blood products used for transfusion. If the hospital can access a blood bank for free, you may not be charged anything, but if they need to purchase blood products for you, you will be charged, at least for the first three units of blood. There are Medigap policies that may help you to pay for your blood transfusions. Please see Chapter 13 for a list of available Medigap plans.

Part A also does not cover private telephone service, television fees, or personal care items such as toiletries, as these are not considered medically necessary.

Rehabilitation and Nursing Home Care

Part A will pay for a stay in a skilled nursing facility (SNF) or rehabilitation center if you meet a qualifying three-day inpatient hospital stay as discussed earlier in the chapter. Skilled nursing and medical care must be required daily or at least five days weekly. This care must be given at a facility that is Medicare certified. This means that the facility has contracted with Medicare to provide a standard of care for its beneficiaries.

 DID YOU KNOW?

The need for skilled nursing facilities (SNFs) increases with age. In 2009, there were 33 SNF stays for every 1,000 Medicare beneficiaries between 65 and 74 years old. That number increased to 222 for those 85 years and older.

Room and board is included, though similar to the hospital stays, rooms are shared unless there is a medical reason to indicate otherwise. Skilled nursing and medical care is covered to include diet therapy, occupational therapy, physical therapy, social services, and speech-language therapy, among other services.

Part A will not pay for custodial care. Custodial care is care for your hygiene and personal needs. This level of care does not require skilled nursing and alone will not be considered sufficient to meet the medical requirements for your stay in a SNF.

Hospice

End-of-life care is essential for quality of life and maintenance of our human dignity. To this end, hospice care is covered by Part A whether that care is provided in the hospital, in a designated hospice facility, or in your own home.

DID YOU KNOW?

In 2012, more than 1.5 million people received hospice care. Care was received 66.0 percent of the time at home, 27.4 percent of the time at a nonhospital hospice facility, and 6.6 percent of the time at an acute care hospital.

In order to qualify for hospice, a physician must evaluate you and determine that your life expectancy is less than six months based on your medical condition. This determination can only be made by a physician, though your primary care provider may be a nurse practitioner after the determination has been made, if you so choose.

When you elect hospice care, you agree to not pursue treatments to try to cure your condition. Instead you choose palliative care and comfort care to provide symptom relief for any pain and suffering you may incur from your illness. Medications, counseling, and therapy services may be included to achieve these goals. You are also assigned a designated hospice team, which includes your primary care provider, that is available to you 24/7. All medical decision-making needs to go through your hospice team. You may elect to discontinue hospice care at any time if you decide that you wish to pursue treatment for your condition.

Part A may also pay for you to return to the hospital if needed for short-term symptom control for your terminal condition or to a nursing facility for respite care. Respite care may be granted if you receive hospice care at home. A short-term nursing facility stay may allow family members and those caring for you a period to rejuvenate as they prepare to continue your care. Your hospice team must approve these short-term stays, or Medicare will not cover the expense.

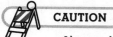

Always ask your hospice team before you make any decisions to go to the hospital for any reason. The team can review your case and medical needs to assure you will not lose your hospice benefits due to any misunderstandings of what is and is not covered.

Medicare will pay for room and board at hospital-based hospice programs but not for hospice provided at other facilities or in your home.

If you require care for a medical condition not relating to your terminal disease, you may be able to seek medical care at a hospital for treatment. Treatments you receive, however, cannot extend to treatment of your terminal illness or you could potentially lose your hospice benefits.

Home Health Care

If you do not have a qualifying inpatient stay to get you into a SNF, you may still be able to access health services in your home. For this to happen, your health-care provider must certify you as home-bound. This means that it is difficult to leave your home without considerable effort or that leaving your home is not advisable without supervision, transportation assistance, or use of special equipment such as a wheelchair.

In the event that your health-care provider does recommend home health care, Medicare will not pay for that care on a full-time basis. Medicare limits eligibility to those who need part-time or intermittent care. They define part-time as care given less than 7 days a week or care for less than 8 hours daily over 21 days.

DID YOU KNOW?

The need for SNFs increases with age. In 2009, there were 1,896 home health care visits for every 1,000 Medicare beneficiaries between 65 and 74 years old. That number increased to 8,974 for those 85 years and older.

As with SNF coverage, custodial care alone does not qualify you for coverage. All services provided must be necessary due to a defined medical condition. Covered care may include home health aide services, skilled nursing care, occupational therapy, physical therapy, social services, and speech-language therapy. Nursing care includes skilled care, medical evaluation, and educating you and your caregivers about how to manage your condition. Care that you or another nonmedical person could perform on your own is not considered skilled nursing care. For example, you may not be able to administer IV medication to yourself, but you may be able to check your own blood sugars if you have diabetes.

The care you receive cannot be supplied by just anyone. Each agency providing care must be approved by Medicare and agree to a set of fees for its services. If you use an agency that is not Medicare-certified, you may have to pay for those services out of pocket.

Your Costs with Part A

Now that you know what Part A covers, understanding what you pay and what Medicare pays can help you prepare for any urgent care needs. Let's break down the costs so you know what to expect.

Monthly Premiums

Whether or not you pay monthly premiums depends on how much you (or your spouse) have contributed toward Medicare employment taxes. If you or your spouse's tax contributions spanned 40 quarters or more, you are eligible to get Part A without any monthly premiums.

If you divorced and remarried, your eligibility for free Part A based on your former spouse's record is variable. If your former spouse is alive, you are only eligible for benefits based on your current marriage. If your former spouse is deceased, you are eligible for free Part A premiums based on either your current spouse or your ex-spouse's record. Eligibility also depends on how long you were married before you were divorced or widowed. Please see Chapter 5 for details.

 TIP

It may be worth working a little longer to earn more quarters of employment. It could save you thousands of dollars a year in Medicare premiums.

For those who worked fewer than 40 quarters, you will pay monthly premiums in one of two dollar amounts. If you paid Medicare payroll taxes for 30 to 39 quarters, you will pay $234 per month as of 2014. If you contributed less than 30 quarters, you will pay $426 per month. That equates to $2,808 and $5,112 per year, respectively.

Late Penalties

Part A penalties accrue for every year you delay signing up for Medicare. You will pay an extra 10 percent toward your monthly premium for twice the number of years you were eligible for Medicare.

The good news is that 10 percent of nothing is nothing. For the majority of Americans who qualify for premium-free Part A, they will not be subjected to late fees.

Using an example of a three-year delay in enrollment, a person who contributes 30 to 39 quarters of taxes would pay $257 per month for six years, while someone contributing fewer than 30 quarters would pay $468 per month for six years.

Benefit Deductibles

What you pay out-of-pocket for Part A coverage is based on *benefit periods*. Your hospital benefit period for an inpatient stay begins the day an inpatient order is placed on your chart, whether that occurs on the first day you are in the hospital or if you are changed to inpatient status on a later date, and extends for 60 days of continued care, whether you are in the hospital or a skilled nursing facility.

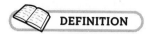

> **DEFINITION**
>
> A **benefit period** is a fixed period of time where your insurer, Medicare or otherwise, provides coverage based on their program guidelines.

You pay a single deductible for each hospital benefit period. As of 2014, that deductible costs $1,216. This dollar amount covers all Part A approved fees for a hospital stay up to 60 days long. After 60 days, you will be required to make daily payments. From days 60 to 90, you will pay $304 per day. For days 91 and over, you will pay $608 per day. These dollar amounts may vary annually.

Medicare will not cover an extended number of days after a 90-day hospital stay. They limit you to 60 lifetime reserve days. This means that Medicare will not pay after you use 60 days for hospitalizations lasting longer than 90 days. For example, if you stay in the hospital for 100 days, you will pay $1,216 for the first 60 days, $304 per day for 30 days, and $608 per day for 10 days. You will have used 10 lifetime reserve days, leaving 50 days for future use.

The hospital benefit period for a SNF stay is 60 days long as previously discussed, though you can receive care at a SNF for up to 100 days. This means that you become eligible for SNF care in the first 60 days but can continue care beyond that. The first 20 days are free. Days 21 through 100 will cost you $152 per day as of 2014.

When you go to the hospital and have a qualifying three-day inpatient stay, you are eligible for SNF care. You can continue SNF care for 100 days. If you leave the SNF before your 100-day benefit ended, you may be able to return to the SNF if needed and use up the remaining days you had left. It depends on when you try to return to the SNF.

- If you return to the SNF within 30 days, your original 100-day SNF benefit resumes.

- If you try to return to the SNF 31 to 59 days after you left, your original 100-day SNF benefit would resume, but you will also require a new three-day qualifying hospital stay.

- If you try to return to the SNF after 60 days, you will require a new three-day qualifying hospital stay and your old 100-day SNF benefit period is considered closed. You will start from scratch.

 ROUND TABLE

George was admitted as an inpatient to the hospital after a heart attack. He required rehabilitation care at a SNF and qualified for Part A coverage after staying 5 days in the hospital. He went to the SNF for 24 days after which time he and his health-care provider felt he could continue care at home. However, George did not do well. He became dizzy and had an unsteady gait. It was recommended that he return to the SNF for continued care. Because he returned within 30 days, he did not require another qualifying hospital stay. He has 76 days remaining on his original SNF benefit (100 minus 24). Each day will cost him $152 now that he has passed the 20 days of free SNF care.

Your home health-care benefit periods are renewable every 60 days. Your health-care provider will receive certification forms from Medicare to report whether or not you require continued care. Qualifying home health-care services are free with the exception of any medical equipment that is needed to provide that care.

Your hospice benefit periods change in duration. Your first two benefit periods are 90 days long. After that, benefit periods shorten to 60 days. Your health-care provider will receive certification forms from Medicare, similar to home health-care forms. It may seem strange that your benefit periods can continue past the six-month life expectancy your health-care provider initially used to qualify you. Prognoses are only estimates, and you may recertify for hospice care as needed. Note you are only able to change providers once per benefit period, and you are required to have Original Medicare in order to access coverage. You should not be on a Medicare Advantage Plan if you wish to receive hospice benefits.

Copays and Coinsurance

There are few copays and coinsurances required for Part A services.

- Any medical equipment that is covered as part of your home health-care services requires a 20 percent coinsurance.

- For hospice care, you will pay 5 percent for respite care stays.

- For hospice care, you will pay $5 for medications needed for pain and symptom control if you receive those medications at home. Part A covers the full cost of those medications if they are administered in an inpatient setting.

Financial Assistance Programs

If you are one of those who need to pay Part A premiums, there may be Medicare Savings Programs that can help you make your payments. These plans are offered to those with low incomes.

In particular, the Qualified Medicare Beneficiary (QMB) Program and the Qualified Disabled and Working Individuals (QDWI) Program may offer assistance in paying your Part A premiums. The details of these programs are addressed in Chapter 19.

Total Annual Costs

Most people will pay nothing for Part A coverage unless they actually require its services.

Part A Premium Cost Summary for 2014

Cost	40 or More Quarters	30 to 39 Quarters	Fewer Than 30 Quarters
Monthly premium	$0	$234	$426
Late penalty	$0	$23	$42
Monthly premium with penalty	$0	$257	$468
Annual cost	$0	$2,808	$5,112
Annual cost with penalty	$0	$3,088	$5,623

Part A Deductible Cost Summary per Benefit Period in 2014

Period	Hospital Stay	SNF Stay
Day 1–60	$1,216 total	NA
Day 61–90	$304 per day	NA
Day 91+	$608 per day up to 60 lifetime reserve days	NA
Day 1–20	NA	$0
Day 21–100	NA	$152 per day

The Least You Need to Know

- Medicare will not pay for services it does not deem to be medically necessary.
- Part A provides coverage for inpatient hospital stays, skilled nursing facility (SNF) stays, home health care, and hospice.
- The two-midnight rule requires that you are expected to have a medically necessary hospital stay that spans at least two midnights.
- To qualify for SNF care, you must first have a three-day inpatient hospital admission.
- Medicare does not pay for custodial care.
- To qualify for hospice, a physician must certify that you have less than six months to live.

Medicare Part B

The truth is you hope you never need to use Medicare Part A. No one wants to be so sick as to need hospital care. Part B is exactly the opposite. Part B offers you care that helps to prevent disease and manage your medical conditions, hopefully to the point that you never need to use the hospital in the first place. You should make the most of Part B services whenever possible.

Services Covered by Part B

Part B services are predominantly for your *outpatient care*. This includes care that is provided to you outside of the hospital, as well as care that is provided to you when you are under observation at the hospital. All health-care provider fees, whether you are inpatient or outpatient, are paid for through Part B.

In This Chapter

- What to expect at your Welcome to Medicare Exam and Wellness Visits
- Part B coverage for counseling and treatment
- Preventive screening services covered by Part B
- Limited Part B medication coverage
- Durable medical equipment coverage
- Understanding your out-of-pocket costs and when you do not have to pay

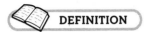

DEFINITION

Outpatient care includes services you receive at a health-care provider's office, testing facilities, or a hospital when you are under observation. It also includes the supplies required to provide these services.

Your Medicare card labels Part B as Medical Insurance. The bulk of your routine medical costs will fall under Part B as you manage your basic health-care needs.

Ambulance Transport

Medicare does cover ambulance transportation, but only if it considers the ride to be medically necessary. Ambulances are not taxis. They cannot be used to bring you back and forth to routine appointments and especially not for nonmedical reasons.

DID YOU KNOW?

Medicare spends nearly $6 billion annually in ambulance costs. The Government Accountability Office reported in 2012 that the cost of an ambulance ride ranged from $224 to $2,204.

Ambulance costs are frequently itemized, sometimes charging not only for the emergent or non-emergent care given on the ambulance but also for each mile that is driven. Mileage costs have even been reported to be more than $100 per mile with different ambulance agencies.

Medicare will only pay for ambulance transportation for emergent medical reasons if another means of transportation is considered to be too high risk for the beneficiary. Also, it will only pay for services to the nearest facility that has the capacity to treat the condition.

For example, if the nearest hospital does not have a trauma center but that service is needed to treat an injury, Medicare will pay for a hospital farther away that does provide this level of care. Likewise, if you request transport to a specific facility but it is further in distance than another Medicare-approved facility, Medicare will not pay the cost of the ambulance ride, not even for the mileage amount that would have brought you to the nearest facility.

Doctor Visits

Any evaluations performed by your health-care providers, whether for primary care or for medical specialty care, whether inpatient or outpatient, are covered under Part B. These examinations should continue at the frequency recommended by your providers. As long as your provider documents the medical needs for these visits and associates them with the appropriate diagnostic codes, Medicare will cover a percentage of costs toward these visits. You will pay a 20 percent coinsurance for each visit.

New visit types have been added to the Medicare roster since the passage of the Affordable Care Act. These are known as the Welcome to Medicare Examination and the Annual Wellness Visit. These visits are free to you, though your health-care provider must accept assignment for this to be the case (see Chapter 15).

Though you may continue to require evaluations for specific medical conditions, the Welcome to Medicare Examination is the only physical examination that Medicare will ever cover 100 percent. The exam has an expiration date. After you enroll in Part B, you have 12 months to have this examination completed or you miss out. If additional testing is done, such as an EKG, those exam components may require coinsurance or copays.

The Welcome to Medicare Examination includes:

Counseling on advanced directives. You will be given the opportunity to discuss your end-of-life wishes with your health-care provider.

Depression screening. Identifying depression can help to improve your quality of life and provide treatment options.

Health risk assessment. Your safety and ability to perform your activities of daily living will be assessed. This may be completed in the form of a questionnaire.

Measurement of vital signs. Your height, weight, and blood pressure will be measured.

Review of your medical history, family history, and social history. This allows your provider to assess any risk factors you have.

Review of your medication history. It is important to make sure your medications are appropriate to your needs and minimize side effects as much as possible.

Preventive screening list. Your provider will review what preventive screening tests Medicare may cover given your medical history and risk factors.

Vision testing. A simple eye chart may be used for this purpose.

 TIP

You may be offered an EKG at your Welcome to Medicare Exam. Unlike for other visits, you do not need to have an underlying medical condition to have the test covered. It may be beneficial to have a baseline EKG on your medical record in the case that you do develop a cardiac issue in the future. It provides additional information for your provider to use as a basis for comparison. Though an EKG may be offered with the Welcome to Medicare Exam, it does require a 20 percent coinsurance.

What is offered as a physical exam may be limited. Medicare does not specify what physical examination components are required in the Welcome to Medicare Examination beyond vital signs. The extent of your examination will depend on what your health-care provider chooses to offer you.

On the other hand, physical examinations are outright not included as part of Wellness Visits, which include the Initial Wellness Visit and Annual Wellness Visits. These are meant to be counseling sessions that review your medical history, medications, and health-risk assessments. They also include measurement of vital signs, screening for cognitive impairment, and an update of any preventive care services you need. Depression screening is also included as part of the Initial Wellness Visit.

You have to be on Part B for longer than 12 months in order to be eligible for the Initial Wellness Exam. The Annual Wellness Exams begin the calendar year after your Initial Wellness Exam.

Counseling

Part B offers a variety of screening and counseling options for those at risk.

Alcohol abuse screening. Alcohol dependence can lead to medical, social, and legal consequences. Screening for alcohol use is free once annually. If alcohol misuse is uncovered during the screening process, Part B allows for further counseling in four one-on-one sessions without your needing to pay coinsurance.

Depression screening. Depression impairs quality of life and has also been associated with heart disease. Screening is offered once annually free of charge.

Diabetes self-management training. If you have diabetes, you can receive training to help you manage your disease. Information may include how to approach your diet, how to check your blood sugar, and how to inject insulin. You are allowed 10 hours of training in your first year. After that, you are permitted 2 hours of follow-up training per year. These sessions will occur in groups of 2 to 20 people and last for at least 30 minutes per session. Each visit will cost you 20 percent coinsurance.

Medical nutrition therapy. You may qualify for one-on-one counseling with a nutritionist if you have diabetes, kidney disease, or had a kidney transplant within the past 36 months. This does require that your provider place a referral to a registered dietician or other certified professional on your behalf. These visits are free of charge. However, if you make the appointment yourself, you may pay for the visit out of pocket.

Obesity counseling. This service is offered only to those who have a BMI greater than 30. Counseling services may include nutritional guidance, activity recommendations, and identification of any medical problems that could be contributing to your weight. If your health-care provider believes that medications may be necessary to address your obesity, those discussions will be covered under these counseling sessions. There is no coinsurance for these visits.

Sexually transmitted infection (STI) counseling. Individuals who are at higher risk for STIs may have counseling sessions with qualified medical professionals twice a year free as long as the health-care provider accepts assignment. Sessions may last up to 30 minutes in duration.

Tobacco-use cessation counseling. Quitting smoking can make a lasting impact on your health. To support your healthier lifestyle, Part B allows you to have one-on-one counseling sessions over a 12-month period to discuss the risks of continued smoking and strategies to help you quit. These visits will be charged at a 20 percent coinsurance.

Therapy

Occupational therapy (OT), physical therapy (PT), and speech-language pathology (SLP) are services frequently required for beneficiaries who have suffered stroke, musculoskeletal injury, rheumatologic conditions, and more. These services aim to strengthen your body and improve your ability to function, both physically and verbally. These services are covered by Part A when you are an inpatient. When they are provided in the outpatient setting, they are covered by Part B.

It had once been the case that you were allowed a fixed number of visits of these therapies per year. This is now changed to a set dollar amount. How much you spend will depend on which therapists you use and what specific services they provide.

Medicare will pay up to $1,920 for PT and SLP combined annually. It also allows for $1,920 for OT every year. You will pay a 20 percent coinsurance for each visit.

Medicare may cover beyond these $1,920 therapy cap limits if your therapist can prove the medical necessity of the care provided in their documentation. However, no matter how well they prove their case, your charts will automatically be audited if you spend more than $3,700 for PT and SLP combined or for OT alone.

Laboratory Tests, Imaging, and Procedures

Part B will cover laboratory tests, imaging, and other procedures if your health-care provider links them to appropriate diagnostic codes and Medicare considers those services medically necessary. This also includes EKGs. Costs typically include a 20 percent coinsurance.

What you need to know about these services is that you may or may not need to pay coinsurance. Before a test is performed, the health-care provider offering that service needs to have you sign an Advanced Beneficiary Notice (ABN). This form is intended to notify you that a service may not be covered under Original Medicare. The ABN does not apply to Medicare Advantage plans since each of these plans is different. The specific procedures in question must be clearly listed on the form. It is your right to be informed before the test is performed so that you can decline the test if you do not wish to risk having to pay for it out of pocket.

Your provider cannot have you sign the ABN after the service has been completed. By then, it is too late. You would have not been given the opportunity to make a decision about payment. In this case, if Medicare declines coverage for that particular service, you are not liable to pay for it. This also applies if the provider simply forgets to have you sign an ABN at all. The provider has to eat the costs because he will now not be reimbursed for care that he provided.

> **TIP**
>
> If Medicare does not cover a service, contact your provider to see if an ABN had been signed for that particular test. You may not need to pay for it if an ABN had not been offered to you that day or if that specific test was not listed on the ABN. Generally speaking, it is helpful to ask for copies of the ABN before you leave the office or health-care facility to keep for your records.

This is why it is so important to read everything before you sign it. If you have questions about a form, you should ask for assistance so you understand what it says. You may otherwise be financially liable for unanticipated costs.

Limited Medications

Part A covers medications you receive in the hospital when you are an inpatient, and Part D covers the bulk of your outpatient medications. Part B also offers medications, however, but only to a limited extent.

> **TIP**
>
> Though some common vaccinations are covered by Part B, Tetanus, pertussis, and shingles vaccinations are covered under Part D.

Vaccinations are partially covered under Part B. Influenza vaccination is offered once each season to everyone. A pneumococcal vaccination against pneumonia is offered to everyone as a one-time dose. Hepatitis B vaccines are only covered if you are considered high risk, for example if you have diabetes, end-stage renal disease, hemophilia, a history of blood transfusions, or if you are a health-care worker who may be exposed to the disease. Hepatitis vaccinations are given in a series of three doses.

Part B may also cover medications that are administered in the home and require durable medical equipment to administer them. Examples of such medications include those used in nebulizer machines to help your breathing and those used in infusion pumps.

The following medications for those with specific diagnoses meeting certain criteria are covered:

- Anti-nausea medication (oral) within 48 hours of chemotherapy
- Anti-cancer medication (oral) if equivalent in strength to an intravenous drug
- Blood-clotting factors for hemophilia
- Erythropoisis-stimulating factor for anemia caused by end-stage renal disease
- Immunosuppressant medications after a kidney transplant
- Intravenous immunoglobulin for primary immune deficiency disease
- Intravenous nutrition
- Medications for post-menopausal osteoporosis
- Tube feedings

Medical Supplies

Part B may pay toward medical supplies if they are medically necessary to treat your condition. A 20-percent coinsurance is often required for this equipment. Examples of covered durable medical equipment are as follows:

- Air mattresses
- Bedside commodes
- Braces
- Canes (but not white canes for the blind)
- CPAP machines
- Crutches
- Feeding pumps
- Hospital beds
- Hydraulic lifts
- Infusion pumps
- Nebulizer machines
- Ostomy supplies
- Prosthetic devices
- Shoe inserts
- Suction pumps
- Walkers
- Wheelchairs (both standard and motorized)

Diabetic supplies are also considered to be durable medical equipment. This includes the glucometer device to measure your sugar, control solution to make sure your glucometer is working properly, lancets used to prick your finger, and test strips used to put your blood into the machine. Part B covers 100 test strips and lancets once a month if you are on insulin. If you are not on insulin, Part B covers 100 test strips and lancets and that supply will be expected to last for three months.

Preventive Screening for Everyone

There are certain preventive screening tests that are offered to everyone under your Part B coverage.

Blood pressure screening. High blood pressure can lead to serious health complications. Not only are heart disease and stroke associated with hypertension, high blood pressure can lead to kidney disease and vision problems. Screening of your blood pressure is free with your wellness visits.

 DID YOU KNOW?

More than 67 million Americans have hypertension. High blood pressure increases the risk for heart disease and stroke, two of the most common causes of death in the United States. In 2010, $93.5 billion was spent to treat hypertension and its complications.

Cholesterol screening. High cholesterol levels can lead to thickening of your arteries and increase your risk for heart disease. Your total cholesterol, your LDL cholesterol ("bad" cholesterol), your HDL cholesterol ("good" cholesterol), and your triglyceride levels can be measured in a standard laboratory lipid panel. Screening is free once every 5 years. If you are found to have abnormalities in your cholesterol screening, more frequent testing may be covered since the study is no longer considered to be for screening purposes. It is being ordered as a follow-up to an identified medical problem.

Colon cancer screening. Screening for colon cancer is recommended starting at 50 years old. The United States Preventive Screening Task Force (USPSTF) recommends screening continue through age 75 for most people. Screening can happen by different techniques. You should discuss the preferred method with your health-care provider. All the colon cancer screening tests listed in the following table are free of charge if your provider accepts assignment. The exception is the barium enema which requires a 20-percent coinsurance.

Frequency of Different Colon Cancer Screening Tests

Test	Frequency for Those at Normal Risk	Frequency for Those at High Risk
Barium enema	Every 48 months	Every 24 months
Colonoscopy	Every 120 months or Every 48 months after a flexible sigmoidoscopy	Every 24 months
Fecal occult blood testing	Every 12 months	NA
Flexible sigmoidoscopy	Every 48 months or Every 120 months after a screening colonoscopy	NA

Preventive Screening for Those at Risk

There are also preventive screening tests that are only offered to those who are considered at risk for certain conditions.

Abdominal aortic aneurysm screening. Men who smoke may be at higher risk for enlargement of their aorta known as an aneurysm. The larger an aneurysm is, the higher the risk the artery will burst and possibly lead to death. Men, but not women, between the ages of 65 and 75 years old who have smoked more than 100 cigarettes in their lifetime are eligible for a free one-time screening by ultrasound. Also, anyone who has a family history for an aortic aneurysm, regardless of gender, may also have this evaluation without cost.

Diabetes screening. Surprisingly, not everyone is eligible for diabetes screening, though its complications lead to a considerable number of hospital stays every year, ranging from 15 to 31 percent of admissions. Medicare does not specify how this screening should be done. It may be done by measuring a fasting sugar level, a hemoglobin A1C test, or an oral glucose tolerance test. The latter test is labor intensive and requires your sugar levels be monitored before and after ingesting a certain amount of glucose. The amount of change determines your diabetes risk or confirms a diagnosis. The risk factors required for Medicare to pay for diabetes screening must include at least one of the following:

- If you have high blood pressure

- If you have high cholesterol or triglycerides

- If you have an episode of elevated blood sugar

- If you have obesity as defined by a BMI greater than 30

- If you meet two of the following criteria: 1) you are age 65 or older, 2) you have a family history of diabetes, 3) you had gestational diabetes or you gave birth to a baby that weighed more than 9 pounds, or 4) you are overweight with a BMI between 25 and 30.

DID YOU KNOW?

In 2012, more than 29.1 million Americans had diabetes. Pre-diabetes was also identified in 86 million people over age 20.

Hepatitis C screening. You may be eligible for screening for hepatitis C if you ever used illicit injectable drugs, had a blood transfusion before 1992, or were born between 1945 and 1965. Screening is allowed one time only unless you continue to use illicit injectable drugs. In this case, screening for hepatitis C is permitted annually.

Human Immunodeficiency Virus (HIV) screening. HIV screening is offered free of charge for anyone at high risk for HIV, pregnant women, or anyone who simply wants to be tested. Risk factors for HIV include unprotected sexual intercourse, sexual intercourse with multiple partners, history of sexually transmitted disease, intravenous illicit drug use, unsterile needle use with tattoos, and blood transfusions occurring prior to 1985.

Lung cancer screening. Medicare has recently approved screening for lung cancer with low-dose CT scans for beneficiaries less than 74 years of age with extended smoking histories. Men or women who smoked at least thirty pack years (the number of packs smoked per day x the number of years of smoking) are considered eligible for the free screening test. Coverage for this screening test will begin in 2015.

Osteoporosis screening. Osteoporosis, the thinning of the bones that makes them brittle, increases the risk for fractures and disability. Osteopenia is weakness of the bones to a lesser degree. Screening for osteoporosis can be done through a test known as a bone density scan. Part B allows for screening every 24 months for those who are considered at risk for the condition. This includes women in menopause, women with other forms of estrogen deficiency, people on medication for treatment of osteoporosis, people on prednisone or other steroid drug use, people with primary hyperparathyroidism, people with X-rays that are suggestive for osteopenia or osteoporosis, or people with X-rays that are suggestive for vertebral fracture.

DID YOU KNOW?

Osteoporosis accounts for 1.5 million fractures and more than $12 billion in health-care costs every year.

Sexually transmitted infection (STI) screening. Medicare does not specifically identify who is at risk for STIs, risk factors include unprotected sexual intercourse outside of a monogamous relationship, with multiple partners, or with a partner who has been unfaithful. Medicare allows for tests that look for the following infections: chlamydia, hepatitis B, gonorrhea, and syphilis. It does not include screening for herpes. Screening may occur once every 12 months and for pregnant women during certain stages of their gestation.

Preventive Screening for Women

Breast cancer accounted for more than 40,000 deaths in 2014, and is the most common cause of cancer death in women for any reason second only to lung cancer. More than 232,000 cases of invasive breast cancer and more than 62,500 cases of noninvasive cancer were diagnosed that year.

 DID YOU KNOW?

In 2014, there were more than 2.8 million women with a history of breast cancer in the United States, some survivors, others actively undergoing treatment.

Controversy exists over mammogram screenings for breast cancer. The United States Preventive Screening Task Force (USPSTF) recommends screening begin at age 50 and end at age 74. The American Cancer Society (ACS) recommends that screening start at age 40. The American College of Obstetricians and Gynecologists (ACOG) recommends screening every 1 to 2 years between 40-49 years of age and annually after age 50.

Medicare allows for annual screening mammograms for women starting at age 40 but does not specify an end date. A baseline mammogram may be performed one time between 35-39 years of age.

The rate of cervical cancer, one of the leading causes for death in women in the 1940s, significantly decreased after screening with the routine Pap smear was established. In 2013, there were 4,020 deaths from cervical cancer.

Recommendations for Pap smear screening are consistent across ACOG, ACS, and USPSTF. Screenings are recommended from age 21, regardless of when sexual intercourse first took place—if at all by that age—to age 65.

ROUND TABLE

Eileen wanted to get up to date with preventive screening services now that she has finally enrolled in Medicare. At 68 years old, she was due for her annual mammogram. She did not require additional Pap Smear screening based on ACS, ACOG, or SPSTF guidelines, so she deferred that examination, though Medicare would still have paid for it. She was also due for screening colonoscopy. She also had alcohol screening, blood pressure screening, cholesterol screening, and depression screening. She was not eligible to have other preventive screening services as she did not meet risk factor criteria.

Medicare covers Pap smears every 24 months for all women but does not specify an end date. Certain women may have evaluations more frequently. Women in their child-bearing years, women who have had an abnormal Pap smear within the past 36 months, and women at high risk for cervical cancer may have evaluations every 12 months. The most common risk factor for cervical cancer is infection with human papillomavirus (HPV).

Preventive Screening for Men

Prostate cancer screening remains controversial. The testing options are not 100-percent perfect and can lead to false positive results. This means that prostate cancer may be suspected in men who do not have the disease, leading them to have unnecessary biopsies or procedures. These procedures in and of themselves may be wrought with side effects and complications.

For 2014, approximately 233,000 cases of prostate cancer were diagnosed and nearly 30,000 men died from the disease. More men die with prostate cancer than from it. Autopsies suggest that 1 in 3 men after age 50 have evidence of prostate cancer on examination.

A screening may be performed with a digital rectal exam where a health-care provider inserts their finger into the rectum to feel the prostate directly. Irregularities on the prostate raise suspicion for cancer and may warrant further investigation. Digital rectal examinations require a 20-percent coinsurance.

Prostate specific antigen (PSA) is a protein secreted by the prostate that can be detected by a simple blood test. A high level of PSA may suggest an abnormality with the prostate, such as a benign tumor, a malignant cancer, or an active infection. An elevated PSA test may require further testing to see if there could be an underlying cancer present. Annual PSA testing is free of charge under Part B. Interestingly, the USPSTF advised against PSA screening.

When Screening Procedures Become Diagnostic

As long as your health-care provider accepts assignment, the majority of your preventive screening evaluations are free of charge as previously noted. This may change, however, if something happens during the study that changes what needs to be done.

The classic example is a screening colonoscopy. During a colonoscopy, an abnormality may be detected. A colon polyp could be a precursor to cancer, and as a result requires biopsy for further evaluation. It would not make sense to delay the biopsy to a later time if the provider is able to perform the procedure then and there. Otherwise, you would need another colonoscopy to do the biopsy. Why go through the bowel prep twice? It would unnecessarily subject you a second time to any possible risks related to the procedure. The biopsies are, therefore, taken at the same time.

This means that your screening colonoscopy is no longer for screening purposes. It is now a diagnostic colonoscopy used to investigate an abnormal finding. Your colonoscopy is no longer free. It now requires a 20-percent coinsurance.

The trick is to know if you signed an ABN that outlined this possible cost change to you before the procedure was done. Sometimes, with colonoscopy especially, these fine details may be written into your informed consent form rather than an ABN. If you signed a document allowing biopsies and interventions on an as-needed basis and you acknowledged there could be a price change because of it, you are liable to pay the coinsurance.

You will also pay a 20-percent coinsurance for diagnostic mammograms. These studies may be indicated to follow-up on any previous abnormal mammogram findings.

Services Not Covered by Part B

Part B does not cover everything. Specific limitations are outlined in Chapter 3. These include dental screening, dentures, hearing aids, vision screening, white canes for the blind, and care required when you are out of the country.

Restrictions will exist on your Part B coverage based on what Medicare determines to be medical necessity. You must take your health-care needs into consideration and investigate whether or not a Medicare Advantage Plan or other supplemental plan may offer additional coverage for services, if you need them, that Part B does not cover.

Cost Summary

As of 2014, Part B has an annual deductible of $147 that must be spent before your coverage benefits kick in.

The majority of coinsurances will cost you 20 percent of the Medicare-approved cost of the service. Many preventive services are free of charge if your health-care provider accepts assignment. If your provider does not accept assignment, you will be responsible for a 20-percent coinsurance.

Monthly Part B premiums vary based on your income. The lowest premium in 2014 was set at $104.90 per month for individuals earning less than $85,000 per year or married couples earning less than $170,000 per year. The highest income bracket was for those earning more than $214,000 as an individual or more than $428,000 as a married couple and would cost $335.70 each month in premiums. That equates to $1,259–$4,028 each year, respectively.

You need to pay Part B premiums whether you participate in Original Medicare or a Medicare Advantage Plan.

Late Penalties

If you miss your Initial Enrollment Period or miss or are ineligible for a Special Enrollment Period, you may be subjected to Part B late penalties that extend for the life of your Medicare benefits. You will be expected to add 10 percent to your monthly premium for every full year you were eligible but did not enroll in Part B.

For example, if you missed your eligibility date by five years, you will pay 50 percent more on your Part B premiums for as long as you have Medicare. If you are in the lowest income bracket, this increases your monthly premium to $157.35 per month with an annual payout of $1,888. If you are in the highest income bracket, your monthly premium will now be $503.55 or $6,043 annually. Annual amounts are rounded to the nearest dollar.

The one exception to the extended Part B late penalties occurs if you were penalized prior to turning 65 years old. Once you meet eligibility criteria by age, you get a clean slate. Your late penalties will be removed.

Financial Assistance Programs

There are multiple Medicare Savings Programs aimed to help you decrease how much you spend out-of-pocket on Medicare. Programs that assist with Part B payments include the Qualified Medicare Beneficiary (QMB) Program, the Specified Low-Income Medicare Beneficiary (SLMB) Program, and the Qualifying Individual (QI) Program. The low-income requirements for each of these programs are outlined in Chapter 19.

Total Annual Costs

The following table outlines the average costs you will pay out of pocket for Part B coverage.

Part B Costs for 2014

Income	Monthly Premium	Deductible	Annual Cost
Single: <$85,000 Joint filing: <$170,000	$104.90	$147	$1,259
Single: $85,000–$107,000 Joint filing: $170,000–$214,000	$146.90	$147	$1,763
Single: $107,000–$160,000 Joint filing: $214,000–$320,000	$209.80	$147	$2,518
Single: $160,000–$214,000 Joint filing: $320,000–$428,000	$272.70	$147	$3,264
Single: >$214,000 Joint filing: >$129,000	$335.70	$147	$4,028

The Least You Need to Know

- Initial and Annual Wellness Visits are consultation visits that do not include a physical examination.
- Screening for alcohol abuse, blood pressure, cholesterol, colon cancer, and depression are offered to all Medicare beneficiaries regardless of risk factors.
- Screening for abdominal aneurysm, diabetes, hepatitis C, osteoporosis, and sexually transmitted infections may be covered but only if you have specific risk factors.
- Certain preventive screening tests may be free, but only if your health-care provider accepts assignment.
- If an abnormal finding is discovered during a free screening evaluation, it may be converted to a diagnostic study that costs you money.
- If you did not sign an Advanced Beneficiary Notice informing you that Original Medicare may not cover a test, you are not liable to pay for that test.

CHAPTER 12

Medicare Part D

It's hard to imagine a health-care program for the elderly that doesn't include a plan for prescription drug coverage, but Medicare Part D did not come into existence until 2006. Part D is optional with its own set of costs. Finding the best Part D plan that fits your needs, medically and financially, takes some know-how. Without this information, Part D can be a hard pill to swallow.

The Drug Business

Your health depends on many factors. Exercise and active lifestyles are one part. What you put into your body is another. Food provides nourishment and essential nutrients and vitamins to keep you healthy. Despite your best efforts to eat well and make healthy choices, sometimes you may need help in the form of prescription medications.

How Formularies Work

There are a limited number of ways to purchase prescription medications. For one, you could purchase directly from the manufacturer. This rarely happens in America since pharmacies frequently act as a middle man. Your next option

In This Chapter

- Understanding how formularies work
- Choosing the right medications for you
- Getting the most out of your Part D plan
- Working your way through the donut hole
- How to reduce prescription drug costs

is to purchase a medication from a pharmacy when you have no insurance—often an expensive proposition. Finally, you may purchase from a pharmacy when you do have insurance. What you pay for the medication will depend on what others have negotiated for you behind the scenes.

Pharmacies and insurance companies work with pharmaceutical companies to offer you medications at a set cost. You may recognize some of the larger pharmaceutical companies by their branding and marketing, while other companies are much smaller in size and make more generic medications.

The drug manufacturer wants to sell its product so it negotiates deals with the pharmacies and insurance companies. The manufacturer sells their medications to them at a discounted rate. The insurance company then offers you a *formulary* with the medications it prefers to use. They prefer to use these medications because they will be less expensive to the company overall, even if you pay a part of the price known as a copay.

 **DEFINITION**

> A **formulary** is a preferred list of medications offered to beneficiaries by a Part D prescription drug plan or other insurer. Medications not included on a formulary may not be paid for by the insurer.

Though a pharmacy needs to offer a wide variety of medications, it stands to make a larger profit if it sells more of the drugs that are purchased at a discount. The pharmacies can sell you the medication at a higher cost than it paid, pocketing the extra dollars for themselves.

An insurance company is less likely to make a profit because it still has to pay for the drug. Instead of having you pay the full drug cost out-of-pocket like the pharmacy, the insurance company shares the cost with you. You pay a portion of the cost and the insurance company pays the rest. By having you use medications it purchases at a discounted rate, the insurer spends less money on your health care than it would otherwise.

This is one of the reasons no formulary has every medication available on it. It would be difficult to negotiate plans with every pharmaceutical company that exists. Also, negotiations with one pharmaceutical company may prevent the insurer from negotiating with that company's competitors.

 DID YOU KNOW?

> More than four billion prescriptions were written in 2011, costing $319.9 billion. Of those prescriptions, 264 million prescriptions were for the antidepressants Zoloft® and Celexa®. Lipitor®, the best-selling brand-name medication that year, resulted in $7.7 billion in medication costs.

Copayments and Coinsurance

The dollar amount you contribute to each prescription is called a copay or coinsurance. The first is a fixed dollar amount you pay toward a prescription. The latter is a percentage of the total cost of a prescription that you are required to pay. The majority of medications require copays, while expensive brand-name products may require coinsurance depending on the plan you use.

Your formulary will be divided into different tiers. Copays and coinsurance are often set based on these tiers. The drugs that will cost the insurance company the least will be in the lowest tiers. These are the medications that are preferred. As you move up to higher tiers, your out-of-pocket costs will increase as the insurance company also must pay more toward more expensive medications.

Because each Part D plan is run by a different insurance company, the cost of your copays will vary depending on which plan you choose. There is no federal mandate to set rates on copays or coinsurance rates for prescription medications.

Promoting Drugs

Pharmaceutical companies do not limit their marketing to just insurers. Far from it. If you watch television, you are constantly bombarded with images without any description of the drug or are otherwise fed the miraculous benefits of the drug with a litany of its side effects.

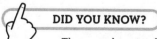 **DID YOU KNOW?**

There are laws in place that regulate pharmaceutical marketing. If a commercial tells you what a drug is used for, it must also tell you about its potential side effects.

While this marketing may encourage you to talk to your provider about a medication, it does not mean your prescriber will or should prescribe it. The pharmaceutical companies know their biggest target is not you or even the insurer. Their target is the source of the written prescription—the health-care provider.

In the past, pharmaceutical companies would try to entice medical professionals with gifts to encourage them to prescribe their products over others. Gifts could be quite extravagant, ranging from money to vacations. Obviously, this practice is strongly discouraged on moral grounds. Your health is not to be bargained with.

To shed light on the issue of gifts, a provision of the Affordable Care Act known as the Physician Payments Sunshine Act has been put into effect. All gifts given to health-care providers from the pharmaceutical industry must be reported to the government and will be disclosed to the public for any individual gifts greater than $10 or any gifts adding up to $100 or more in a given year. Medication samples, vouchers, and rebate cards are not considered to be gifts as they are intended to benefit the patient, not the provider. Failure to report gifts accordingly will result in considerable fines.

On September 30, 2014, CMS unveiled its Open Payments portal. Did your doctor accept gifts from pharmaceutical companies? Visit portal.cms.gov/wps/portal to find out.

Free Samples

Free samples sound like a win-win situation, but do not be falsely reassured. They are still a way for the pharmaceutical companies to make sales.

Of course, free samples are the least expensive way to get your hands on medication. However, they are only available for brand-name products, and these are the most expensive medications on the market. These medications also do not have generic options available. What happens when the samples are no longer available?

 DID YOU KNOW?

You cannot use medication rebate cards or coupons when you use your Part D plan. The same applies to any medications purchased through a government plan. This includes Medicaid and Tricare.

The pharmaceutical companies aim to get you started on an expensive medication for free so that when samples are no longer available you will want to continue the drug and purchase it. The pharmaceutical company is investing in its future sales when it offers free samples.

If you respond well to a medication, it seems a shame to change it to something that you are not sure will work as well, or even at all. The stability of your health is always at risk when you change from a medication that you know works well for you to one with which you do not yet have experience. However, it may be in your financial interest to do just that.

Changing medications could be a smooth transition or one where you face side effects and multiple trials of different medications until you find the most cost-effective one that gives you the most benefit. The best medical option is to start with a low-cost generic option to treat your condition so that you will be able to afford your medications in the long run.

Do not be fooled by the illusion of free samples. You always end up paying more in the end, whether it is with dollars, time, or your health.

Choosing the Best Medications

Reliance on medication rises with age. The average American over age 65 is given 28.5 prescriptions every year, including refills. For those over 75 years old, expect to take five or more regular medications daily. Understanding which drugs are best will reduce your health-care spending.

Classy Drugs

Medications may be more alike than you realize. Medications that have similar chemical composition and work via the same biologic pathways may be part of the same drug class. This often means that switching from one drug to another within the same class will have similar effects on your body.

 DID YOU KNOW?

> Changing from one drug to another in the same drug class does not necessarily mean you will have the same response. You could have a negative reaction to one medication based on its chemical composition even if you responded well to another drug in the same class.

To this end, it does not make sense to be on more than one drug in any given class. If they work the same way, you are not gaining any benefit. On the other hand, you could benefit from being on two drugs for the same medical problem if the drugs are from different classes. In this case, the two drugs are attacking the medical condition in different ways and could better control the problem.

For example, there are many different classes of drugs used to treat hypertension. There are angiotensin receptor blockers, beta-blockers, calcium channel blockers, and more. Being on two beta blockers would not be beneficial and would actually increase your risk for side effects. Being on a beta blocker and a calcium channel blocker together would reduce your blood pressure in different ways and improve your overall blood pressure control.

Not every medication has another drug available in its class. Some drugs are the first of their kind. In this case, the drug is often a brand-name product and can be quite expensive without other drugs as competition.

Generic vs. Brand-Name Medications

Questions often arise about whether brand-name medications are better than generic ones. There are several factors to consider.

DID YOU KNOW?

U.S. drug patents last for 20 years. Because it may take several years for a medication to go through clinical trials, it may only have a portion of years left on its patent once it is finally put on the market.

Brand-name medications are more expensive than generic ones. This is because brand-name medications are covered by patents. A pharmaceutical company holds the rights to a patent for a number of years. Once the patent runs out, other pharmaceutical companies can begin to produce and market the medication under the chemical name. The original company maintains the rights to the trademarked name.

With more versions of the medication on the market, costs decrease as the manufacturers compete for sales. The brand-name manufacturer will continue to charge more than the generic, though the costs are generally lower than when they had the only version on the market. The brand-name companies continue to engage in competitive marketing, often claiming that their product remains better than the generics.

If there is a generic version of a brand-name medication on the market, why would you choose to pay more if it is based on the same active ingredient? There should be no chemical difference between the products, and the mechanism of action of the product remains the same. Generic medications usually cost 80 to 85 percent less than brand-name products.

The only question becomes one of purity. Depending on how the drug is manufactured, there could be impurities in the product that make it less effective for you or cause you to have an unwanted reaction, though this is rarely the case.

DID YOU KNOW?

The average drug takes a minimum of 7.6 years before it hits the marketplace. Preclinical trials may take 1 to 6 years. Clinical trials may last 6 to 11 years. The FDA must then approve the drug application, a process that may take up to 2 years.

Some people get excited when a new drug is introduced on the market. New does not mean best. Many brand-name medications have been withdrawn from the market after high hopes when they first came out. They were withdrawn even after going through the long, drawn-out process of gaining FDA approval for safety.

Brand-Name Drugs Withdrawn From the Market Before Generics Were Available

Name of Drug	Years on the Market	Reason for Withdrawing
Baycol (for cholesterol lowering)	3 years (1998–2001)	Rhabdomyolysis (muscle breakdown), kidney failure
Bextra (for pain relief)	3.3 years (2001–2005)	Heart attack, stroke, gastrointestinal bleeding, skin reactions
Duract (for pain relief)	1 year (1997–1998)	Liver toxicity
Lotronex (for irritable bowel syndrome)	0.8 years (2000)	Ischemic bowel (loss of blood flow to the colon)
Micturin (for bladder incontinence)	2 years (1989–2001)	Cardiac toxicity
Omniflox (an antibiotic)	0.3 years (1992)	Low blood sugar, kidney failure, hemolytic anemia
Posicur (for hypertension)	1 year (1997–1998)	Fatal interactions with more than 25 other drugs
Raxar (an antibiotic)	2 years (1997–1999)	Cardiac arrhythmia
Redux (for appetite suppression)	1 year (1997–1998)	Heart valve disease
Rezulin (for diabetes)	3.25 years (1997–2000)	Liver failure
Vioxx (for pain relief)	4 years (1999–2004)	Heart attack, stroke
Zelnorm (for irritable bowel disease)	4.6 years (2002–2007)	Heart attack, stroke, unstable angina

Sometimes a medication with a generic option is the better bet. The medication has been around for at least the 20 years it was on patent and then for however many years have passed since then. The drug stands the test of time.

There may be times when you have no choice but to use a brand-name medication, for example when the brand-name is the only medication in its class and you have not had the desired response to other available therapies.

Choosing the Best Plan

Part D plans are an optional component for Medicare coverage. They are not managed directly by Medicare, though CMS does set criteria for the standard plan.

Similar to Medicare Advantage Plans, Medicare contracts with private insurance companies to offer these plans to you. Medicare pays a monthly fee to the insurance company, and you pay monthly premiums to the insurance company. In the end, you have your pick of a variety of prescription drug plans.

 TIP

You may elect to choose a Medicare Advantage Plan that also offers Part D to expand your coverage.

With so many different Part D plans available, how do you choose the one that is right for you? If you are lucky, a plan will be available that addresses all of your medical and financial needs. Oftentimes, you will need to weigh the benefits of one plan versus another because that perfect plan may not exist.

Drug Exclusions

You must understand that Medicare may not cover all of your medications, even if you pick a very extensive Part D plan. There are specific exclusions that Medicare will never pay for.

For one, Medicare does not cover any over-the-counter medications you may need to purchase. In the event of a cold, you are out of luck. Even if your health-care provider prescribes you the medication for cold relief, Medicare will not cover those expenses.

Medicare also does not deem it medically necessary to cover the cost of drugs used for cosmetic conditions, erectile dysfunction, fertility, or hair growth.

As for vitamins, Medicare will only cover prenatal vitamins and fluoride preparations as indicated. A daily multivitamin will be an out-of-pocket expense.

Medications for anorexia, weight loss, and weight gain will only be considered for those with AIDS, cancer, or other advanced-stage diseases that can cause physical wasting.

At one time, Medicare would not cover benzodiazepines or barbiturates. These medications are sedatives that have a risk of harm to seniors. Medicare lifted the exclusion to these drugs in 2013 with a caveat. While these medications are technically covered, they are only allowable for medically approved conditions. Insomnia, one of the most common uses for benzodiazepines, may not be considered an approved use of the medication since other medication alternatives are available.

Choosing the Best Formulary Based on Need

There is no one way to choose a Part D plan, but I advise you do not open to a page blindly and just pick one. You want to make an informed decision. Doing otherwise could cost you considerable dollars. You will want to look at both medical needs and costs to find the best fit for you.

Review your current medication list. You may want to select a plan that covers the majority of medications you currently take. In an ideal situation, you will not want to change your current medications if they have worked well for you to this point. Using medications that are not on your Part D formulary will cost you.

Review your current medical conditions. If your medical conditions have been stable for years, you may not need to consider a plan that offers much more drug coverage than what you currently use. However, if you are newly diagnosed with a condition or you have a condition that is unstable or worsening, you may want to keep your options open. You may be prescribed new medications in the coming year, and you will want to consider plans that will give you proper coverage.

Review your family history. Some medical conditions do not present themselves until you get older. You may want to review histories with your family members, if you have not already. You may want to consider broader prescription coverage in the case that you may be at risk for certain medical conditions.

These three factors may help to guide you to a Part D plan that will best meet your needs.

The Donut Hole

The hard truth is that personal finances have entered the equation. If you cannot afford a Part D plan, even if it is the best medical option for you, you may have to decide if it is worth pursuing. Balancing medical needs with expenses is essential to be cost efficient while obtaining adequate coverage.

The harder truth is that Part D coverage drops off after a certain amount of spending has occurred on your plan. You will be forced to pay a much higher proportion of drug costs in what is known as the *donut hole*.

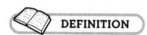 **DEFINITION**

The Medicare **donut hole** is not a tasty treat. It is a coverage gap in Part D prescription drug plans that occurs after you and your Part D plan have spent a certain dollar amount. During this coverage gap, your out-of-pocket costs increase until you reach another set dollar amount.

Before the donut hole begins, you will pay an annual deductible, monthly premiums, and copays and coinsurance for each drug you are prescribed. Your Part D plan pays the remaining cost for your prescriptions. Your Part D plan will continue to do so until you reach the donut hole threshold. In 2014, this dollar amount was $2,850.

Any amount you spent on your monthly premiums does not count toward this threshold amount. Also, any money spent on medications not covered by your Part D plan are excluded. Medications purchased out of the country also do not count.

Once you are in the donut hole, you will pay much more than you did before. Copays are not available. You will pay coinsurances of 47.5 percent for any brand-name medications you take and 72 percent coinsurance for any generic medications. Your Part D plan will pay the remaining 52.5 percent and 28 percent, respectively. This will continue until you and Medicare have spent $1,700. You will continue to pay your monthly premiums, though again your monthly premiums and uncovered medications do not count toward this dollar amount.

 TIP

When you are in the donut hole, this is the only time you are eligible to use medication rebate cards and coupons for any drugs you purchase out-of-pocket.

The average monthly price of a generic medication in 2008 was $35.22, nearly four-fold less than the average brand-name drug at $137.90. However, this does not reflect medications specifically used to treat chronic medical conditions that tend to affect those over 65 years of age. In 2009, the average brand-name drug for such conditions averaged $1,400. That is a mighty big difference.

To show how this may impact your wallet, consider the example of a brand-name prescription drug. Before the donut hole, you would pay a fixed copay for your medication. We will assume a copay here of $50, though in reality your costs would likely be lower. Now your monthly cost for this same drug would be increased to $665, 47.5 percent of $1,400. Your monthly costs have increased more than thirteen-fold, and that is for only one medication.

After you and your Part D plan have spent $1,700 to get out of the donut hole, you will then enter a new phase of your plan known as Catastrophic Coverage. Your prescription costs will be reduced to $2.55 for generic medications, $6.35 for brand-name medications, or 5 percent of the total medication cost, whichever is higher. These values will change annually.

Looking again to our example, you paid $665 last month, but you may only pay $6.35 this month—more than 100 times less!

Breaking Part D Coverage Down into Phases

Phase of Your Part D Plan	What You Pay	What Medicare Part D Pays
Pre-Donut Hole	Deductible Monthly premiums Copays/coinsurance	Total drug cost – copay/coinsurance
Donut Hole	Monthly premiums 47.5% cost of brand-name medications 72% of generic medications	52.5% of brand-name medications 28% of generic medications
Catastrophic Coverage	5% of drug costs or $6.35 copay for brand-name medications $2.55 copay for generic medications (whichever is greater)	95% of drug costs or Total drug cost – copay (whichever is lesser)

The financial burden of the donut hole leaves many seniors struggling to make ends meet. Careful cost planning is essential to allow you to have viable drug coverage when you need it. You should not be forced to decide between paying for food, shelter, or medications. They are all essential to keep you safe and healthy.

Closing the Donut Hole

The intent of the donut hole was to incentivize health-care providers to prescribe less-expensive generic medications over more expensive brand-name products. It was also seen as a way to decrease the influence pharmaceutical companies had on a provider's prescribing patterns.

The unintended consequence of the donut hole was leaving millions of seniors without a means to afford their needed medication regimens. Many of these seniors have multiple chronic medical conditions and require multiple medications. Many may have trialed generic medications that did not work for them. There may be medically necessary reasons why they need to be on more expensive medications. In the end, they are being penalized for their health status. Moral issues abound.

The Affordable Care Act has mandated that the donut hole will eventually be phased out. By 2020, beneficiaries will have to pay only 25 percent for both brand-name and generic medications. This may still be higher than copays in most Part D plans, but it is better than what currently exists.

Mail-Order vs. Local Pharmacy

Another way to achieve cost savings is to use a mail-order pharmacy for your prescriptions. Mail-order pharmacies can fill your prescriptions in bulk, up to 100 days at one time. You pay one copay for a three month supply, the same copay you would have spent for a one month supply at your local pharmacy. Instead of going to the pharmacy, your medications will be delivered to your home.

 TIP

Do not use a mail-order pharmacy for your prescriptions until you are on a stable dose of your medication. If your health-care provider continues to make adjustments to your dose, you may be caught with too many pills at the wrong strength. This could lead to confusion when it comes time to take your medication.

Many insurers have negotiated discount rates with mail-order pharmacies. It is cheaper for your Part D plan to purchase medications in bulk. For this reason, your plan may require you, or strongly encourage you, to use mail-order pharmacies for all of your prescriptions. You could be charged more for the same prescriptions if you do not comply with their recommendations.

Not everyone will be on the same page. You may prefer to support your local pharmacy. Kudos to supporting your local economy, but understand that you may be paying a bit more.

Where to Go for Help

You are not alone in this. There are resources you can access to help you decide which plan will work best for you.

You should speak with your health-care provider about your medical condition. Also, it will be important to see if any changes are anticipated in your prescription regimen or if it would be appropriate to transition you from brand-name to generic medications to reduce overall costs. Understanding your medical needs may help to steer you toward the best Part D plan.

Your pharmacist can also be a valuable source of information. He will know not only the ins and outs of the industry but may be able to make suggestions for plans that have good reputations. He may be able to suggest plans that would cover the medications you use.

The Medicare.gov website is a wealth of information. Visit Medicare.gov/find-a-plan to compare different plan options in your area. Chapter 8 reviews tips on how to navigate the site and to set up the best plans for comparison.

ROUND TABLE

Loraine has a decision to make. She has to select a Part D plan now that she is eligible for Medicare. She knows if she waits after her Initial Enrollment Period to sign up, she could face late penalties. She does not have chronic medical conditions, although her parents did have a history for diabetes. She eats a healthy diet, and her doctor measured her sugars in the normal range. She chooses the standard benefit Part D plan to keep costs down because she does not anticipate the need for more extensive drug coverage.

Cost Summary

Costs for Part D plans will be variable since they are managed by private insurers. You will be responsible for an annual deductible, which is set across the board at $310 for 2014. You will also pay different amounts for monthly premiums, copays, and coinsurance whether you are in or out of the donut hole.

Based on your earnings, you may also have to pay an additional fee known as the Part D income-related monthly adjustment amount (IRMAA). Depending on your income, you may not be on the hook for IRMAA or may pay up to $69.30 extra per month. These additional fees are not paid to your insurance company but directly to Medicare. You will receive the bill through Medicare to make payments as needed. If you do not pay your IRMAA accordingly, you will lose your Part D plan coverage, even if it is part of a Medicare Advantage Plan.

You will also be charged a late penalty if you sign up for Part D after your Initial Enrollment Period for Medicare. You will be charged 1 percent for every month you were eligible for Medicare but did not sign up for a plan. That is the case unless you had creditable coverage during that time. Creditable coverage means you had coverage that is as good as the standard benefit plan offered by Part D plans. If you lose your creditable coverage for any reason, you have 63 days to sign up for a Part D plan to avoid the late penalty.

Your late penalty is not based on your monthly premium, because that would not necessarily be fair for those who elected for a more expansive plan. If that were the case, it could actually be a disincentive for beneficiaries to choose those plans.

To standardize the late fees, the penalties are calculated as a percentage of a national base beneficiary premium (NBBP), set at $32.42 in 2014. For example, if you signed up for a Part D plan 10 months after your Initial Enrollment Period, you would pay 10 percent of the NBBP in fines (1 percent for each month), resulting in $3.24 added to your particular monthly premium.

These penalties are paid as long as you have Medicare, with one exception. If you became eligible for Medicare and enrolled late in Part D before you turned 65 years old, your Part D penalties will be discontinued when you turn 65 years old.

Low-Income Subsidy

If you are unable to afford a Part D plan or have difficulties during the donut hole, there is financial assistance available. You should not go without your medications. Your health is at stake.

The Medicare Extra Help program offers a Low-Income Subsidy (LIS) for those meeting certain financial criteria. Not only do you get assistance in paying your annual deductible, monthly premiums, copays, and coinsurance through the program, but you get to avoid the donut hole altogether. You may be able to save as much as $4,000 in any given year.

> **TIP**
>
> Apply for the Medicare Part D Low-Income Subsidy through your local Social Security office, online at socialsecurity.gov/extrahelp, or by phone at 1-800-771-1213 (TTY 1-800-325-0778).

The LIS program takes both your income and your assets into consideration. You may be eligible if you earn less than $17,235 as an individual or less than $23,265 as a married couple. Income limits may be higher for people living in Alaska and Hawaii. If your income exceeds the limit, you may still qualify if you support other family members who live with you.

Assets less than $13,440 for an individual or less than $26,860 for a married couple are also needed to qualify. The house where you live, your car, and any insurance policies you hold (e.g., life insurance) do not count toward those assets. Assets that would be considered include bank accounts, cash, IRAs, mutual funds, stocks, bonds, and real estate other than the home where you live.

The Least You Need to Know

- Formularies are a list of preferred medications offered to you through your Part D or other prescription drug plan.
- You cannot use medication rebate cards or coupons to purchase medications through a government sponsored program such as Medicare Part D, Medicaid, or Tricare.
- The coverage gap known as the donut hole will be closed by 2020.
- Using a mail-order pharmacy may save you money in copays.
- Financial assistance is available through a Medicare Low-Income Subsidy to help you pay for your prescription medications.

Medicare Advantage Plans and Medigap

Original Medicare provides many offerings in its health-care plan for those who qualify, but as discussed in Chapter 3, there are limitations to what it can do. With an expanding number of beneficiaries, financial constraints keep the program from expanding to cover more and more services.

These gaps in coverage do not have to remain exposed. You can close them by opting for supplemental insurance. Employer-sponsored health insurance, union benefits, and retiree benefits may do this for you, but not everyone has those options. When you retire, you need to know that you have access to programs that can give you the extra care if you need it. This chapter will discuss two types of plans that provide additional health-care coverage, namely Medicare Advantage Plans and Medigap policies

Medicare Advantage Plans

Medicare Advantage Plans are an official part of Medicare, though participation in these Part C programs is optional. These plans are intended to offer you additional coverage beyond Original Medicare if you so choose. As an optional program, they are not free and require their own monthly premiums and other costs.

How Medicare Advantage Plans Work

The U.S. government has contracted with private insurance companies to develop and offer you Medicare Advantage Plans. Medicare makes monthly payments to the insurers who provide you the plan. You pay your monthly Medicare Advantage premiums and other health-care costs, i.e. coinsurance, to the insurance company. You continue to pay Part B premiums directly to Medicare. The care you receive remains under Medicare's umbrella, but the money is used in a different way.

The federal government sees Medicare Advantage Plans as a way to slow down expenditures from the Medicare Trust Fund. The slower the Trust Fund is depleted, the longer Medicare can remain a viable program. In theory, Medicare will pay less to an insurance company than it would have paid if a beneficiary had needed to access expensive health-care services, such as hospital stays. These plans shift expenses to the private sector while offering you more services.

 DID YOU KNOW?

The theory behind Medicare Advantage Plans has not yet played out in practice as it seems the government is spending more on these plans than on Original Medicare! That will change in coming years as reductions in payments to Medicare Advantage Plans are in the works.

The insurance companies benefit in several ways. First, the insurance companies have access to a larger population than they would have had otherwise. Generally speaking, a large portion of the elderly population has limited financial income and does not have the means to purchase traditional coverage through private companies.

Second, private insurance companies receive monthly payments from Medicare in addition to premiums paid by their beneficiaries. It is a for-profit venture. There is debate as to whether these plans will remain as robust in the future when Medicare pulls back on Medicare Advantage payments.

Because Medicare Advantage Plans are run by private companies, their cost can be quite variable. The insurers have the freedom to set their own rates. Medicare does not regulate the costs of these plans.

What Medicare Advantage Plans Cover

Medicare Advantage Plans must cover all services that would be available through Original Medicare and can also offer you additional coverage options. In fact, many Medicare Advantage Plans also offer you Part D plans as well.

CAUTION
Part D late penalties still apply even if your Part D plan is covered under a Medicare Advantage Plan.

Medicare Advantage Plans may be able to offer services that you cannot get with Original Medicare. Depending on the plan you choose, you may be able to access coverage for dental care, vision screenings, and hearing aids, among other common services frequently needed by a senior population.

You will be responsible to pay all your own deductibles, coinsurance, and copayments.

Types of Plans

There are a variety of different types of plans to choose from. Understanding the basic principles of how each one works may help you to make the best decision based on your needs.

Health Maintenance Organizations (HMO) come in two flavors. The first allows you to only use health-care providers and hospitals within a designated network. The second, an HMO-POS (point of service), allows you to use this in-network group but also allows you to access providers and hospitals outside of the network for certain services, though at higher cost. In either type of HMO plan, you cannot be charged higher fees for care that is required in an emergency situation, even if such care is out-of-network.

Preferred Provider Organizations (PPO) also have in-network and out-of-network providers. You pay less when you use in-network services. This allows you wider access to care options. There are also fewer restrictions related to referral requirements. These plans tend to cost more than HMOs.

Private Fee-for-Service (PFFS) plans work in a different way. These plans determine how much you pay for each service and they will cover the difference. Costs will vary depending on the type of care provided. There may be in-network providers that always agree to accept payment from a PFFS plan, but other providers may or may not accept the terms of the plan, even if they have seen you before. Out-of-network health care will cost you more. An out-of-network provider may choose to accept payment for one visit and not another. These plans can be tricky because there is no guarantee for care. The benefit is they may cost you less in premiums and deductibles.

Special Needs Plans (SNP) are tailored to those with particular medical conditions such as ESRD, dementia, diabetes, heart failure, and HIV. Because these plans target specific diseases, the covered services best meet the needs for these conditions, including specialists and medications commonly required to manage the health of the beneficiary. These plans are not uniformly available. Only those living in health-care facilities, those getting nursing care at home, those on Medicare or Medicaid, or those with conditions covered by the SNP may be included. Care is only covered for in-network services unless emergency care or out-of-area dialysis is required.

Requirements for Different Types of Health-Care Plans

Type of Plan	Do You Need a Primary Care Provider?	Do You Need a Referral?
HMO	Yes	Yes
HMO-POS	Yes	Yes
PPO	No	No
PFFS	No	No
SNP	Yes	Yes

Everyone will have different preferences. Certain restrictions may make it difficult to access care that you may need or to access specialty care in a timely manner. That said, plans with more restrictions may cost less. You have to weigh the pros and cons for your situation.

The key is to shop around. Different insurance companies may offer all or only some of these options, and at different costs. Before you dive into one plan, arm yourself with information. A strategy to find the best health-care plan for you is outlined in Chapter 8.

Enrollment Options

You are eligible to enroll in a Medicare Advantage Plan during your Initial Enrollment Period and during the annual Open Enrollment Period that occurs from October 15 to December 7. Benefits kick in on January 1.

Once you choose a plan you are generally stuck with it until the next Open Enrollment Period, so choose wisely. Exceptions include the following:

Cancellation. If your plan gets cancelled for any reason, you are given a Special Enrollment Period in which you can enroll in another plan.

Five-star plans. You may elect to join a five-star plan at any time.

Relocation. If you move to a new area, you may lose access to your Medicare Advantage Plan and will be able to sign up for a new one during your Special Enrollment Period.

Trial period. If you try a Medicare Advantage Plan and decide it is not for you, you may return to Original Medicare within 12 months of your Initial Enrollment Period.

See Chapters 7 and 8 for more detail on enrollment periods.

Medigap Policies

Do not let the name fool you. Medigap is not an official part of Medicare. These policies, also referred to as Medicare Supplemental Insurance, may be purchased to help cover costs that Original Medicare leaves on the table.

Even though the government regulates and standardizes what these plans can cover, Medigap policies are entirely priced by private insurance companies. The government pays no money to private insurance companies that offer these Medigap policies.

How Medigap Policies Work

Depending on the state where you live, there are 11 Medigap policies to choose from. These plans must meet certain requirements set by the government. Because the plans are standardized, the only difference between individual plans is cost. Massachusetts, Minnesota, and Wisconsin work a little differently, as you will see later in this chapter.

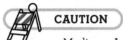

CAUTION

> Medicare Advantage Plans and Medigap policies do not go hand in hand. You must choose one or the other. Also, you cannot have a Medigap policy if you are on Medicaid.

You must have both Parts A and B to purchase a Medigap policy. Original Medicare will pay any claims first, and any leftover costs are submitted to your Medigap policy to pay its part.

You do not get additional care services under a Medigap policy, only help toward paying off costs that Original Medicare doesn't cover. This means you do not gain access to dental, vision, or hearing benefits that were not offered as part of Original Medicare. Long-term nursing home stays and private nursing care are still not covered.

Prescription drug coverage is no longer included though it had once been an option prior to 2006. You may well need to purchase a Part D plan in addition to a Medigap policy to add these benefits.

Types of Policies

Though Medigap policies are standardized based on what they can cover, how much they cost will vary quite a bit depending on what type of plan the private insurance companies provide. Understanding these plan types can help you to anticipate how much your Medigap policy will cost you in the future.

There are three types of plans insurance companies may offer you:

Community-related policies. These policies charge the same rate no matter how old you are. This could be good and bad. If you are younger, you may be charged more than if it were an age-based policy. If you are older, you could benefit from the averaging of the costs.

Issue age-related policies. These policies charge you based on how old you were when you first signed up for the policy, and premiums stay the same over the course of the policy.

Attained age-related policies. These policies charge you based on how old you are now, and premiums increase as you get older.

This does not mean that costs do not change at all. Monthly premiums may be adjusted based on inflation. If you have limited income, you may want to consider a plan that has fixed premiums.

Alphabet Soup

Medigap policies come in different flavors and those flavors taste like alphabet soup. With each letter down the alphabet, a plan offers increased coverage. Some plans may have higher out-of-pocket expenses than others. Specifically, plans K and L require you to pay expenses out of pocket of $4,920 and $2,470, respectively, as of 2014, before each kicks in to cover its listed benefits. Plan F also has an alternative available, a high-deductible option where coverage does not kick in until $2,140 has been paid out of pocket.

Summary of Medigap Policy Benefits

Medigap Benefits	A	B	C	D	F	G	K	L	M	N
Part A deductible		X	X	X	X	X	50%	75%	50%	X
Part A hospice coinsurance	X	X	X	X	X	X	50%	75%	X	X
Part A hospital coinsurance up to 365 days after Medicare exhausted	X	X	X	X	X	X	X	X	X	X
Part A SNF coinsurance			X	X	X	X	50%	75%	X	X
Part B deductible			X		X					
Part B coinsurance	X	X	X	X	X	X	50%	75%	X	X
Part B preventive coinsurance	X	X	X	X	X	X	X	X	X	X
Part B excess charges					X	X				

Medigap Benefits	A	B	C	D	F	G	K	L	M	N
First 3 pints of blood	X	X	X	X	X	X	50%	75%	X	X
Foreign travel emergency coverage			X	X	X	X			X	X

You may notice a few letters missing from the preceding table. Plans E, H, I, and J are no longer available.

 TIP

Visit medicare.gov/find-a-plan/questions/Medigap-home.aspx to explore your Medigap options.

All insurance companies that sell Medigap policies must offer Plan A and either Plan C or F. Beyond that, they can offer any of the other letter policies they choose. Please note that not all policies will be legally available in your state.

Massachusetts, Minnesota, and Wisconsin do not care for alphabet soup. They prefer to mix their own ingredients, though Minnesota does allow the F (high-deductible version), K, L, M, and N plans.

	Massachusetts	Minnesota	Wisconsin
Part A deductible	Supplemental plan only	Available in certain plans	Available in certain plans
Part A hospital coinsurance	Yes	Yes	Yes
Part A hospice	Yes	Yes	Yes
Part A inpatient mental health stays	60 days (120 days for supplemental plan)		175 days after Medicare exhausted
Part A SNF coinsurance	Supplemental plan only	120 days	
Part B deductible	Supplemental plan only	Available in certain plans	Available in certain plans
Part B coinsurance	Yes	Yes	Yes
First 3 pints of blood	Yes	Yes	Yes

continues

continued

	Massachusetts	Minnesota	Wisconsin
Foreign travel emergency	Supplemental plan only	Available in certain plans	Available in certain plans
Home health services			40 visits (may increase up to 365 visits with certain plans)

This table is meant to provide a brief overview of the main coverage options in these states. Specific details may be found by reviewing information from your state's State Health Insurance Assistance Program (SHIP). A state by state directory is available at seniorsresourceguide.com/directories/National/SHIP/.

Another option available in certain states is Medicare SELECT plans. These plans are also standardized but limit their coverage to a network of providers. If you use an out-of-network provider or hospital, this type of plan may not pay anything towards your care. Since they offer you less coverage, Medicare SELECT may be less expensive than a traditional Medigap policy.

Remember that Medigap policies are not part of Original Medicare and they certainly are not equivalent to a Medicare Advantage Plan. If an insurance agent tells you otherwise, be on high alert.

Companies are also not allowed to offer you a Medigap policy in the following situations:

- If you have a Medicare Advantage Plan and do not plan to change to Original Medicare
- If you already have a Medigap policy and are not planning to cancel it
- If you are on Medicaid

If any of these situations occur, these companies must be reported for fraud and abuse. Reach out to your State Health Insurance Assistance Program.

Enrollment Options

Timing is everything when it comes to signing up for a Medigap policy because your costs will jump if you miss your window of opportunity.

Your Medigap Open Enrollment Period begins once you sign up for Part B. You have six months to sign up. Most states require that you also be 65 years old, but some states do allow for Medicare beneficiaries under 65 years old with disabilities to apply as well. This enrollment period is special because it does not allow the policy to refuse coverage or delay care based on pre-existing conditions.

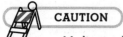

CAUTION

Medigap policies may cost you more if you have pre-existing conditions and apply after the one-time Open Enrollment Period.

Pre-existing conditions are a hot-button item. A pre-existing condition is a medical problem you had before you applied for the plan. The Affordable Care Act requires pre-existing conditions to be disregarded for applicants of insurance in the health-care marketplace. However, those ACA protections do not extend for those 65 and older. You could still be denied coverage based on a pre-existing condition if you apply for Medigap outside of the Open Enrollment Period.

When you apply late for Medigap, the private insurance company can refuse or deny coverage to you based on your medical history. Expect to be charged more, too. If you have pre-existing conditions, then there will commonly be a six-month pre-existing condition waiting period before your Medigap coverage benefits kick in. This waiting period can be waived if you had creditable health insurance coverage for at least six months without any gaps longer than 63 days preceding your Medigap application.

Your Medigap coverage begins on the first day of the month after you apply, i.e., if you apply on August 19, your benefits will begin on September 1.

Swapping Coverage

Swapping one Medigap policy for another has its own set of rules. It depends on how long you've had your current plan and whether or not you have pre-existing medical conditions.

If you've had your current Medigap policy for less than six months and you have pre-existing conditions, the insurance company can go back to their medical underwriters and charge you more, or even deny you coverage for another plan. When and if they accept your application, you may be caught with another six-month pre-existing condition waiting period before benefits kick in.

If you've had your current Medigap policy for more than six months and you have pre-existing conditions, you may or may not be on the hook for those pre-existing conditions. It depends on whether or not you are choosing a plan that has the same benefits as your current policy. If you elect for a higher letter plan, your pre-existing conditions could result in another six-month pre-existing condition waiting period.

TIP

Your insurance agent cannot cancel your Medigap policy for you. You must submit a written request to the insurance company for this. Always confirm that the request has been received and approved so you know when benefits will end.

It may cost you a bit more to change policies, too. It is recommended that you take advantage of a 30-day free-look period on the new plan. If you don't like the new plan, you can go back to your old one at the same rates. The catch? The "free-look period" isn't free.

You have to pay premiums for both plans while you make your decision. When you decide which plan you want to keep, you must cancel the policy on the other plan. If you opt out of the free-look period but then decide you want to go back to the old plan, you will be back on the hook for any pre-existing conditions for that plan as well as any resulting higher premiums.

Guaranteed Coverage

You may lose your Medigap coverage if the company selling your plan closes for any reason, bankruptcy or otherwise, or if you stop paying your premiums. Otherwise, it will depend on whether or not your plan is guaranteed renewable. Plans purchased after 1992 are guaranteed renewable, meaning that your coverage cannot be cancelled based on any health conditions you have. Even if you purchased your plan prior to 1992, your plan may be guaranteed renewable if it was purchased in one of the following states:

California	Mississippi
Colorado	Missouri
Connecticut	Montana
Delaware	New Hampshire
Florida	New Jersey
Georgia	New York
Hawaii	North Carolina
Illinois	Oklahoma
Kansas	Oregon
Louisiana	Pennsylvania
Maine	South Dakota
Maryland	Tennessee
Massachusetts	Texas
Michigan	Vermont
Minnesota	Wisconsin

If you apply for a Medigap policy outside of the Open Enrollment Period, you may still be offered some protection against medical underwriting for pre-existing conditions but only if you meet certain criteria:

Your Medicare Advantage Plan is no longer available to you and you want to change to Original Medicare. This may be the case if the private insurance company no longer offers the plan, the company has closed its doors, or you relocate outside of the service area for the plan. If you use your Special Enrollment Period to switch to Original Medicare as reviewed in Chapter 8, you are eligible to apply for a Medigap policy without restrictions put on your health status. You are limited to select from the following plans: A, B, C, F, K, or L, if they are available in your state.

You want to switch from a Medicare Advantage Plan to Original Medicare within the first 12 months of your initial eligibility. This is considered a trial right. You have from 60 days before to 63 days after the end of your coverage to add the Medigap policy of your choice.

You lose access to a non-Medicare supplemental policy. This may be the case if you were relying on an employer-sponsored health plan or COBRA to cover benefits and those plans have ended. You must apply for a Medigap policy within 63 days of losing those benefits. You are limited to select from the following plans: A, B, C, F, K, or L, if they are available in your state.

You lose access to your Medicare SELECT plan due to relocation. You may apply for a Medigap policy from 60 days before to 63 days after your loss of Medicare SELECT coverage. You are limited to select from the following plans: A, B, C, F, K, or L, if they are available in your state.

You want to switch back to a Medigap policy after switching from a Medigap policy to Medicare Advantage Plan. You have a trial right to return back to your original Medigap policy with the same company. If the particular plan is no longer offered, you may be able to choose from the following plans offered by any insurance company: A, B, C, F, K, or L, if they are available in your state.

Your Medigap policy ends through no fault of your own. You have 63 days to apply for a new plan after your loss of coverage.

Choosing Between Medicare Advantage and Medigap

You cannot have both a Medicare Advantage Plan and a Medigap policy. You will have to make a decision as to whether one or the other of these supplements to Original Medicare will work in your situation.

ROUND TABLE

Loraine has reached the age for Medicare eligibility and must decide whether or not to choose a Medicare Advantage Plan or a Medigap policy to supplement her care. She is relatively healthy with the exception of some mild hearing loss. She does not require frequent doctor visits and has never been hospitalized, other than for the birth of her children.

Since she does not utilize health-care services frequently, a Medigap policy that helps pay for deductibles and coinsurance is unlikely to provide as much benefit in her situation as a Medicare Advantage Plan that may offer hearing tests and assistance in purchasing costly hearing aids in the future.

Does Medicare Advantage Have the Advantage?

Pros:

- You may gain extra health-care benefits not offered by Original Medicare, such as dental care, vision screening, hearing aids, nursing home coverage, and private nursing care.

- You may be able to include prescription drug benefits in your plan selection.

Cons:

- Depending on the plan you select, the health-care providers or hospitals you can access for care may be limited.

- Medicare Advantage Plans still require out-of-pocket expenses, including deductibles, monthly premiums, and copayments.

Does Medigap Fill the Gaps?

Pros:

- You maintain access to all providers and hospitals that accept Medicare for payment.

- If you have medical conditions that require frequent medical evaluations or hospitalizations, a Medigap policy may save you the most money by covering costly deductibles and coinsurance.

Cons:

- If you have pre-existing medical conditions, you could be on the hook for higher payments if you sign up late or want to change to a different plan.

- You do not gain extra health-care benefits beyond what Original Medicare offers.

- You may have to purchase a Part D plan, adding an additional premium to what you pay every month.

The Least You Need to Know

- The federal government pays money toward Medicare Advantage Plans but not Medigap policies.
- Medicare Advantage Plans may cover additional health services, while Medigap policies do not add additional coverage beyond what Original Medicare offers.
- Medigap policies are not part of Medicare.
- Medigap policies are standardized according to federal guidelines but can vary in cost depending on the particular plan and which company you use to buy them.
- Medigap policies can penalize you for having pre-existing conditions.

Employer-Sponsored Health Plans

Medicare may only be one part of your overall health-care plan. If you (or your spouse) have not yet retired, you may also have access to employer-sponsored health care through your current job. Many factors must be taken into consideration to understand when that insurance will work in conjunction with your Medicare plan and when it will not.

Do You Need Both?

The first question you have to ask yourself is whether or not you need Medicare when you still have access to another health insurance plan. The answer will depend on your financial resources and your medical needs.

Most people will want to avoid paying two premiums a month instead of one. There needs to be a good reason to make the added cost worthwhile. Let's consider your options.

In This Chapter

- How to decide whether or not to enroll in Medicare when you have employer-sponsored health insurance
- Understanding how the size of your employer affects your benefits
- Securing your health-care insurance in times of family or medical need
- Your rights under Workers' Compensation insurance
- When Medicare will pay your bills

Employer-Sponsored Health Insurance Alone

Employer-sponsored health plans may provide coverage not only for you but also for your spouse and dependents. Medicare is not a shared plan and can only be accessed by you as the beneficiary. If your family relies on you for health-care coverage, you may prefer to hold onto your employer-sponsored plan as long as possible.

If your employer-sponsored coverage meets your current needs and you are satisfied with its service, you may choose to keep that plan. Adding Medicare may or may not add additional services to the roster depending on how extensive your current plan is. If you do not require the added coverage, you may choose to defer Medicare.

In the case of Medicare, whether or not you defer coverage will depend on where you work. If your job makes you eligible for a Special Enrollment Period (see below) and you do not currently need the extra health-care coverage, you may put Medicare on hold until you leave your job without facing monetary penalties.

Employer-Sponsored Health Insurance with Medicare

You like your current health plan. You need a means to provide health care for your dependents. Choosing to stay with your employer-sponsored plan may make sense, but you may still need to consider enrolling in Medicare on top of that.

If you are not eligible for a Special Enrollment Period based on your current job, not signing up for Medicare could cost you significant dollars in the future. Though you may pay higher premium costs now for the two plans, you will pay less later if you enroll in Medicare when you first become eligible.

You must keep in mind that Medicare's late penalties, depending on whether they are for Parts A, B, or D, may extend for years or even as long as you have Medicare. Late penalties are discussed in detail in Chapter 7.

It may also be the case that you could benefit from additional health-care coverage, especially if your employer-sponsored plan is limited. Adding Medicare services to your employer-sponsored plan may give you additional coverage options if you have increased medical needs.

Medicare Alone

Taking all the previous arguments into consideration, you may need to consider putting all your eggs into the Medicare basket for financial reasons. Not everyone can afford to pay premiums for multiple plans every month. If your current employment does not make you eligible for a Special Enrollment Period, deferring Medicare will cost you more money down the road. It may save you money to choose Medicare over the employer-sponsored plan.

Medicare may also provide all the benefits you need. Having both plans available may be unnecessary. You will have to take a close look at your health situation to see where your needs lie. Only you can make that decision.

When Bigger Is Better

I have said it before, and I must say it again. Size does matter, in certain situations. The size of the company you work for will decide whether or not you are eligible for certain benefits.

DID YOU KNOW?

Small businesses have been key to pulling the United States out of the Great Recession. From 2009 to 2012, small businesses employing fewer than 20 employees increased job opportunities by 4.7 percent, whereas larger businesses only did so by 1.9 percent.

This is not to say that working for a small company is bad. The exact opposite is true. Small companies are the backbone of the American economy. They strengthen communities and local economies by not only offering jobs but by delivering innovative concepts. They are better aligned to address the changing needs within a geographic area and build lasting relationships. Larger companies may also rely on smaller businesses to succeed.

Also, let us not forget that many big businesses had to get their start somewhere. Amazon, Disney, Google, Hewlett-Packard, Mattel, and Microsoft are all businesses said to have begun in a garage.

Special Enrollment Periods

You may be granted a Special Enrollment Period for enrolling in Medicare if your employer employs at least 20 full-time employees or the equivalent in part-time employees with those employees working more than 20 weeks in the preceding calendar year. Self-employed individuals do not count toward the required 20 employees. In addition, the 20 weeks do not have to be consecutive. If your employer meets this criteria, you can wait to sign up for Medicare without penalty.

The Special Enrollment Period based on your employment status extends from the time you leave your job or lose your employer-sponsored health coverage, whichever comes first, and extends up to eight months thereafter.

DID YOU KNOW?

Businesses employing fewer than 20 employees accounted for 98 percent of all U.S. firms in 2012.

Companies with fewer than 20 full-time equivalent employees may provide excellent job opportunities, but they cannot protect you from these regulations. The Tax Equity and Fiscal Responsibility Act (TEFRA) of 1982 set this standard, and it is unlikely to change in the future. The longer you wait to sign up for Medicare after you are eligible, the higher the late penalties will be.

If you are uncertain how many employees work for your company, be proactive and investigate. Your employer needs to report any changes regarding changes in TEFRA status. It is better to be safe than sorry. Assuming you have a Special Enrollment Period when in fact you do not will cost you in retirement, when your income will likely be fixed or reduced.

Family Medical Leave Act

Your employer-sponsored health insurance could be at risk if you need to take time away from work to care for a sick or elderly family member, including yourself. That is unless your employer is required to follow regulations set forth by the Family Medical Leave Act (FMLA) of 1993.

FMLA requires your employer to provide you unpaid leave from your job for up to 12 weeks within a 12-month period for medical or family reasons. That time off may be continuous or intermittent, meaning your daily or weekly work hours could be reduced short-term, you take repeated shorter intervals of time off, or you take time off on an as needed basis. In some cases, your employer may require that you first use up your earned paid time off, such as sick or vacation time, before FMLA kicks in.

This legislation provides job security for you so that you still have a job when you return from your leave. It also allows your employer-sponsored health insurance to continue without interruption. You may be required to continue payment of your monthly premiums during your absence.

DID YOU KNOW?

Thirteen percent of employees took FMLA leave in 2012, with the average leave lasting 27.8 days. Reasons for FMLA leave that year included 57 percent for personal illness, 22 percent for birth of a child, and 19 percent to care for a family member.

Protections are given to employees who work for state, local, and federal agencies. Private businesses may also be held responsible to these standards. For the private sector, size again comes into play. Two requirements must be met for a company to comply with FMLA. First, an employer must have 50 or more full-time employees or an equivalent working for them in a given year. Second, these employees must work at least 20 weeks to count toward the requirement. For example, if a company hired an employee full time but the employee quit after 15 weeks, he would not count toward the 50 employee requirement. The FMLA requirement will be enforced if the company had the qualifying number of employees in the current or past year.

Even if your employer is obligated to offer FMLA, your employer may not be required to offer it to you. To be afforded FMLA protections, you must have worked at your current job for at least 12 months, and also must have worked at least 1,250 hours in the last 12 months.

Your employer may require proof about the reasons necessitating your leave. This may require your health-care provider to examine you or your family member to complete the designated paperwork. If your employer disagrees with the health-care provider's recommendation for any reason, they may request a second opinion, but they must pay for it. Your employer may also request progress reports over the course of your leave to ensure that you are on track to return to work as expected.

Understanding how FMLA works is important because if your employer is not eligible or your personal work history does not qualify under the legislation, you could lose your health benefits. Take a close look at your medical history and that of your family.

- Do you have a chronic illness that could lead to future work absences?

- Are you anticipating surgery that requires an extended rehabilitation?

- Do you have a family member who is currently in need?

- Will you be responsible to care for an aging parent or family member in the future?

If your job is not protected under FMLA, you may want to sign up for Medicare when you can to make sure you have access to health-care coverage when you need it. Otherwise, you may be forced to go without benefits for a period of time before you can apply. Depending on what time of year this happens, it could be months before coverage starts. You may need to wait until the annual General Enrollment Period from January 1 to March 31 to apply for benefits, and your Medicare benefits will not begin until July 1. Alternatively, if you are eligible for other health-care coverage, such as a private insurance plan or a plan through the ACA Health Insurance Marketplace, you may wish to pursue those at this time.

COBRA Considerations

Retiree benefits and union benefits aside, employer-sponsored health insurance does not last forever. Your rights to continue that health plan after you leave your job may depend on the size of your employer.

The Consolidated Omnibus Budget Reconciliation Act (COBRA) of 1986 applies to businesses that employ more than 20 full-time equivalent employees. Furthermore, those employees must work for at least 50 percent of all business days from January 1 to December 31 the preceding year. COBRA requires that such employers offer extended coverage on your employer-sponsored health plan when your or your spouse's job changes for one of the following qualifying reasons:

- You or your spouse, whoever is the covered employee, leaves the job voluntarily but not for reasons of misconduct.

- You or your spouse, whoever is the covered employee, loses the job involuntarily but not for reasons of misconduct.

- You or your spouse, whoever is the covered employee, has work hours reduced.

- Your spouse, if he or she is the covered employee, dies.

- You divorce or separate from your spouse, whether you or he or she is the covered employee.

- Your child is no longer considered a dependent.

Benefits may not be limited to just you. Your spouse and dependents may be eligible as well.

The cost of the health-care plan offered to you under COBRA is less expensive than it would have been if you paid for a health plan directly from the insurance company. You get the discounted rate negotiated between the insurer and your employer. Only now, you foot the whole bill whereas during your active employment, your employer paid a portion of the cost.

You have 60 days from the date you would have lost your health-care coverage to decide whether or not to sign up for COBRA benefits. If you choose this option, you may have benefits for 18 months or longer if you meet certain criteria.

The maximum duration for COBRA coverage is 42 months if you qualify for an extension. You may be eligible for an 18-month extension for a total of 36 months if you have a second qualifying event, like those listed previously, and notify the plan within 60 days of the qualifying event and before the initial 18-month period has ended. All beneficiaries will be granted a 24-month extension, for a total of 42 months, if the covered employee dies.

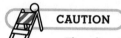

CAUTION

Though employment by a company that provides COBRA benefits may qualify you for a Special Enrollment Period with Medicare, COBRA coverage itself does not. If you wait longer than the eight months from the time your job ended to enroll in Medicare, as dictated by your SEP, you will face late penalties no matter how long you have been on COBRA.

Another qualifying event may occur if the covered employee becomes eligible for Medicare within 18 months of the initial qualifying event. The coverage for all covered beneficiaries is extended to 36 months minus the number of months the employee had been eligible for Medicare. For example, if you became eligible for Medicare six months before you leave your job, you, your spouse, and your dependents could have COBRA benefits for 30 months (36 months – 6 months). This qualifying event does not require that you actually enroll in Medicare.

Disability is another reason that COBRA benefits may be extended. An additional 11 months may be allowed for a total of 29 months of COBRA benefits if you or your family member is determined to have a disability by the Social Security Administration (SSA) that is expected to last throughout the 18 months of the initial COBRA benefit period. The disability must be confirmed within the first 60 days of your COBRA benefits to be eligible.

The Trade Adjustment Assistance Reform Act (TAA) of 2002 enables eligible individuals to earn tax credits for payment of COBRA premiums. Certain workers and retirees whose employer-sponsored health coverage is lost because of increased imports or trade-related relocation are eligible. TAA also offers you tax credits to purchase non-COBRA insurance, such as coverage from a spouse's employer if the employer pays less than 50 percent of the premium, or a private policy purchased within 30 days of your leaving your employer. TAA tax credits will cover for 65 percent of eligible premiums.

COBRA has its place in the health-care schema. Sometimes it is the only means you may have to access health insurance when you have not yet met eligibility for Medicare. If you are eligible for Medicare, you must decide when to enroll. COBRA coverage can be very costly in comparison to Medicare premiums. Unless you need to provide health-care coverage to your family, it may be more cost effective to sign up for Medicare and decline COBRA.

Workers' Compensation

Your employer should be prepared to assist you if you sustain an on-the-job injury. To this end, you make an agreement, known as a compensation bargain, with your employer not to sue them for any injuries that occur as a result of your job. In return, your employer provides you with workers' compensation benefits.

The compensation bargain is beneficial to your employer for obvious reasons. For one, it removes the subjective "pain and suffering" component from a possible costly settlement. It is beneficial to you because the legal process can usually be long and drawn out. By removing litigation from the equation, you will get faster recompense and are guaranteed rights; whereas if you lost in court, you may get nothing.

DID YOU KNOW?

Every state runs a workers' compensation program. Federal laws have established programs for federal employees under the Federal Employment Compensation Act, for railroad workers under the Federal Employment Liability Act, for seamen under the Merchant Marine Act, and for coal workers under the Black Lung Benefits Act.

Workers' compensation will cover you for any medical expenses and a percentage of any lost wages beyond three to seven days after the inciting injury. It may even cover for anticipated loss of wages in the future. A settlement may be agreed upon for any long-term consequences from the injury. In the event that you die from the injury, your spouse and dependents may be offered wage benefits.

You will only receive benefits once your case has been reviewed by a health-care provider who performs an independent medical examination (IME). You must be evaluated by a provider who participates in your workers' compensation insurance plan. If your employer or insurance company disagrees with the outcome of the IME or believes your injury was not job-related, they may contest the case in a court hearing.

If you are on Medicare, any medical expenses relating to a work injury must be billed first to your workers' compensation insurance. Medicare will not even consider offering payments until at least 120 days have lapsed from the time your workers' compensation plan had been billed, and even then, they may only pay in certain situations.

DID YOU KNOW?

Workers' compensation paid out $29.9 billion for medical expenses in 2011.

Your workers' compensation insurance company may need additional time to review your case before they will decide whether or not to cover your expenses. Until you get the green light, your bills will not be paid. Medicare may step in during this waiting period to offer conditional payments for your medical expenses, but only for services usually covered by Medicare, so services like vision screenings may not be covered.

If your case is later approved for workers' compensation, you must reimburse Medicare for any payments it made on your behalf. In some states, you will not be given the full settlement amount until you reimburse Medicare. Any funds you receive through workers' compensation should be used for this purpose.

If your case is denied workers' compensation, Medicare will cover its share of costs as if it were a nonworkers' compensation case. Again, Medicare will only cover services under its umbrella.

Your workers' compensation insurance may also limit or only offer partial payments if it believes your injury was related to a medical condition that existed before you started your current job. Your past medical records would document that your job did not cause that medical condition. If your medical records were limited, it may be difficult to support your case. That does not mean your job did not exacerbate your condition. Workers' compensation will acknowledge this and pay a percentage of the costs, leaving the rest to you. Medicare may pay its share towards any remaining costs.

When you receive your workers' compensation settlement, it may include funds to be used for any future medical expenses that arise from the injury. You may put these funds into an account known as a Workers' Compensation Medicare Set-Aside Arrangement (WCMSA). You can use these funds to help Medicare pay for health care relating to the injury in question. Medicare will return to usual payments for this condition once you exhaust all funds from the WCMSA account. Medicare will usually only approve use of a WCMSA if your settlement is larger than $25,000 or if your expected lost wages due to the injury are more than $250,000.

Who Pays First?

Having Medicare does not mean that it will be first in line to cover your health-care costs. In order to reduce how much money is spent from the Medicare Trust Fund, protocols have been put in place so that Medicare is often set up to pay second on any claims when you have another source of health insurance. The term used to describe this is Medicare Secondary Payer (MSP).

Your employer-sponsored health plan may be first on the docket. It is important to know your rights for payment.

When Medicare Pays First or Second

Type of Health Insurance	Medicare as Primary Payer	Medicare as Secondary Payer
COBRA	You are 65 years of age or older. or You are disabled by a condition other than End-Stage Renal Disease (ESRD). or Your 30-month coordination period for ESRD has ended.	You are in the 30-month coordination period for ESRD.
Employer-sponsored health insurance if you have a disability other than ESRD	Your or your spouse's employer has less than 100 full-time equivalent employees.	Your or your spouse's employer has 100 or more full-time equivalent employees.
Employer-sponsored health insurance if you have ESRD	Your 30-month coordination period for ESRD has ended.	You are in the 30-month coordination period for ESRD.
Employer-sponsored health insurance for those 65 years of age and older	Your or your spouse's employer has less than 20 full-time equivalent employees.	Your or your spouse's employer has 20 or more full-time equivalent employees. or You are self-employed and covered by another employer or your spouse's employer that has 20 or more full-time equivalent employees.
Retiree health benefits	You are 65 years of age or older.	You are less than 65 years of age.
Workers' compensation insurance	Your claim is covered by workers' compensation.	Your claim is denied by workers' compensation. or Your claim is only partially covered by workers' compensation due to a pre-existing condition.

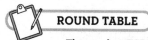

ROUND TABLE

Thomas has ESRD and is newly enrolled in Medicare. He also has employer-sponsored health insurance made available through his spouse's job. His spouse's health plan will cover his ESRD benefits as the primary payer for 30 months during the coordination period for ESRD, and Medicare will take over as primary payer after that.

The Least You Need to Know

- You could lose your job and health benefits if you require time away from work for family or medical reasons and your employer is not required to participate in FMLA.
- COBRA benefits do not qualify you for a Special Enrollment Period with Medicare.
- Medicare pays toward job-related injuries only when your case is denied by workers' compensation insurance or you receive only partial payment based on a pre-existing condition.
- Medicare may pay your claims before your private health plans if the size of your employer is sufficiently small or if you meet certain age or disability requirements.

PART 4

Living with Medicare

Once you are enrolled in Medicare, you will likely have even more questions. How do you pick the right health-care provider? How do you decipher your bills? When and to whom do you make payments? How do you report a complaint? How do you prevent medical identity theft?

Navigating the daily goings-on of Medicare can sometimes be confusing, but it is something you will need to master, or at least know where to turn when you need help. After all, your health is part of your everyday life! You need to know your rights as a Medicare beneficiary, and this part will lead you down the path to making the most of your benefits.

Selecting Health-Care Providers

Knowing what services Medicare provides and how to enroll in the program are key concepts for you to understand. It may be even more important to recognize who should be providing that care and where it can be performed. You will cross paths with many different types of health-care providers in your lifetime—doctors, nurse practitioners, physician assistants, midwives, and more. How you select your medical providers will make a difference for your health-care experience.

What Providers Count

Everyone should have a primary care provider (PCP) to coordinate and provide preventive medicine. For years, the phrase PCP had been synonymous with primary care "physician," but due to the increasing numbers of other trained professionals practicing in primary care fields, the phrase was generalized to primary care "provider." You may consider a nonphysician provider as your PCP if they provide the bulk of your care, but does Medicare agree?

In This Chapter

- The differences among health-care providers
- Choosing a health-care provider who works with Medicare
- How Medicare sets physician fees
- The impending physician shortage and how it is being addressed

The Path to Doctoring

The road to becoming a physician may be different for each person. All physicians practicing in the United States have completed medical school, whether in the United States or abroad. For those taught in the United States, there are two different training paths, allopathic and osteopathic.

Allopathic medical schools are the traditional medical schools you have come to learn about in the television and movies. There are 136 allopathic medical schools across the country accredited by the American Medical Association. Education occurs over four years with didactic training in the basic medical sciences and clinical rotations for hands-on experience. A graduate from an allopathic medical school becomes a medical doctor (MD).

Osteopathic schools provide the full scope of medical training that allopathic medical schools do but also include osteopathic manipulative medicine (OMM) as a key tenet. OMM focuses on hands-on techniques to manipulate your muscles and joints as an approach to diagnosis and treatment. There are 26 osteopathic medical schools accredited by the American Osteopathic Association. A graduate from osteopathic medical schools is referred to as a DO, a doctor of osteopathy. Despite their training in medical school, only a fraction of DOs practice OMM in clinical practice.

 DID YOU KNOW?

Medicare provides a portion of the funding for residency training via direct medical graduate payments (DMGP) to teaching hospitals. Medicaid, the Department of Veterans Affairs, and the Department of Defense are other federal sources of funding for residency training. The funds are used towards resident salaries, faculty salaries, and institutional overhead costs. Limits on the number of residents Medicare will approve for DMGP payments were set in 1997 by the Balanced Budget Act and has not been increased since that time.

After medical school, future practicing doctors must enter a residency in the medical field of their choice. These programs vary in length depending on the specialty but are at a minimum three years in duration. Some of the residency slots may be slated specifically for allopathic graduates or osteopathic graduates. Graduates of foreign medical schools may also apply for residency programs. In order to practice clinical medicine in the United States, training in an American residency program is required.

Through residency training, the doctor in training must pass a series of examinations known as the United States Medical Licensing Examination (USMLE), of which there are three parts. This testing allows each physician to demonstrate their clinical knowledge and application of key principles. Physicians can then apply for licensure in their state(s) of choice. At this point they are legally clear to practice medicine.

Beyond medical licensure, many physicians will then certify in their specialty with yet another examination. Some private insurers, including Medicare, will only allow coverage for services provided by *board-certified* physicians. Those physicians who are *board-eligible* may have limited insurance options that will accept them for coverage.

DEFINITION

> **Board-eligible** and **board-certified** are not the same thing. A board-eligible physician is one who has completed a residency program but has not yet taken, or perhaps has even failed, the certification examination in his specialty. The term board-eligible can be used up to seven years after residency. Board-certified means the physician has met the certification requirements, including passing of an examination, in their specialty.

Taken together, your Medicare doctor will have completed 11 years of training—four years of undergraduate training, four years of medical school, and at least three years of training in residency with four in-depth examinations—plus Drug Enforcement Administration (DEA) licensure for prescription of medications.

Nurse Practitioners

Nurse practitioners (NPs) go through a lengthy training process as well, and have done so since 1965. Training requires completion of a four-year bachelor's degree in nursing followed by a two- to four-year program in which they specialize as a nurse practitioner. The latter program generally results in a master's degree, but some may earn a doctoral degree, specifically a Doctor of Nursing Practice. There are 350 NP training programs available at colleges and universities across the country accredited by the American Association of Nurse Practitioners (AANP). Similar to medical school trainees, NP students undergo an extensive series of lectures and clinical rotations during their training. Training beyond high school averages six to eight years.

An NP must then complete an examination for national licensure known as the National Council Licensure Examination (NCLEX-RN) and also apply for licensure in the state where they will practice. After all these steps are taken, Medicare then requires that an NP be certified in their field before they will accept him for coverage. The AANP and the American Nurses Credentialing Center (ANCC) are two organizations that offer approved certification.

The scope of practice of an NP is generally similar to that of a physician, diagnosing and treating conditions. Certain areas of expertise may be limited depending on differences in training. The majority of states require physician supervision of an NP though the doctor may not necessarily have to be physically present to meet guidelines in certain states; being accessible by telephone or online also qualifies. If you live in one of the following 17 states or the District of Columbia, an NP can practice with full authority without requiring physician supervision.

- Alaska
- Arizona
- Colorado
- Hawaii
- Idaho
- Iowa
- Maine
- Montana
- Nevada
- New Hampshire
- New Mexico
- North Dakota
- Oregon
- Rhode Island
- Vermont
- Washington
- Wyoming

As a Medicare beneficiary, you can select an NP as your PCP if you are in hospice, but a doctor must be the one who diagnoses you as having a terminal illness. In this case, a physician-NP team is essential.

Similar to doctors, an NP will require a DEA number if they intend to prescribe medications; additional licenses for drug dispensing may or may not be needed depending on the state. Many states allow NPs to prescribe medications, some with limitations on controlled medications (Alabama, Arkansas, Florida, Georgia, Louisiana, Missouri, Oklahoma, South Carolina, Texas, and West Virginia), and some outright not allowing for prescription management (Florida). As to U.S. territories, Puerto Rico does not allow an NP to write prescriptions and there are marked restrictions on what an NP can write in the U.S. Virgin Islands.

DID YOU KNOW?

There have been decades of debate about whether nonphysician providers should be considered qualified to be primary care providers (PCP). Physician organizations such as the American Medical Association have argued that nonphysician providers do not have adequate training to offer this level of care. Multiple states have acknowledged the expertise and quality care given by these nonphysician providers by allowing them to practice without restriction.

Medicare pays NPs differently than doctors but you, as a beneficiary, will be charged the same. The program usually pays them only 85 percent of the usual physician fee unless they meet the "incident-to" provision. This specifically states the NP is working under direct supervision of a physician who is on the premises or the NP is providing follow-up care to a condition first diagnosed and treated by a physician. If "incident-to" criteria are met, an NP may be reimbursed for the full cost of the care provided.

Physician Assistants

The first physician assistants (PAs) graduated from Duke University in 1967. As of 2012, there were 86,700 PAs in the United States and the number is rising, with 181 accredited training programs under the Accreditation Review Commission on Education for the Physician Assistant.

There are different routes a PA could take to complete training. If training is started immediately after high school, one could opt for an accelerated PA program which would take five years to complete. Otherwise, one would complete a bachelor's degree that satisfies certain prerequisites in the meantime, and then apply to a PA program which generally requires an additional two years to complete (for a grand total of six years).

To qualify as a provider under Medicare, a PA must be licensed in the state they practice as well as certified by the National Commission on Certification of Physician Assistants.

There are similarities and differences between NPs and PAs. With regard to medication management, state regulations limit controlled medication prescribing in Alabama, Arkansas, Arizona, Florida, Georgia, Hawaii, Louisiana, Maine, Missouri, Montana, Oklahoma, South Carolina, Texas, and West Virginia; and do not allow for any prescriptions in Florida or Kentucky. Puerto Rico and the U.S. Virgin Islands also disqualify PAs from prescribing these medications. Payments to a PA are reduced to 85 percent of what a physician would be paid but Medicare may pay 100 percent of the charges if "incident-to" provisions were met.

A PA never has the full authority of care that has been allowed for NPs in certain states. PAs must be part of a physician team and have an assigned physician documented as their supervisor. This physician must work in the same state and must be readily accessible to guide diagnostic and treatment care plans even if they are not present on the premises. A PA also cannot be assigned as a PCP to a Medicare beneficiary who is on hospice.

Picking the Right Provider for You

It would be wonderful if you could pick whatever health-care providers you liked and be assured that they would accept your insurance and give you the best in quality care. More and more providers are making choices about whether they will accept Medicare for payment. This could affect your bottom dollar. There are key aspects you have to understand about your provider that will help you to make an educated decision.

Accepting Providers

Your health-care provider has a choice to make—whether to opt-in or -out of Medicare. Those who opt-in are called *accepting providers*. If your provider does not accept Medicare for payment, you are out of luck. Even if the services he provides or orders, such as laboratory studies or X-rays, would otherwise be covered by Medicare, Medicare will not pay. A contractual agreement needs to be in place between the federal program and your provider for any payments to exchange hands. Medicare will also not reimburse you separately for services.

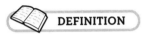 **DEFINITION**

An **accepting provider** has signed an agreement with Medicare to accept their policies in order to receive payment.

The exception would be if a nonaccepting provider referred you to another provider for care who did opt-in to accept Medicare. The referral visit would be covered.

Physicians who do not accept Medicare will often have you sign a contract agreeing to their terms and conditions, including that they do not accept Medicare for payment. You must know that it is against the law for them to put any limitations on emergency care in these contracts. It would be outright unethical for them to turn you away for care for any reason, including their nonaccepting status, if you walked into their office in a medical emergency.

It is in your financial interest to find a provider that accepts Medicare, if you need it, but sometimes that may not be possible. You could live in an underserved area with a limited selection of primary care providers or specialists that accept Medicare.

Numerous reasons exist why a provider may choose to not accept Medicare, though they may not seem all that reassuring from your perspective. To circumvent Medicare's increased red tape and regulatory requirements, to avoid the high costs of routine board examinations and certifications, or to have increased control over what they can charge are just a few examples.

Participating Providers

Accepting Medicare for payment is only one piece of the puzzle. Your health-care providers must also decide if they will participate in Medicare as a *participating provider*. Though the terms accepting and participating sound similar, they mean different things.

 **DEFINITION**

A **participating provider** is an accepting provider who also agrees to Medicare's fee schedule. A **nonparticipating provider**, while also an accepting provider, agrees to accept only some of the fee schedule or none at all.

Participation does not relate to accepting Medicare for payment, but to agreeing to a plan that sets fixed fees for services. This is also referred to as "accepting assignment." Assignment only applies to Original Medicare and not Medicare Advantage Plans.

This pre-set list of fees determines what a provider can charge you for services. This means your provider cannot then go behind Medicare's back and ask you to pay the difference for what they think is their fair share. They can bill you the amount that Medicare recommends and not a penny more. This leaves you to pay only your deductible and coinsurance or copays as dictated by your Medicare plan. Working with health-care providers who accept assignment saves you from being overcharged and saves you money. The Medicare Physician Fee Schedule is set every year for all services that Medicare may contribute payment but is not as straightforward as you would think. Then again, how many federal programs are? The fee schedules are based on complicated calculations that require conversion factors that take into account where you receive those services. Still, it offers a way to standardize charges across a geographic area. It's meant to be fair.

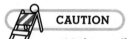

CAUTION

Medicare offers free preventive screening tests such as mammograms and colonoscopies but they will only be free if your provider accepts assignment.

You should ask your provider if they accept Medicare. However, do not ask if they participate in Medicare. Some offices may misunderstand that they are "participating" because they accept "some" of the fee schedule when they are technically nonparticipating for that very reason. It is an all or none deal. Don't let the lingo confuse you.

Instead ask specifically if your health-care provider accepts assignment. If they do not accept assignment, ask them if it is for all services or certain services. It is up to you to make a decision about the odds of your needing those services or not. Ideally, you would prefer a provider who accepts assignment to save yourself the most money.

Limiting Fees

Providers who do not accept assignment still have to contend with Medicare. In order to receive payments, they still have to agree to some terms and these are defined by a limiting charge. This allows a nonparticipating provider to charge up to 15 percent more than the Medicare Fee Schedule. In this case, Medicare pays the same amount they would have otherwise paid (80 percent of the Medicare Fee Schedule price) and the extra charges go to you (20 percent coinsurance + 15 percent limiting charge). If you had not already spent the amount of your deductible during the year, the deductible would also be included toward your expense for the service.

ROUND TABLE

Loraine had been travelling when she developed severe dizziness. With her primary care doctor a hundred miles away, she needed to seek care at a local clinic. There were two clinics to choose from; both accepted Medicare patients, the first accepted assignment but the second did not. Assuming Medicare set the cost of the visit at $100, Loraine would pay $20 at the first clinic (she pays a 20 percent coinsurance while Medicare pays 80 percent). At the second clinic, she would pay $35. This is because the second clinic added a 15 percent limiting charge to their fee, increasing the cost to $115. Since Medicare only recognizes their set cost for the visit, the first $100 in this case, she would be left to pay for the difference herself. Which would you choose?

Limiting charges do not apply to nonparticipating suppliers of medical equipment. They can charge you whatever they want, so check with the company about assignment before you make any purchases. You are more likely to get a better deal if you use a participating supplier that has accepted assignment.

It would seem that a nonparticipating provider gets a better deal than a participating one, making up to 15 percent more for every service. In the end, however, their patients suffer by losing access to what would have otherwise been free preventive screening services under the Affordable Care Act. These tests would still be available to these beneficiaries, but they would be obligated to pay a coinsurance, typically 20 percent of the cost. This provides an incentive for primary care physicians to accept assignment, and indeed the majority do.

Getting a Second (or Third) Opinion

There are times when you may feel like you need an extra set of eyes on your health situation. A recommendation for nonemergency surgery is one of those times. Sometimes a second opinion will help you to make an educated decision about how to proceed.

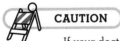

CAUTION

If your doctor believes you need emergency surgery, there is no time to wait. Holding out for a second opinion could risk your health and even your life.

Medicare will only pay toward a second or even a third opinion only if the surgery is recommended for a medically necessary reason. Cosmetic surgery, for example, is off the table.

Generally speaking, you should seek your second opinion from a medical office separate from the one where you had your initial evaluation. Surgeons from the same group may review your case together and this may not offer you an objective second opinion. To save money, you should also have all tests and study results forwarded to the new provider for review. Medicare may not cover the cost of a repeat test in such a short period of time unless it was reasonably expected to have changed since the first one was completed, again a determination of medical necessity.

Of course, you should select a second opinion from a health-care provider who opts-in for Medicare and hopefully accepts assignment. Know that requesting a second opinion does not obligate you to change providers for the long haul. You can always return to the original provider for care if you choose.

Are There Enough Doctors?

It may be harder to find a doctor as time marches on. A physician shortage is expected by 2020 due to multiple factors:

- Of the 830,000 physicians in the United States, nearly half of them are in their 50s. Based on their age, one-third of doctors are expected to retire in the next decade.

- Passage of the Affordable Care Act has added more than 30 million people into the system that would not have previously had access to health care, increasing demands on providers.

- Baby boomers are reaching Medicare age at a rapid rate. With age comes more complicated medical issues and increased demand for services, both primary care and subspecialty.

- The number of residency training positions for physicians has not changed since 1997 because the federal government has not increased the necessary funding.

- According to *The Journal of the American Medical Association*, more internal residency graduates are going into specialties compared to primary care at a rate of 5:1.

The Association of American Medical Colleges (AAMC) projects that by 2020, there will be a shortage of 91,500 physicians—45,400 in primary care and 46,100 in subspecialties. By 2025, that shortage will escalate to 130,600, with primary care providers contributing to 65,800 (50.4 percent) of that deficiency.

To compensate, existing medical schools have started to take on more students and new medical schools are on the horizon. There has even been talk about decreasing the length of medical training to get doctors into the workforce sooner.

Without sufficient residency positions to complete their training, however, it will make little difference. These fresh-faced medical school graduates cannot train the rigorous hours of a residency for free, and this intensity of training is necessary to build experience and expertise in their respective fields. More residency positions are needed but there has yet to be action taken by the government.

With further cuts being made to how Medicare pays doctors and hospitals, fewer doctors may opt-in for Medicare. This could exacerbate the physician shortage for the elderly and those with disabilities.

The Least You Need to Know

- All health-care providers must be licensed and certified in their respective fields to be compliant with Medicare.
- Nonphysician providers are reimbursed at a lower rate than physicians unless they meet "incident-to" criteria, where a physician is involved in the care of the patient.
- Only physicians and nurse practitioners can be primary care providers for hospice patients.
- Choosing a provider who accepts assignment will decrease your costs and allow you access to free preventive services.
- Medicare contributes funds toward training of resident physicians, but the number of available residency positions has remained fixed since 1997.
- America is approaching a health-care crisis with an impending physician shortage.

Using Medicare Cards

You should carry a piece of Medicare with you wherever you go. Whether you put it in a purse or a wallet, your Medicare card holds the information that will get you the care you need. It is important to understand what information is accessible on your card and how to safeguard that information from identity theft.

When and How to Use Your Card

When you receive your card in the mail, hold on to it with care. Your Medicare card is your ticket to health care, and you should have it on you at all times in case of a medical emergency. It not only signifies that you are entitled to the program but holds a great deal of information about you, if you know how to read it. Let's learn how it works.

When to Expect Your Card

If you are automatically enrolled in Medicare, your card should arrive in the mail approximately three months before your sixty-fifth birthday. At this point, your card will document enrollment in both Part A and Part B. You will need to decide whether or not to keep your Part B coverage.

In This Chapter

- Making sense of your Medicare card
- Protecting your health information
- How medical identify theft happens
- What to do if your identity is stolen

You must be actively receiving Social Security benefits at age 65 years of age or be qualified for Medicare based on disability to be automatically enrolled in Medicare.

> **TIP**
>
> Interestingly, the Social Security Administration manages your Medicare card, not Medicare. If you have an issue with your Medicare card, you can call Social Security's toll-free number at 1-800-772-1213 or contact your local Social Security office. If you have a question about Medicare benefits, then you should call Medicare at 1-800-MEDICARE. You may also check their respective websites at socialsecurity.gov and medicare.gov.

If you are not automatically enrolled in Medicare, your card will not arrive until you apply and qualify for coverage. Your card will usually arrive in the mail within 30 days.

If you do not receive your card within the expected timeline, take action. It could be lost or stolen. Make a call to the Social Security Administration and report it as soon as possible.

Starting to Use Your Card

You do not need to activate your card per se, but understanding when coverage begins is important information. If you are automatically enrolled in Medicare, your coverage begins on the first day of your birth month with one exception. If your birthday lands on the first of the month, your coverage begins the first day of the month before your birthday, i.e., someone with a birthday on March 23 would begin coverage on March 1 but someone with a birthday on March 1 would begin coverage on February 1.

Your initial enrollment period begins three months before and ends three months after your sixty-fifth birthday. If you apply during the first three months of your initial enrollment period (IEP), these rules also apply. If you apply during your birth month, one month after your birthday, or in the final two months of the IEP, your coverage will begin on the first day of the first, second, or third month after you apply, respectively.

If you missed the initial enrollment period, you have other opportunities to sign up. There is a General Enrollment Period (GEP) every year from January 1 through March 31. If you sign up during the GEP, your coverage will begin on July 1. If you enrolled during a special enrollment period (SEP), your coverage begins on the first day of the month after you apply. Enrollment periods are discussed in Chapters 7 and 8.

Paper or Plastic?

Your Medicare card is double-sided and arrives in paper form, not a plastic card as you would usually receive from a credit card company. Because paper can be easily damaged, it is encouraged that you make a copy of your Medicare card and store the original card in a safe place. In this way, you will always have a copy of this valuable document. You can carry the photocopy around with you to use for insurance purposes.

Some people choose to laminate their Medicare cards. This is perfectly acceptable so long as it does not obscure any data on the card. If there were a problem with the lamination process, the card could possibly be damaged.

Basic Information

Most of the information on your Medicare card is relatively straightforward. On the front side of the card, your name will be listed as the "Name of Beneficiary." Your gender will be listed under "Sex" and your eligibility for "HOSPITAL (PART A)" and "MEDICAL (PART B)" are listed under "Is Entitled To" with the "Effective Date" of enrollment listed to the right. There is also a place for your signature at the bottom of the card (make sure you sign the card prior to photocopying or laminating).

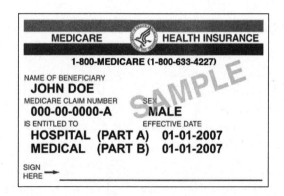

The back side of your Medicare card reports the importance of having your card available at all times and also gives a notice warning against fraud and abuse.

There is an option to decline your Part B coverage, "medical insurance." You check the open box and sign the back of the card in the designated area in the presence of a witness who also signs the card. The witness must provide their contact information as a means for Medicare to verify the authenticity of the requested change, if needed. You must then mail this back to the CMS address listed on your card. This process must be done before the effective date of coverage listed on the card or you may be required to pay for Part B services for that benefit period. If you do opt out of Part B coverage, you will be sent a new card by Medicare that limits you to HOSPITAL (PART A) insurance coverage.

TIP

Contact information for CMS is listed on both sides of the card to answer any questions you may have.

It is important to note that your Medicare card does not designate whether or not you have elected to participate in a Medicare Advantage Plan or Medicare Part D coverage. You will receive separate cards for these programs from the private insurer who sold you the plan. These cards may differ in appearance.

Keeping Your Social Security Number Secure

Locate the Medicare Claim Number on the front of your card. This is your Medicare identification number and will likely look very familiar to you. For most beneficiaries, this number is your social security number (SSN). In the case where it is not your personal SSN, it will be the number of a spouse, your parent, or your dependent, whoever made you eligible for the Medicare or Social Security benefits. Still, it will always be someone's SSN.

Concern has been raised about having your SSN exposed in this way, as it increases your risk should the card ever be stolen. The SSN is the most common identifier used by people to apply for credit cards, bank accounts, and other programs. A stolen SSN can provide criminals a direct path to your financial accounts and, once you are on Medicare, your health coverage. Medical identity theft is a rising problem as will be discussed further in this chapter.

The CMS is hesitant to change the Medicare Claim Number to another numerical or alphanumerical identifier because it would cost them too much money to do so. With tens of millions of Medicare beneficiaries on the roster and more to come, CMS estimated it would cost $300 million to make these changes in 2011 and has increased that expected dollar amount to $845 million in 2013. The United States Government Accountability Office (GAO) has since advised that CMS spearhead an information technology (IT) project to develop an effective plan to change from use of SSN's to a new Medicare identification system in the future. Only in this way can Medicare beneficiaries be protected.

Understanding What the Letters and Numbers Mean

Next to your identification number on your Medicare card is a letter designation, sometimes followed by a number or a second letter. This is where your Medicare card becomes a wealth of information that is rarely appreciated. Those letters and numbers are essentially code generated by the Social Security Administration to document your Social Security status, including whether you qualify or are receiving Social Security benefits. It also specifies your eligibility for Medicare.

This system of letters and numbers can be confusing because the nomenclature does not always relate to Medicare even though it is printed on your Medicare card. As a point of interest, these letters never make their way to your Social Security card.

Twelve different letter headings are used as categories, with the most common designations noted here. Please note these letters have nothing to do with Medicare Parts A, B, C, or D.

A: You are a retired primary claimant. This means you are Medicare-eligible based on your own wage earnings and are also receiving Social Security benefits. There are no subcategories for "A."

B: You are the spouse of a primary claimant. In this scenario, both you and your spouse receive Medicare and Social Security.

> B—Wife over 62 years old
>
> B1—Husband over 62 years old
>
> B2—Wife younger than 62 years old caring for a child
>
> B3—Wife over 62 years old (second claimant)
>
> B5—Wife younger than 62 years old caring for a child (second claimant)
>
> BY—Husband caring for a child

C: You are a child of a primary claimant. In this case, you are on Medicare and receive Social Security benefits based on your parent's status. The number designation after the "C" specifies your birth order, i.e., if you were the oldest child you would be C1 and if you were the fourth child you would be C4.

Hopefully, you can see the trend here. Because each letter is printed on a Medicare card, you have Medicare eligibility. Why else would you even have a Medicare card? If there are stipulations to that coverage, the letter system may explain that. How you qualify for Social Security benefits becomes the major focus of the designation.

D: You are a widow or widower.

> D—Widow over 60 years old
>
> D1—Widower over 60 years old
>
> D2—Widow over 60 years old (second claimant)
>
> D3—Widower over 60 years old (second claimant)
>
> D6—Surviving divorced wife over 60 years old

E: You are a widowed parent to the primary claimant.

> E—Widowed mother

> E1—Surviving divorced mother

> E4—Widowed father

> E5—Surviving divorced father

F: You are the parent of the primary claimant.

> F1—Parent (father)

> F2—Parent (mother)

> F3—Stepfather

> F4—Stepmother

> F5—Adopting father

> F6—Adopting mother

H: You are eligible based on disability.

> HA—Disabled claimant

> HB—Wife (over 62 years old) of a disabled claimant

> HC—Child of a disabled claimant

J and K: You are a "special beneficiary." This is based on how many quarters you paid into both Medicare and Social Security.

> J1, J2, K1, and K2 qualifies for free Medicare Part A

> J3, J4, K3, and K4 qualifies for paid Medicare Part A

M: You are not eligible for free Part A coverage but are enrolled in Part B.

> M Uninsured—Pays for Part A coverage

> M1 Uninsured—Qualifies for but declines Part A

T: You are eligible for Medicare benefits but not Social Security benefits.

> T Uninsured—Qualifies for Medicare based on age or kidney disease; or qualifies for Medicare but elects only Part A

TA—Medicare Qualified Government Employment (MQGE)

TB MQGE—Aged Spouse

W: You are a disabled widow of the primary claimant.

W—Disabled widow

W1—Disabled widower

W6—Disabled surviving divorced wife

WA—Railroad retirement

As lengthy as this list is, it is in your best interest to understand what your Medicare card says about you and to verify that this information is true and accurate. You would not want to have your full benefits denied due to a card error.

Correcting Errors or Replacing Your Card

When you see errors on your Medicare card or you want to replace a lost or damaged card, you need to know how to proceed, and fast. Inaccuracies are not your friend. More importantly, you need an accurate card on hand for health-care purposes.

CAUTION

> Before you do anything, be sure the Social Security Administration has your most up-to-date contact information. They will mail your Medicare card to the last listed address in their system. You do not want your Medicare card sent to a wrong address. This increases the chance it could be stolen or abused.

The procedure to follow is quite simple. If you follow these steps, you will receive your new card in the mail within 30 days.

First, gather your information. This will keep the process moving. At a minimum, you will need your name as listed on your most recent Social Security card, your birth date, your SSN, your place of birth, your mother's maiden name, your last Social Security statement, and the exact dollar amount paid to you on your last statement if you received Social Security benefits within the past year.

Next, you need to contact the Social Security Administration. They run the show for your cards, both Medicare and Social Security cards. There are three ways you can choose to reach them to get the job done.

Face-to-face. Heading down to your local Social Security office is an effective way to make sure you have everything taken care of, especially if you have unusual circumstances that need to be addressed. This may be the case if you are changing information, namely those pesky letter codes. Sometimes the most effective way to get the point across is to speak with someone in person. You can locate your nearest field office by an online search at secure.ssa.gov/ICON/main.jsp.

Online. The Social Security website allows processing of simple requests, e.g., replacing cards, during designated business hours, 5 A.M. to 1 A.M. on weekdays, 5 A.M. to 11 P.M. on Saturdays, 8 A.M. to 10 P.M. on Sundays, and holidays from 5 A.M. to 11 P.M. The website has multiple security features in place to protect your information from getting into the wrong hands. A Secure Sockets Lock (SSL) application is used with your internet browser and your data is encrypted during transfer to make it unreadable to anyone trying to access the system. The online site also logs you out every 30 minutes to make sure you do not forget to log off when you are done. If it takes you longer to complete the application, you may need to log in again.

Telephone. If you come across tasks you cannot complete with the online system, such as changing your identification letter code, or if you prefer to address an issue with a representative by phone, you can always call the Social Security Administration directly at 1–800–772–1213 to review your case.

Everyone will have a preferred approach to complete the task. Be thankful there is more than one option to get the job done!

Stolen Cards and Identity Theft

When people think of identity theft, they tend to think about credit cards. Criminals may hack into computers or go *dumpster diving* for information, essentially stealing someone's financial identity and using it for their own gain. It doesn't take long before credit cards are charged to the hilt or bank accounts are cleared of all cash. With an SSN, someone can even file a tax return with your information and claim your income tax refund! Your life assets can disappear in an instant.

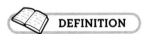 **DEFINITION**

> **Dumpster diving** is exactly what it sounds like, though few people have dumpsters where they live. It is a concept that applies to people who scavenge information and items from discarded materials, items such as bank statements and other documents with identifying information. They may rummage through your discarded personal property for data or from companies where you work or do business. It is far too easy for bad guys to access your financial records by reviewing information that has been thrown away carelessly. To protect yourself, you should properly dispose of confidential documents by shredding or otherwise making them illegible.

Medical identity theft is just as ominous to its victims, and your Medicare card could be the key. Instead of limiting themselves to your finances, thieves also gain access to your health-care accounts and may impersonate you to garner physician care, medical supplies, and drugs. Unlike financial records, which can be cleared and corrected, there is often fear of medical liability that prevents medical professionals from removing information from your health records. It becomes difficult to tease apart the real you from the imposter. Your long-term health, and your wallet, is at stake.

The Identity Theft Resource Center (ITRC) reported 269 health-care breaches in 2013. There were 222 data breaches in the health industry through August 2014, an increase of 26.8 percent compared to the previous year. Of these, 6,880,835 records were affected, accounting for 42.6 percent of all data breaches that year, with other breach categories including banking/financial, business, education, and government/military. Numbers don't lie. Medical identity theft is a growing threat to you and your health.

Protecting Your Information

The Health Insurance Administration Portability and Accountability Act (HIPAA) was passed into law under the Clinton administration in 1996 but had not been put into full effect until 2003. The law was intended to protect your health information by developing strategies to secure the exchange of electronic health data referred to as protected health information (PHI).

You would be surprised how many people could come into contact with your health information, not only health-care providers but hospital networks and insurance companies, as well as businesses that work in concert with those networks, even if they are not medically oriented.

All of these entities need to comply with federal regulations to maintain the confidentiality of your information. This requires not only technology to protect your information from being viewed by outsiders, but established workflows to train the staff who enter and use that information to perform their jobs. Failure to safeguard your information could result in penalties and fines from as little as $100 for a single offense to as much as $1.5 million for repeat offenders.

Medical Data Breaches

What exactly is a data breach? It means that your information has been stolen either in paper or electronic form, and there has likely been a failure to adhere to HIPAA regulations.

The types of data breaches are variable from accidentally mailing letters to the wrong sets of patients to malicious thievery and computer hacking. One case in 2014 occurred because data was literally lost in the mail when a delivery by UPS went missing. Unfortunately, the delivery was a CD sent from Jersey City Medical Center that contained unencrypted data for Medicaid patients, including names, SSNs, and health information. Too many times breaches occurred because data was not properly encrypted on electronic devices.

The most threatening breaches occur when SSNs are procured. This allows criminals access to your credit history as well as Medicare and Social Security benefits. The largest breach in history occurred in 2014 when 4.5 million patients had their names, birth dates, and SSNs stolen by computer hackers in China. The health network that was breached, Community Health Systems, provides services in 29 states across 206 hospitals. It was believed the hack was made possible due to vulnerabilities posed by the *Heartbleed* security bug.

 **DEFINITION**

> **Heartbleed** is a security bug found in an internet cryptographic software library called OpenSSL. This vulnerability allows hackers to access user passwords and track their key strokes on the internet. The security bug was identified in 2014 and affected millions of websites.

Identity theft is becoming all too pervasive. You have to understand that it exists, that you are not immune, and that you must remain on high alert to protect yourself.

What to Watch For

It may be difficult to stop a criminal from stealing computers out of your doctor's office, but sometimes you have a front row seat to the action. Some of those criminals come directly to you, trying to manipulate vulnerabilities or insecurities you may have on a personal level. They often do this by appealing to your need to save money or your kindness in wanting to help others. You can prevent theft if you know what to look for.

No one should ever ask you for your Medicare card or number outside of a medical office or professional setting.

- Be wary of health surveys over the phone if they request this information.

- Be wary of telemarketers who say they want to offer you free services but first require your information; if it were truly free, they wouldn't need your information anyway.

- Be wary of product vendors trying to sell you products outside of a professional medical setting.

 **ROUND TABLE**

George went to a local park to watch his grandchildren play. As an amputee, he has relied on a wheelchair for years. The one he currently had was on its last wheels, so to speak, and a man approached him in the parking lot, offering to help him push the wheelchair over a curb. It so happened the man sold motorized wheelchairs! If George would show him his Medicare card, he may even be able to get him one for free. As tempting as it sounded to get a fancier piece of equipment, George was smart and made a mental note to call his doctor when he got home to find a way to replace his old chair. When the man persisted, George rolled away, right over the man's foot.

You need to verify the authenticity of these people before you commit to anything. Do not hand over your information if there is even the slightest doubt.

Some people will brazenly outright ask you to borrow your Medicare card in exchange for services. Perhaps you need someone to do your groceries or to drive you places. Don't do it! First of all, it is illegal to share your Medicare benefits in this way, and second, it puts your medical identity and future at risk.

How to Report Suspicious Activity

Medical identity theft is not always obvious at first. A successful scam often goes undetected for long periods, taking smaller dollar amounts at a time as opposed to larger chunks all at once. This approach makes these crimes much harder to detect unless you know what to look for:

- Are there duplicate charges on your bills?

- Are there charges for services or medical supplies on your bills you did not receive? Do these charges correlate with dates that you actually received care?

- Have you reached the Medicare Part D donut hole earlier than you expected based on the medications you use?

- Has your supplemental insurance notified you that you have reached annual spending limits, if these apply, earlier than you expected?

These are all signs of possible fraud and abuse. If you keep careful receipts of your medical visits and expenses, you may be able to catch any suspicious activity. To support your cause, you can also request copies of your bills and medical records from your health-care provider to review as well. Your provider must legally allow you access to your medical record content within 30 days, though some offices may require you to pay the cost of printing the record.

If you suspect you are a victim of medical identity theft or that your SSN has been stolen, you must act immediately. You should:

- Contact the big three credit-reporting agencies—Equifax (1–800–525–6285), Experian (1–888–397–3742), and TransUnion (1–800–680–7289)—to report that your SSN is stolen, to request copies of your credit reports, and to have a credit alert placed on your account.

- Notify the IRS, 1–800–908–4490 or irs.gov/uac/Identity-Protection.

- Notify the Internet Crime Complaint Center, ic3.gov.

- File an identity theft report with the Federal Trade Commission, 1–877–ID–THEFT or consumer.ftc.gov/features/feature-0014-identity-theft.

- File a report with your local police.

CAUTION

Changing your SSN may not solve all of your problems and may actually give you new ones. With a new SSN, you may have to rebuild a credit history from scratch. This means having a more difficult time opening accounts and often paying higher interest rates.

Changing your SSN is a daunting if not impossible feat and requires that you have had prolonged complications from theft of your original number. The government often denies the request to change an SSN, even if you are at risk for bankruptcy, but you should still contact the SSA to review your options. Every case is different. Your best bet is not to have to change your SSN in the first place. Protect yourself.

The Least You Need to Know

- Your Medicare card holds key information about your Medicare and Social Security status and should be safeguarded at all times.
- HIPAA rules and regulations require health-care agencies and their partners to protect your personal and health information.
- Medical identity theft is a serious crime increasing in America.
- If you suspect your SSN has been stolen or that you may be a victim of medical identity theft, report it to the appropriate authorities immediately.

CHAPTER 17

How to Read Your Medicare Statements

Once you become a Medicare beneficiary, you will receive different kinds of documents from CMS. Understanding what these statements mean and how to respond to them is essential not only to keep your Medicare coverage in good standing but to make sure you are not overpaying for services. Knowing how to review your statements may also help to protect you from medical identity theft.

You've Got Mail

If you are like most Americans, you never want to find a bill in your mailbox. For most of us, it is an unavoidable reality. Know what you have to pay for and how to do it.

Medicare Charges

Medicare charges monthly premiums for Part A and Part B coverage. Monthly premiums for Original Medicare are discussed in Chapters 4, 10, and 11.

Medicare Advantage Plans are managed by private insurance companies, and you will not receive bills from Medicare regarding these plans.

In This Chapter

- Receiving and paying your Medicare bills
- Breaking down your Medicare Summary Notice
- How medical codes affect billing
- Where to get help with your questions

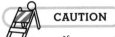

CAUTION

If you receive a bill directly from Medicare for specific services you received, contact CMS immediately. This document is likely falsified and could be someone trying to swindle funds from you. Medicare pays your health-care provider their share of the medical costs, usually at 80 percent of the agreed Medicare Fee Schedule, leaving the health-care provider to bill you for the difference, the 20 percent coinsurance. Your health-care provider, not Medicare, bills you for the coinsurance fees.

Medicare Part D also comes into play. Though you pay your monthly plan premiums directly to the drug plan you selected, Medicare will bill you separately for the mandated added costs based on your income. As discussed in Chapter 12, this charge is known as the Part D-Income Related Monthly Adjustment Amount (Part D-IRMAA).

If you receive free Part A services and decide to opt-out of Part B, you will not receive a bill unless you are required to pay Part D-IRMAA. You can skim through this section to learn about your options in case your situation changes in the future. For everyone else, here is how it works.

If you have free Part A and opt-in for Part B or if you pay for both Part A and Part B, you will be responsible for monthly premiums. Remember that if you are ineligible for free Part A and wish to purchase coverage, you are required to also sign up for Part B.

Payment Options

How you pay Medicare is only partially a matter of choice. If you receive Social Security or Railroad Retirement Board benefits, your premiums will be automatically deducted from those benefits on a monthly basis. Otherwise, you will receive a monthly bill if you pay for Part A or Part D-IRMAA, or you could be billed quarterly for Part B. When Medicare requests payment, it includes all charges on a single billing statement.

Medicare offers you different ways to pay for your benefit coverage. You may choose to pay directly though their Medicare Easy Pay system, which can take payments directly from a designated checking or savings account of your choice. It usually takes 30 to 60 days before your first payment can be processed through the system. There is no service charge to use this payment method, even if you do not sign up when you are first eligible for Medicare.

Alternatively, you may pay by sending a check, money order, or credit card authorization through the mail. The proper mailing address will be listed on your billing statement.

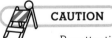

CAUTION

Pay attention when mailing your payments to Medicare. The address to pay your bills is different from the address listed on your Medicare card. Sending your payment to the wrong address may delay processing and could possibly result in discontinuation of your coverage if the payment is received too late or gets lost.

Late Payments

Medicare works like any other health insurance plan. If you don't pay, you won't get coverage. The program offers you multiple opportunities before it will discontinue your coverage, and it does so by sending repeated copies of the bill to your door. Three strikes and you're out.

First notice (first bill): Your bill is now due.

Second notice (reminder bill): Your bill is 60 days late.

Delinquency notice (final bill): Your bill is 90 days late.

Overdue statements will be mailed to you monthly, and you are responsible to pay them by the twenty-fifth of the month. In other words, if your billing statement is dated January 10, your payment will be due on January 25; if the statement is dated for the January 27, it will be due on February 25.

This means that you may actually get up to three months to pay for a premium due for a specific month. For example, if you were due to pay a premium for January, you may receive a first notice in January, a second notice in February, and a delinquency notice in March. If you do not pay by the twenty-fifth of the designated month (March or April, depending on the date of the billing statement), you will lose your coverage.

 **CAUTION**

If you travel to different parts of the country for extended periods of time during the year, you could miss your billing statements and risk missing payments. It may be in your best interest to utilize Medicare's Easy Pay system to have fees automatically deducted from your bank account. Otherwise, have your mail forwarded or change your address with Medicare to be sure you receive your statements.

Please note that you are not off the hook for premiums that would have been due since your first notice. Your statement clearly delineates "Current amount due for Part A and/or Part B" (most current monthly premium due) and "Past due amount for Part A and/or Part B" (overdue premium amounts) with the corresponding dates listed. If we use the example above, not only would you be due for January's premium, but you would also be due to pay the premiums for February and March.

If you do not pay your Part-D IRMAA fees before the final deadline, you will lose Medicare Part D coverage even if it is part of a Medicare Advantage Plan.

There are no late fees associated with late premium payments. You will simply lose your coverage if you do not pay by the final due date. You are responsible to pay for all premiums due to Medicare even after you lose coverage. This also applies to overdue bills after you die. Medicare will collect payment from your estate. If your estate does not have sufficient funds to cover these costs, Medicare will eat the remaining costs. Your health-care providers, however, may continue to pursue collection through the person or group that has taken on legal responsibility for your estate.

If you became eligible for Medicare based on your spouse's employment record, you will not lose your coverage if your spouse does not pay his or her premiums. Each Medicare beneficiary is responsible to pay his or her own premiums.

In order to get your coverage back, you will have to wait until the General Enrollment Period which opens January to March every year. Even so, your coverage will not begin until July 1 of that year. One delinquent payment can leave you without health-care coverage for an extended period of time.

Medicare Summary Notice

Medicare also sends you information quarterly that reviews any services you received during that time. These Medicare Summary Notices (MSN) are not bills but summaries designed to provide you a quick overview of your coverage and expenses. They can provide valuable insight into how much you and Medicare have contributed to your health-care expenses. They can also alert you to possible fraud and abuse.

Breaking Down the MSN

You will receive separate MSNs for Part A and Part B coverage. Though they may provide different financial information, the two documents have several similarities. They are both usually four pages each, though they can be longer based on the number of services you receive. You ought to look for the following information on each statement.

The CMS logo. This will be located in the header portion of the statement on Page 1 and signifies the authenticity of the document.

Your name, address, and Medicare number. If there are any errors or discrepancies with your personal information, these must be addressed immediately with CMS. This information is located on the upper half of Page 1.

"Making the Most of Your Medicare." This Page 2 subject matter provides instructions on how to read the statement, offers advice on how to avoid and mitigate fraud, and gives contact information should you have questions.

"How to Handle Denied Claims or File an Appeal." This important form is located on the final page of the MSN. Appeals must be filed in writing, and this form is your ticket to the process. The details of appeal processing are discussed in Chapter 18.

Outpatient Services

Medicare Part B covers a wide range of services. Information on your MSN can let you know whether or not you have been fairly charged for those services according to the Medicare Fee Schedule. Where do you look?

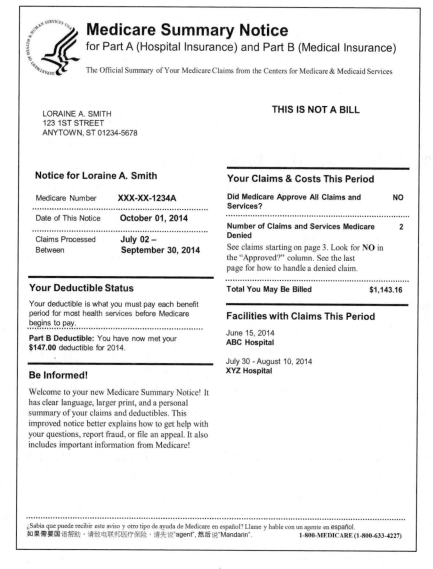

In the left column of Page 1, your deductible will be listed. The total amount of your deductible will be given, $147 for 2014, as well as the amount you have already paid toward that deductible. Medicare will not start covering services until you have paid the full deductible amount, even though you continue to pay monthly or quarterly premiums.

The right hand column shows "Your Claims & Costs This Period." There are three important subheadings listed below:

1. Did Medicare approve all services?

2. Number of claims and services Medicare denied

3. Total you may be billed

With a simple glance, you can see whether or not there have been any issues with coverage. If Medicare has denied payment for services ordered by your provider, you will want to know which ones and investigate why. The details of all services, both covered and uncovered, are outlined on Page 3.

Before you flip to Page 3, there is one other key bit of information you need to review on Page 1. "Providers with Claims This Period" will be listed at the bottom of the right-hand column with the dates of service for Part B services and "Facilities with Claims This Period" for Part A services. Make sure you are familiar with any providers listed here. You should also verify the dates of service listed match care that you actually received.

If there are unfamiliar provider names listed here, you have to ask yourself why. Could this be the name of another provider in an office that cared for you? Was another provider covering for your usual doctor in his absence? Does your doctor work in multiple offices? In these cases, the charges could be legitimate. Regardless, you should never assume. Double check with that office if you have any questions.

 TIP

When you are admitted to a hospital for care, things can happen at a whirlwind pace. You will be faced with many new names and faces, and it may be difficult to keep them straight. Each provider who provides a service will be billed under Part B, not Part A. This can potentially fill your Part B MSN with unfamiliar names. If possible, you or a loved one should keep a notebook listing the names of each provider you meet during a hospital stay. This will make your record keeping easier down the line. You may also ask the nurse to prepare a list for you before you are discharged from the hospital.

If you cannot corroborate the information in your Part B MSN with your provider's office, it is possible you did not receive the service in question but Medicare was billed regardless. This could be a case of fraud and abuse or it could be medical identity theft from a criminal outsider. You should contact CMS to review your concern.

After reviewing Page 1, you will want to get into the meat of the services charged. Each service will be listed under an appropriate service date on Page 3. The name of the service, whether the service was approved for coverage by Medicare, how much the provider charged, the Medicare approved amount based on the Medicare Fee Schedule, the amount Medicare paid, and most importantly the maximum that you could be billed will be divided up into easy to read columns.

THIS IS NOT A BILL

Your Outpatient Claims for Part B (Medical Insurance)

Part B Medical Insurance helps pay for outpatient care provided by certified medical facilities, such as hospital outpatient departments, renal dialysis facilities, and community health centers.

Definitions of Columns

Service Approved? This column tells you if Medicare covered the outpatient service.

Amount Facility Charged: This is your facility's fee for this service.

Medicare-Approved Amount: This is the amount a facility can be paid for a Medicare service. It may be less than the actual amount the facility charged. The

facility has agreed to accept this amount as full payment for covered services. Medicare usually pays 80% of the Medicare-approved amount.

Amount Medicare Paid: This is the amount Medicare paid the facility. This is usually 80% of the Medicare-approved amount.

Maximum You May Be Billed: This is the total amount the facility is allowed to bill you and can include a deductible, coinsurance, and other charges not covered. If you have Medicare Supplement Insurance (Medigap policy) or other insurance, it may pay all or part of this amount.

June 15, 2014
ABC Hospital, (555) 555-1234
123 Main Street, Anytown, ST 01234-5678
Referred by John Doe

Service Provided & Billing Code	Service Approved?	Amount Facility Charged	Medicare-Approved Amount	Amount Medicare Paid	Maximum You May Be Billed	See Notes Below
Anesth correct heart rhythm (00410)	Yes	$269.50	$56.72	$45.38	$11.34	A

Claim #12345678901234CTA

Notes for Claims Above

A This service is paid at 100% of the Medicare approved amount.

As discussed in Chapter 15, Medicare sets a cap on how much a provider or facility can charge you for services. This explains the "Medicare Approved Amount" on the statement. The "Amount Medicare Paid" and the "Maximum You May Be Billed" will usually add up to this dollar amount. If the sum total adds up to a larger amount, it may be that your provider has not accepted assignment for that particular service. In this case, their contract with Medicare allows them to bill you up to 15 percent above the cost recommended on the Medicare Fee Schedule but no more. This is known as a limiting charge. When Medicare declares the maximum you will have to pay, they are taking this into consideration.

It may happen that the provider charges in excess of the "Medicare Approved Amount." You need not be overly concerned about this. Based on contractual agreements made with Medicare, your providers have agreed to accept Medicare's recommended charges for payment. You do not need to pay more than the maximum amount Medicare advises.

This is where being proactive means everything. You will want to gather any bills you received from your provider and see if they charged you more than the dollar amount listed for that particular service. If they billed you more, you can contest the added charges.

If a service is denied coverage by Medicare, however, you will be billed the full cost of the service by your provider. You may or may not be liable for paying these costs. Your provider must have notified you in advance if there was a chance that Medicare would not pay for the service. They do this by having you sign an Advanced Beneficiary Notice (ABN) before the service is rendered as discussed in Chapter 11. If you did not sign an ABN, you do not have to pay. If you are uncertain whether or not you signed an ABN, ask your provider for a copy.

Inpatient Services

To understand Part A statements, you need to first understand the concept of a benefit period. Benefit periods are periods of time that originate with an inpatient hospital stay or a skilled nursing facility stay and extend for 60 days after services have not been used. You would be responsible for a deductible in each benefit period. The details surrounding benefit periods are discussed in Chapter 10.

Part A MSNs and Part B MSNs have similar presentation styles but different content. Whether or not you have met any deductibles will be noted in the lower left-hand column on Page 1. Since each benefit period has its own deductible, there may be multiple listings here. For 2014, the deductible was $1,216.

The right hand column with "Your Claims and Costs This Period" is also present, but with different subheadings as listed below:

1. Did Medicare approve all claims?

2. Total you may be billed

Again, with a simple glance, you get the sense if there is a possible problem or not. If Medicare has denied coverage, you have to ask yourself why.

Instead of "Providers with Claims This Period," Part A MSNs note "Facilities with Claims This Period." Even though you may have encountered several providers over the course of a hospital or skilled nursing facility stay, the statement does not list them separately. Why? Because provider charges are not paid by Part A in the first place. They are covered using your Part B plan.

Again, if you do not recognize a facility name, or if dates do not correspond with the dates of service you received, you should first call the facility to clarify and then call CMS if your concerns are not addressed to your satisfaction.

The coverage details are outlined for you on Page 3. The dates of the benefit period, number of benefit days used, noncovered charges, amount Medicare paid, and the maximum amount you can be billed are clearly listed in column format.

Similar to Part B, you may be billed the full charge by the facility if Medicare denies coverage for a particular service. For services that Medicare does approve coverage, you cannot be billed more than the maximum amount allowed by Medicare. Compare your billing statement from the facility to your MSN to be sure you have not been overbilled for services.

Unlike Part B, the "Medicare Amount Approved" rarely equals the sum of "Amount Medicare Paid" and "Maximum You May Be Billed." In fact, the approved amount is often much higher than what gets paid out. This is because hospitals are paid differently than providers.

In 1983, a law came to pass that changed how Medicare paid hospitals for their services. Though hospitals could bill each service separately as an itemized component, each one with its own Medicare Approved Amount, Medicare began to pay fixed amounts for diagnosis-related groups, or DRGs, regardless of how many services were provided for that medical problem.

For example, if Medicare only paid $1,500 for diagnosis X but the hospital performed services costing $3,000 to treat diagnosis X, even if Medicare approves coverage for each of those services, Medicare would limit its payment to $1,500. The Medicare Approved Amount would be $3,000 but Medicare would only pay $284, the amount left over from $1,500 after you paid your deductible of $1,216 for that benefit period. This legislation significantly cut payments to hospitals and saved Medicare a lot of money.

Because these grossly mismatched numbers confused many beneficiaries, Medicare changed their Part A MSN and removed the "Medicare Approved Amount." Now, you only see what Medicare pays and what you should pay, not what the Medicare Fee Schedule would have otherwise dictated. If you are reviewing an older statement, you now understand what those numbers mean, but this should not confuse you on statements looking forward.

Looking for Duplicate Charges

Whether you are reviewing your Part A or Part B MSN, you should always be on the lookout for what appear to be duplicate charges. These could be justified or made in error. For example, multiple doses of a medication may be administered in one day. These may appear to be duplicate charges but may in fact be appropriate bills for each dose provided. Similarly, if repeated laboratory studies were drawn on the same day, this may also occur.

Duplicate charges are not always benign. If made in error or maliciously by someone trying to commit fraud or abuse, it costs not only you but Medicare money. If you do not remember having multiple services performed in the same day (this is less likely to occur when you are an outpatient), you ought to request a copy of your medical records for review to verify whether or not the services were in fact completed. If it is not documented, it didn't happen, at least from a legal perspective. You may not have understood the services being provided to you at the time, and discussing this with your provider may also help to clarify things.

 ROUND TABLE

Loraine went to see her doctor last month for a persistent cough that her doctor suspected was pneumonia. Laboratory studies and an X-ray were ordered to assess her condition. It was indeed pneumonia, and she was treated with antibiotics. When she received her Part B MSN, she found two bills for chest X-rays performed on the day in question. She remembered they had to take extra X-rays in the Radiology Department to "get a better view" but they never said she would have to pay more. When she looked into it, she learned that a second chest X-ray had not been performed in full. One of the original images was inconclusive and had to be taken again, all part of the same evaluation. After she raised her concerns, the Radiology Department removed the charge for the second X-ray.

If you still feel an error has been made, you should contact CMS. Approaches to preventing fraud and medical identity theft are reviewed in Chapter 16.

Understanding Diagnostic Coding

It can be frustrating to find out that Medicare has denied coverage for a service that your provider has ordered. This costs you money, and isn't Medicare supposed to help you save money?

Sometimes, there is little that can be done about it. After all, Medicare makes it clear that certain types of tests are not covered, no matter the situation. Chapter 3 provides a partial list of these services. At other times, there are things your health-care provider can do to encourage Medicare to make payments on your behalf.

Changing Medical Codes

Every medical service that is ordered, whether it is an examination, laboratory test, imaging study, or otherwise, requires that a provider associate a diagnosis code with it. Without a diagnosis code linked to it, Medicare cannot know if a test is being ordered for a medically necessary reason, at least not without reading the medical note for that patient. Quite frankly, Medicare does not have the time or resources to check a beneficiary's medical chart every day. The most cost effective way for them to assess medical need is achieved with proper coding.

This may sound easier than it actually is. Medical coding has gotten complicated over the years. Do you have high blood pressure? If there were one code, it would be easy. Instead, it depends on many factors. What caused the blood pressure? Is it associated with heart or kidney disease? The number of possible codes starts to add up and fast.

Now think of all the possible medical conditions that exist. The number of possible codes can be staggering. How does your provider know which one to choose?

What adds to that complexity is that Medicare may only approve certain diagnostic codes for coverage. If your coverage has been denied by Medicare, it may be that they will approve coverage if your provider selects another diagnostic code. It is worth contacting your health-care provider's office or billing department to see if they can submit the bill with another medical code.

> **TIP**
>
> Your health-care provider may be willing to change diagnostic codes to meet Medicare requirements for coverage. However, this can only be done if the provider feels it is medically appropriate. It would be fraud for your provider to use diagnostic coding that did not match your medical history.

More Codes (and Confusion) to Come

A system for medical coding was devised in 1893, initially managed by the International Statistical Institute and subsequently the World Health Organization in 1948. Known as the International Statistical Classification of Diseases and Related Health Problems (ICD), it is currently in its tenth revised edition.

The problem is that the United States is not on the same schedule as everyone else. ICD-10 has been in use worldwide since 1994, but the United States remains in ICD-9 mode, at least through 2015. WHO already has revisions for ICD-11 ongoing through 2017. Where will we be then?

It is not that America wants to lag behind. Sharing the same diagnostic codes with other countries may allow us to better standardize and share data as we learn about and research different medical conditions.

HIPAA regulations require transition to ICD-10, but the deadline date has been postponed for several years in a row. CMS currently has mandated that the transition be made to ICD-10 by October 1, 2015, but not after a lot of heated debate.

Why is it a big deal? Transitioning from the list of five digit codes in ICD-9 to the list of seven digit codes in ICD-10 would dramatically increase the number of available medical codes from roughly 17,000 to 155,000. And we thought we were confused before!

The American Medical Association has expressed multiple concerns on behalf of physicians. Specifically, there are fears that the change will slow down health-care providers. Taking longer to complete administrative tasks and charting will decrease efficiency in offices. There is also increased risk that services will be denied payment by Medicare and private insurers because the preferred medical code was not selected. Surely, providers will have a learning curve that will affect reimbursements. Also changing electronic health records to adapt to ICD-10 changes could be costly for medical offices, especially solo and smaller practices. The argument goes that it could be more fruitful to wait for ICD-11 and transition with the rest of the world. For now, a 2015 deadline looms. Only time will tell if there will be another postponement.

When You Have Questions

You are not alone in this. If you have questions, you should not hesitate to reach out to your primary care provider. They are a first-line resource to help you sort out what services have been performed. They can provide you with medical records should you need them to compare to your MSN, and they have copies of your ABN ready to review as well.

You also have the option of hiring a third-party medical bill review company to review your bills and statements. These companies essentially act as a middle man between you and Medicare. Many of these companies have trained staff in medical billing and coding to review your records, and some even have a legal team to help you correct any errors they find along the way. Unfortunately, none of this is free, of course. The services offered by these companies can be expensive but could potentially save you a lot of money if an error were detected. You would have to weigh the cost of paying for the service versus how much you might expect to save based on your individual situation. It is probably best to utilize these services only when you find something suspicious on your statement rather than to have them screen all of your bills.

If you have difficulty accessing information from your providers or you suspect your Medicare account has been compromised, you may need to contact CMS directly to address your concerns. The appeals process is discussed in the following chapter.

The Least You Need to Know

- Medicare will send you three notices to make a payment; if you do not pay after your final notice, you lose your coverage and will have to reapply for Medicare.
- Understanding your billing statements and Medicare Notice Summaries can help to prevent fraud and abuse.
- If Medicare denies coverage for a service, your provider may be able to help by changing the diagnostic code attached to that service.
- If Medicare denies coverage for a service, you may be responsible to pay the full cost. The one exception is if you did not sign an Advanced Beneficiary Notice.

Complaints About Medicare

Health care is an expansive topic unto itself, and Medicare's web of rules and regulations adds an extra layer of complexity to it. No one is perfect and the U.S. government is no exception. It is not surprising that errors sometimes creep into the network. If you disagree with services provided by or declined by Medicare, you have a right to voice your concerns. This chapter outlines how you should proceed in different scenarios to hopefully swing things in your favor.

In This Chapter

- Your right to express concerns to Medicare
- What constitutes a grievance
- When and how to file a claim
- Understanding the five levels of appeals

Filing a Grievance

We live in a world where customer service reigns supreme. If you feel that your health-care experience has been inappropriate in any way, you have a right to speak up and file a complaint. These complaints are referred to as *grievances*.

Depending on the type of grievance, there may be different protocols to follow. Most grievances can be placed by contacting 1-800-MEDICARE or by filling out the Medicare Complaint Form online at medicare.gov/MedicareComplaintForm. There is an option available to expedite reviews of your complaints if needed. Medicare will determine if the case warrants expedition and will usually tell you within 24 hours if it will be able to speed up the process in your case.

DID YOU KNOW?

Medicare handles tens of thousands of grievances every year. Grievances concerning hospital care approach 16,000 annually while grievances related to nursing homes, hospice programs, and home health agencies add an additional 18,000 annually to the fray.

Customer Relations

You deserve to be treated with respect at all times. Human dignity depends on it. If someone has been rude or you do not feel you have been treated fairly, such behavior must be addressed to prevent it from happening again. Sexual harassment or discriminatory conduct against age, race, gender, or sexual orientation also fall under this category. This applies whether you were treated this way by a health-care provider, a receptionist, or even custodial staff. Anyone who works in a facility where you receive health care must be appropriate in their interaction with you.

Location, Location, Location

You may have concerns about a facility (i.e., hospice center, hospital, nursing home, skilled nursing facility) where you received care. Overall cleanliness of a facility may be an issue, or you may be put at risk by hazardous conditions or poor security. Electrical hazards, water damage, fire safety issues, poor temperature control, and even poor quality of food preparation at a given facility are all examples of how location can have an impact on your overall health-care experience. These issues may be remediated if brought to the attention of the proper authorities.

Each of these facilities has a designated official, known as an ombudsman, assigned to address and remediate patient concerns. Your grievances may first be placed with the ombudsman, and then with Medicare if further attention is required.

Quality of Care

While the previously covered issues are indeed important to your health-care experience, they do not inherently relate to the actual quality of medical care you receive. Grievances about the quality of care you receive are addressed through Quality Improvement Organizations (QIO).

The QIO Program is run by CMS and is responsible to assure that the care you receive meets certain standards of care, medically and professionally. In the past, each state had its own QIO, but concern had been raised about conflicts of interest due to ongoing relationships between facilities and their state-run organizations. For this reason, CMS restructured and streamlined the QIO program to improve efficiencies and to reduce undue influence by outside parties. These changes took effect on August 1, 2014.

DID YOU KNOW?

QIOs significantly improved quality of care from 2011 to 2014. Their efforts decreased pressure ulcers in nursing home residents by 34 percent and reduced hospital infections by 54 percent.

QIOs have been redefined, now referred to as Beneficiary and Family-Centered Care Quality Improvement Organizations (BFCC-QIO). The 50 states, District of Columbia, and certain U.S. territories have been divided into five discrete areas. Two contractors have been hired to address the needs of patients in their assigned areas.

The first company, Livanta (livanta.com), based in Maryland, covers quality of care concerns for Alaska, Arizona, California, Connecticut, Hawaii, Idaho, Maine, Massachusetts, Nevada, New Hampshire, New Jersey, New York, Oregon, Pennsylvania, Puerto Rico, Rhode Island, Vermont, U.S. Virgin Islands, and Washington. The second company, Ohio-based KePro (keproqio.com) addresses the remaining U.S. states as well as the District of Columbia. Aside from Puerto Rico and the U.S. Virgin islands, no other U.S. territories have CMS-regulated BFCC-QIO coverage.

Quality of care issues should be voiced to the BFCC-QIO in your state or U.S. territory or to Medicare directly. Common complaints addressed by a BFCC-QIO may include but are not exclusive to the following:

- You are unable to get an appointment within a reasonable amount of time.

- You are made to wait an excessive amount of time at your appointment.

- You were not offered appropriate treatments.

- You were offered and/or given treatments that were not necessary.

- You suffered complications from a failed treatment or surgery.

- You were prescribed the wrong dose, strength, or frequency of a medication.

- You were prescribed a medication that is contraindicated in your situation, either based on allergies you have or based on interactions you could have with your other medications.

- You were given the wrong medication at the pharmacy.

- You were released too early from the hospital.

A formal BFCC-QIO review follows a careful procedure to assure the case has been reviewed from all angles.

1. **Receipt of a written complaint.** You are required to submit your complaint in writing; a telephone call alone will not suffice. The BFCC-QIO will acknowledge receipt of your complaint in writing. It is all about leaving a paper trail.

2. **Medical record request.** In order to determine whether or not you received appropriate care, your medical records need to be reviewed. You will need to sign a release form so that this information can be accessed by the BFCC-QIO. If your health-care provider fails to release the required medical information as requested, there could be serious repercussions. Medicare could even cancel their contract agreement with your provider so he can no longer participate in the program.

3. **Quality case review.** Your case is reviewed by the BFCC-QIO. An initial determination will be made as to whether or not your grievance warrants further investigation. If the treatment you received followed appropriate standards of care, the case may be closed at this stage. You will receive documentation about the decision and investigation.

4. **Re-review process.** If Medicare believes quality care was not rendered, your health-care provider will be contacted and allowed to add additional documentation for review. This essentially becomes his opportunity to defend himself.

5. **Notice of disclosure.** Medicare will notify your health-care provider of their decision based on all information received. Your provider is offered a final opportunity to comment and can decide whether or not to allow the BFCC-QIO to disclose his documentation to you, the claimant. Not disclosing documentation is not a sign of wrongdoing.

6. **Response to claimant.** You will receive the final case report outlining any findings by the BFCC-QIO and their plans to rectify the grievance.

As you can see, the process is thorough but could take considerable time. You would not want someone to breeze through the case and not give it proper attention. That said, you do not want it to take *too* long. If the case is *concurrent*, cases may be processed over 38 to 83 days. If a case is *retrospective*, cases could take as long as 85 to 165 days to complete. These estimates predate the establishment of the BFCC-QIO program.

 **DEFINITION**

> **Concurrent cases** are related to health care that you are currently receiving. For example, you are staying in a facility and receiving treatment. **Retrospective cases** are related to health care you have received in the past, and the course is completed. You are no longer staying in the facility, and you are no longer receiving that specific manner of treatment. Concurrent cases are seen as more urgent given there may still be time to make changes to care you are currently receiving.

Cases that were begun prior to August 1, 2014, under state-run QIOs should have been forwarded to the appropriate BFCC-QIO for final processing. If you placed a grievance during that time and are not sure if it is receiving proper attention, you may contact Livanta or KePro accordingly to address your concerns.

Kidney Disease

Kidney disease is increasing not only in the United States but worldwide. Grievances related to treatment of kidney disease can be placed in many ways. Concerns may range from quality of care to scheduling issues. Though you may report your grievances to your health-care facility or to Medicare directly, local End-Stage Renal Disease Networks have also been established to address patient concerns about care you receive at dialysis or kidney transplant centers. State Survey Agencies once worked in concert with these networks but have since been replaced by BFCC-QIOs.

When you file a grievance about a dialysis center you can choose to remain anonymous, but even if you do not, you will not face any repercussions from the facility if you continue to receive care there. That would be illegal.

Medical Equipment

Durable medical equipment could be damaged or even be inappropriate to your situation. Such equipment may also be unfairly expensive when compared to equivalent offerings through other agencies. If you have received equipment or supplies that you feel do not meet quality standards, you must report your grievance to the supplier within five calendar days. They must respond to you with a written response, and hopefully a solution, within 14 days of receiving the initial complaint.

If the supplier does not follow this protocol, you may report it to Medicare or your BFCC-QIO to address your concern. A Medicare representative may then forward your grievance to the Competitive Acquisition Ombudsman (CAO) as needed to address the issue.

Medicare Advantage and Part D

Grievances for Medicare plans run by private insurers follow a different timeline. For Medicare Advantage and Part D plans, you have 60 days from the time of the inciting event to place your concern with the insurance company. Your grievance must be reviewed and addressed within 30 days.

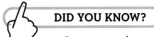

DID YOU KNOW?

Approximately 30,000 grievances and appeals are placed against Medicare Advantage Plans every year.

Each private insurance company will have their own protocols on how to address grievances. If your concerns are not reconciled as expected, you may contact Medicare in writing or by telephone at 1–800–MEDICARE.

Filing a Claim

Being a patient is hard enough without you needing to send your own bills to Medicare. In the majority of scenarios, your health-care provider will send bills to Medicare on your behalf. Exceptions may occur under rare circumstances, but they do occur. Know how to proceed so that you are not shortchanged in the end.

In order for Medicare to pay their share of any services you receive, they need to receive *claims* in a timely manner. If they don't, you are on the hook for the whole payment. Claims must be filed within one calendar year from when you received the service. For example, if the service was rendered on July 11, 2014, your provider has until July 11, 2015, to file the claim.

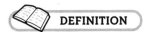

DEFINITION

A **claim** is a bill to Medicare or other insurance provider requesting payment for services provided.

You pay your premiums for a reason. Make sure you get your full money's worth.

Delayed Filing

Your provider may not have an efficient billing department, in which case they may delay sending claims to Medicare for processing. This can be problematic in many ways.

Your health-care provider can still bill you the amount that Medicare would have expected you to pay if the claim had been filed on time. This is usually a 20 percent coinsurance for Part B services. If you have not not yet spent the amount on your deductible that year, you could also be billed that dollar amount as well.

If a claim is not filed, Medicare will not acknowledge that you already paid money toward your deductible, even if the services would have been covered. This means you will still have to pay that amount toward your deductible when you need another service in the future. You want to make sure Medicare credits any money you spent out-of-pocket on your deductible. They can only do this if there is a proper claim on your record.

 **CAUTION**

Claims are processed faster by Medicare when they are sent by your health-care provider. It is in your best interest to nudge your provider to file the claim before you send one in yourself.

The best you can do is call your provider to request they process the claim. If worse comes to worst, you may have to file the claim yourself. You may contact 1–800–MEDICARE or access the Patient's Request for Medicare Payment form, also called the CMS-1490S form, at cms.gov/ Medicare/CMS-Forms/CMS-Forms/CMS-Forms-Items/CMS012949.html. There are detailed instructions on how to process the claim available in both English and Spanish. You will need to have copies of all bills and receipts for the care you received in order to proceed.

Nonparticipating Providers

Your health-care provider may accept Medicare for payment, but he may not accept all the bells and whistles. If you have selected a nonparticipating provider as your care giver, you may be put at higher risk for sending your own claims to Medicare.

As discussed in Chapter 16, nonparticipating providers agree to accept Medicare for payment but do not accept assignment. Accepting assignment means that the provider does not agree to part or any of the Medicare Fee Schedule. This allows him to bill you more than the Medicare recommended amount for certain or even all services. In this case, he may or may not choose to send those claims to Medicare. This would leave you responsible to get the necessary information to Medicare for processing.

If you are on Original Medicare, participating providers are required by law to submit claims on your behalf for any covered services.

Advanced Beneficiary Notices

Advanced Beneficiary Notices (ABN), discussed in Chapter 11, protect both you and your provider financially. If your health-care provider thinks there is a chance Medicare will not pay for a certain test or service, he must notify you of this before the test is performed by having you sign this ABN. This protects the provider because he has it in writing that you agree to cover the costs of any service not covered by Medicare. This protects you, because if you are not asked to sign an ABN for a service that is not covered by Medicare, you are not liable to pay for any charges associated with that service.

Because your provider thinks Medicare might not cover something does not mean that it is necessarily true. Medicare could surprise you! It is always worth submitting a claim because without a claim in effect, you do not even have the option to appeal a decision. It could well be the case that you could make a strong argument to have a certain test covered. The appeals process is discussed later in this chapter.

There is a check box on the ABN form asking whether or not you want your provider to submit a claim to Medicare for that service. Always check YES. Otherwise, your provider, whether they are participating or nonparticipating, does not have to submit a claim for services it does not believe Medicare will cover. Make your life easier. Have your provider do the leg work.

Medicare Advantage and Part D

You will never file a claim with Medicare for a Medicare Advantage or Part D plan. This is because Medicare pays those private insurance companies on a monthly basis already. If you have to file a claim, it will be through the insurance company directly. Each company may have their own policies in place regarding how to submit claims.

While each insurer will be different, it is not uncommon for you to come across this issue when accessing out-of-network providers. If you receive care from a provider who does not have a direct affiliation with your insurance company, they may charge you directly for any services rendered, and you will have to submit claims for the insurance company to make payments to that provider or to reimburse you if you paid for that care out-of-pocket. In-network providers generally submit claims on your behalf.

If You Suspect Fraud

If a participating provider refuses to bill Medicare for covered services and requires you to pay out-of-pocket for services before your appointment, you should be on high alert. Put simply, your provider should not be asking you to pay what Medicare would pay. This is against the law and sanctions could be taken against that provider.

You should contact Medicare immediately to address any concerns you have about suspicious billing activity by your provider. You may also need to notify administrators at the facility where the provider works, the state medical licensing board, the state Attorney General's office, and even your local Medicare Administrative Contractor (MAC). CMS provides an interactive list of MACs by state on their website.

The Appeals Process

Though both are types of complaints, an *appeal* is different than a grievance because it addresses the financial as opposed to the technical aspects of your care. If you feel that Medicare ought to cover a test but this coverage was denied, you can file an appeal. Likewise, if you feel that Medicare did not pay enough toward the cost of a service or test, you can appeal. You have a right to express your concerns. The process can be quite lengthy and requires you to be thoughtful in gathering your documentation.

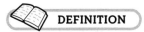

DEFINITION

> An **appeal** is a complaint made against Medicare or other insurance provider when you disagree about what should be covered and paid for under your health plan.

The Medicare appeals process is divided into five stages. Each stage is summarized in the following pages. Differences will be addressed as they apply when appealing to Original Medicare or another Medicare Health Plan.

Level 1: Redetermination and Reconsideration

After your provider (or, if you're unlucky, you yourself) sends a claim for Original Medicare, it is reviewed by a Medicare contracting company to determine whether a service will be covered and for how much. You will receive the determination on your Medicare Summary Notice (MSN). As discussed in Chapter 17, you receive MSNs quarterly.

If you disagree with the initial determination, you may place a Level 1 appeal. Information on how to place an appeal will be clearly outlined on your MSN. You only have 120 days to appeal a decision after you receive the MSN. The same Medicare contracting company will review your case but a different individual will be assigned to look at the information.

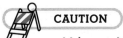

CAUTION

> Make sure Medicare has your most up to date address. If an MSN is sent to the wrong address, you may not receive the document in a timely manner, if at all, and may not be eligible to make an appeal on your case within the allotted time.

A Level 1 appeal for a Medicare Advantage Plan is referred to as a "request for reconsideration" and must be placed within 60 days of the plan declining coverage. You will hear back from the insurer in 30 to 60 days depending on whether your appeal addressed a requested service or payment concern. If your case is denied at this level, your appeal will be automatically bumped to Level 2.

Similar to a Medicare Advantage Plan, a Level 1 appeal for a Part D plan, a "request for redetermination," must be placed within 60 days. Turnover is much faster with a decision made within seven days. If your case is denied a second time, your appeal will be automatically bumped to Level 2.

Level 2: Independent Contractors

Whereas private Medicare plans are automatically forwarded to a Level 2 appeal, you must decide on your own whether to continue the appeal process for Original Medicare. This is referred to as a "request for reconsideration." The lingo becomes confusing as this is the same phrase used to define Level 1 Medicare Advantage appeals.

For Original Medicare, you have 180 days after receiving your Level 1 determination to make a Level 2 appeal. At this stage, the Medicare contracting company is now replaced by a Qualified Independent Contractor (QIC) who hires health-care professionals available to review the medical necessity of your case. The process for appealing and contacting the QIC will be clearly outlined on your Level 1 determination letter. A decision should be made by the QIC in 60 days.

For a Level 2 review, you want all your ducks in a row. You need to write a letter explaining why you are making a complaint and the reasons why you feel the service or charges should be covered. You want to have any additional supporting information forwarded to the QIC for review at this time. It may be difficult to add this information at later levels of appeal unless there are extenuating circumstances.

ROUND TABLE

Thomas' claim for laboratory studies to investigate a possible diagnosis of rheumatoid arthritis was denied coverage by Medicare. Since he uses Original Medicare, he filed an appeal within 120 days, and his case was reviewed by the Medicare contracting company that first saw his case. Unfortunately, his claim was not deemed medically necessary, and he appealed to a Level 2 Qualified Independent Contractor within 180 days. Because his health-care provider forwarded additional information, including a detailed letter, on his behalf, Medicare approved the coverage of these tests, leaving Thomas to only pay his usual coinsurance.

Private Medicare health plans use an Independent Review Entity (IRE) to determine medical necessity at this stage. For Medicare Advantage, Level 2 appeals are called a "reconsidered determination" and for Part D a "request for reconsideration." For Medicare Advantage, you should receive a result within 60 days, and for Part D within 7 days.

Level 3: Hearing

Regardless of the type of Medicare plan you have, all Level 3 appeals are processed the same and must be submitted in writing. There is no automatic entry into this stage. You must actively appeal the case within 60 days of your Level 2 determination, and you can only proceed if there is $140 or more in debate. The requisite dollar amounts may change over time. This value is from 2013.

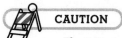
CAUTION

There is a tremendous backlog in the system. As of April 2014, more than 357,000 cases were awaiting Medicare appeals with an Administrative Law Judge. It is estimated this could lead to a delay as long as 28 months before your case is heard.

This level requires that you present testimony before an Administrative Law Judge (ALJ) at a hearing. Experts in a given field may also be asked to testify. Your hearing will take place via video-teleconference (the majority), telephone, or in-person. In the case where the findings are clearly in your favor, a hearing may not be required at all. That said, it rarely occurs that your case would have been denied this far into the appeals process if it were really a slam dunk.

You will be notified at least 20 days before the hearing. Once you are notified of the hearing date, you must respond within 5 days that you accept the assigned date. After the hearing, you will receive a determination within 90 days, though again the deadline could be extended depending on the case.

Level 4: Medicare Appeals Council

If your Level 3 appeal was denied, you have 60 days from receiving your hearing results to advance to a Level 4 appeal under the Medicare Appeals Council (MAC). There is no contested dollar threshold required to enter this stage of appeals.

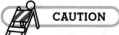
CAUTION

This is where abbreviations go wrong. Medicare Administrative Contractors and the Medicare Appeals Council are both MACs. When you see these abbreviations, keep them in context.

The MAC is part of the Department of Health and Human Services and is not associated with the ALJ as this would be a conflict of interest. After reviewing all the testimony from your hearing, a determination will be made about your case in 90 days though, again, extended deadlines may occur.

Level 5: Taking It to the Courts

Sixty seems to be the magic number for Medicare appeals. You have 60 days to apply for a Judicial Review by a Federal District Court if your Level 4 claim is denied, but you may only proceed to this level if the contested amount is at least $1,400 using 2013 data.

After this, there is no further action you can take. If your case is denied at Level 5 (or even Level 4 if you did not meet qualifying dollar amount to enter Level 5), you will be responsible for any payments charged to you.

Expediting Your Case

There may be situations where you cannot sit around waiting for an answer on your appeal. While we may all feel that way, there are specific situations that may expedite your request. If you are actively receiving or requiring the care in question and your medical health is at immediate risk, your case may be expedited. This is the case for both Original Medicare and private Medicare health plans, but expedition can only occur at Levels 1 and 2. The process for expedition will be outlined in your appeal forms.

The Least You Need to Know

- You have a right to express concerns about any experience you had with your health care, medical or nonmedical.
- A Medicare claim must be filed within one calendar year of the service provided.
- If a claim is not filed with Medicare, you will not get any credit for any money you may have spent toward your deductible.
- Nonparticipating providers do not have to submit claims to Medicare on your behalf but participating providers do.
- If you disagree with Medicare's decision not to cover or pay for certain services, you can appeal their decision using a five-level process.

Fixed Incomes

Everyone is subject to the realities of life. Unemployment rates rise and fall, and job loss can strike at any time. Although money cannot buy happiness, it may very well buy some of life's essentials like food, shelter, and health care. We may not always be able to control our lot in life, but we can learn to make the most of what we have. This chapter outlines resources to help you cope with financial hardships.

Family Considerations

The Affordable Care Act mandated that health insurance coverage be extended to dependents as old as 26 years of age. This saved a lot of college-aged children from getting dropped by their parents' employer-sponsored insurance plans, college-aged children who otherwise may not have had the employment opportunities or finances to access health insurance on their own.

However, this ACA protection does not extend to Medicare. Medicare is not a shared plan. Each individual must meet eligibility qualifications on his own in order to benefit from the program's offerings. Families, in Medicare's eyes, do not count.

In This Chapter

* Medicare's limitations for families
* Financial assistance programs for veterans
* How to get more of your health-care costs covered
* Strategies to save money at home

Grand Families

American families do not necessarily follow the nuclear model comprised of two parents and their dependent children. There are also many other family structures, including single-parent families, extended families where many relatives live together, blended families where one or both parents have children from previous relationships, and grandparent families where grandparents raise their grandchildren. Families in this last group are often referred to as "grand families." This is where Medicare's failure to include dependents can make a significant impact on your wallet.

> **DID YOU KNOW?**
>
> The U.S. Census Bureau reported that 2.4 million grandparents were raising their grandchildren in 2000.

The number of children raised by grandparents is considerable. It is estimated that one in four children will be raised by their grandparent. The reasons for this may vary but could include death of the parents, parental incarceration, parental travel for employment, or even abandonment. Sometimes the parents are involved in the care of the child but rely on the grandparents for the bulk of child care. Regardless, the responsibility of raising a child adds financial burdens to grandparents who are approaching or who have even reached retirement age.

Insuring Dependents

Children need access to insurance as much as their grandparents to promote healthy lifestyles and prevent disease. Because Medicare does not offer coverage to dependents, grandparents are left to find ways to get health-care coverage for their grandchildren. This may mean working past retirement age to maintain access to employer-sponsored health plans that do have those ACA protections. The problem is that not everyone may be physically able to work past retirement age.

COBRA plans remain another option for some grandparents, since coverage can include dependents up to 26 years of age and can extend up to 36 months after you leave your job. While COBRA may be less expensive than purchasing private health insurance out of pocket, it can still be quite costly. COBRA issues are discussed in more detail in Chapters 5 and 14.

> **DID YOU KNOW?**
>
> According to Medicaid.gov, more than 43 million American children are covered by Medicaid and the Children's Health Insurance Program combined.

If certain low-income criteria are met, you may be able to apply for Medicaid as a means to provide health care to your grandchildren as old as 21 years old. Medicaid is funded by the federal government but managed on a state level, therefore different income thresholds for eligibility may exist depending where you live. Generally speaking, federal guidelines set the baseline recommendations at $44,700, so families that earn less than this amount will likely be eligible for the program.

TIP

Visit insurekidsnow.gov to access information about Medicaid and CHIP plans for children.

For those who do not qualify for Medicaid but still cannot afford to pay for private health insurance, the Children's Health Insurance Program (CHIP) may be of benefit. Similar to Medicaid, federal funds support the program but it is run by each state individually. Some states may require you to pay a monthly premium, but it cannot exceed 5 percent of your income. Some states even allow parents and pregnant women to be covered under the program. Coverage of tests may be similar to that of Medicaid but may differ based on how each state set up its program.

Grandparents who meet Medicare eligibility by age do not want to delay signing up for the program, even if it means having to pay Medicare premiums in addition to premiums for a second health plan that covers their dependents. Not signing up on time for Medicare could result in late penalties.

Social Security Insurance

If a child has a disability, be it physical or mental, he may qualify for Social Security benefits but only if the family meets a low-income threshold. To be considered disabled, the child's disability must be expected to last at least 12 months. Social Security will review cases every three years to reassess disability status. For infants meeting criteria for disability based on low birth weight, a case review will happen by the first birthday.

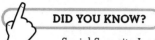

DID YOU KNOW?

Social Security Insurance (SSI) covers 1.3 million children and contributed over $10 billion in benefits, $1.3 billion more than did the nation's welfare programs, in 2013.

After 18 years of age, the child's case is generally reviewed as an adult with disability. This means that the family's income no longer comes into play. The child will meet criteria based on their disability and their individual earnings. However, child benefits may be extended to age 19 if the child is a full-time student.

Qualification for SSI benefits automatically qualifies your dependent for Medicaid though you still have to actively apply for the program.

Temporary Assistance to Needy Families

There are other resources for grandparents raising grandchildren and low-income families to turn to when they cannot afford all their basic needs. One of these programs is the Temporary Assistance to Needy Families (TANF) program. Federal funds may be available to families with children under 18 years of age (or up to 19 years of age if their children are full-time students) if they meet certain income criteria. Additional requirements for participation include U.S. citizenship, active participation in school for students aged 6 to 17 years old, and immunization for preschool children. The latter may limit financial resources for families who opt out of routine vaccinations for their children.

 DID YOU KNOW?

TANF may have assisted in decreasing dependence on our nation's public assistance programs. Within the first four years of the program, the number of American welfare recipients decreased by 6.5 million to the lowest levels since 1969.

The program which started in 1997 is run by the U.S. Department of Health and Human Services and is a short-term welfare program. TANF aims to provide resources for families so that they can become self-sufficient. This is achieved by a work requirement for adults who must work or participate in training programs for at least 30 hours per week. Adults with children younger than 6 years old may only need to commit to 20 hours weekly.

TANF also has a child-only benefits option where the adults in the family do not receive any benefits if the child alone meets criteria. Regardless of the TANF option, family or child-only, benefits will only be available for 48 months. This is a decrease from 60 months when the program was first enacted.

You and/or your dependents automatically qualify for Medicaid if you are accepted into the TANF program.

Foster Care and Guardianships

If you are raising your grandchild, you may need to arrange for custody of the child in order to get legal protections. There are different options that may help you to increase your income.

Foster care programs are one option but only if the child has been removed from a parent's care by the state. Foster care is intended to be temporary until long-term placement can be established. Since you are a blood relative of the child, this is known as kinship foster care.

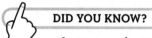

DID YOU KNOW?

In 2012, nearly 400,000 children were in foster care, and 28 percent of them were placed into foster family homes with relatives.

In order to receive monthly payments from the foster care system, the state will require you to participate in routine evaluations and home visits. As part of a kinship foster care arrangement, you can opt-out of these state interventions, but then you will not receive payments.

Alternatively, you may choose to take your case to the courts. You may elect for legal custody, though this may not be a long-term solution if the parent wishes to take back custody rights in the future. It could be the case that a parent initially deemed unfit may have turned her situation around so she is better equipped to care for her children.

Guardianship is similar to legal custody in that you must go to court, but you may also gain financial benefits. The Fostering Connections to Success and Increasing Adoptions Act of 2008 allowed Social Security to fund guardianship assistance programs (GAP) for relatives to take children out of foster homes and give them long-term homes. Once approved into a GAP, benefits may be granted at foster care rates and the children are eligible for Medicaid. Payments continue until the child reaches 18 years of age or the guardianship ends. Unlike with foster care, you are not required to participate in state interventions to maintain these benefits.

Finally, you may claim all parental rights by adopting the child. This dissolves any rights the biological parents may have had.

Tips to Save on a Fixed Income

You do not have to be actively raising a family to benefit from financial assistance programs. Many retirees have limited dollars available to them, relying on Social Security and their savings to make ends meet. Sometimes this is not always enough. Knowing where to turn when you cannot afford your basic needs will help you through those hard times.

Medicare Savings Programs

If you have limited income and are having difficulty paying your medical expenses, you may be eligible for one of the following four Medicare savings programs. You can apply for these programs through your state Medicaid program.

Qualified Medicare Beneficiary (QMB) Program. You may apply for this program if you earn less than $993 per month as an individual, or less than $1,331 per month as a couple. This program offers the most benefits contributing payments to Medicare for Part A premiums, Part B premiums, deductibles, coinsurance, and copays.

Specified Low-Income Medicare Beneficiary (SLMB) Program. You may apply for this program if you earn less than $1,187 per month as an individual, or less than $1,593 per month as a couple. This program may help you pay your monthly Part B premiums.

Qualifying Individual (QI) Program. You may apply for this program if you earn less than $1,333 per month as an individual, or less than $1,790 per month as a couple. Similar to the SLMB program, you only receive assistance with Part B premiums.

Qualified Disabled and Working Individuals (QDWI) Program. You may apply for this program if you earn less than $3,975 per month as an individual, or less than $5,329 per month as a couple. You only receive assistance with Part A premiums.

The dollar amounts above are those set for 2014 and may change on an annual basis. Also, income limits tend to be higher in Alaska and Hawaii.

Medicaid

Medicare offers many essential health services, but one of the most needed is left uncovered for the elderly—nursing home care. While Medicare does allow for stays in skilled nursing facilities after a hospitalization, that care is limited in its duration. Medicare does not offer any coverage for those who are weak, debilitated, or cognitively impaired due to age-related conditions and unable to care for themselves. Even if you are deemed to be unsafe to live on your own and those safety issues risk your health, Medicare will not step in. The burden of cost is put on the beneficiary to pay out-of-pocket costs.

 DID YOU KNOW?

Nursing home care is expensive. Costs averaged $6,235 per month ($74,820 per year) in 2010 if you shared a room with another person, and averaged $6,965 per month ($83,580 per year) for private rooms.

The cost of nursing home care is out of reach for most Americans, not just senior citizens. The median salary in the United States is $51,000. Annual stays in a nursing home facility may cost as much as $80,000, burning up your retirement funds rapidly. It does not take long before you may find yourself eligible for Medicaid based on your low-income. You may qualify for Medicaid long before you would ever need nursing home care, if you ever do. Research the Medicaid eligibility requirements in your state so you can apply for those extra resources when you need it.

Medicaid does allow coverage for long-term nursing home stays. It also provides other health-care benefits not offered by Original Medicare, including hearing and vision care. Costly hearing aids and glasses may be covered. Medicaid programs in some states may also offer dental care.

Seventeen percent of all Medicaid enrollees are also on Medicare. This is known as being *dually eligible.* That equated to 8.3 million people in 2014. For those who are dually eligible, Medicare is charged first for appropriate health-care claims, and Medicaid pays second, including some or all of your deductibles, coinsurance, and copays left behind by Medicare. This does not mean that all your costs will be covered in full, but it sure helps to save you money in the big picture.

Program of All-Inclusive Care for the Elderly

The Program of All-Inclusive Care for the Elderly (PACE) is a program that may be able to offer you additional health-care resources at low cost. Not all states offer the program, but if you live in a state that does, you may want to look into a possible application. Since the majority of states do offer coverage, the following is a listing of the few states that do not.

Alaska	Maine
Arizona	Mississippi
Connecticut	Nevada
Georgia	New Hampshire
Hawaii	South Dakota
Idaho	Utah
Indiana	Washington, D.C.
Kentucky	West Virginia

Eligibility for PACE is based on both age and medical needs. You may be able to apply through your local Medicaid program if you meet all of the following:

- You are at least 55 years old
- Your state certifies you as needing nursing home care
- You are medically stable to live in the community
- You live in an area serviced by PACE

The goal of the PACE program is to keep people out of nursing homes for as long as possible. By identifying those at higher risk for needing a nursing home, the program keeps you active and living in your community by tailoring service to your needs. Only 7 percent of people who use the program actually live in nursing homes. When and if you do eventually require nursing home care, PACE will cover the costs of the stay, a significant benefit not provided by Medicare.

The PACE program uses a capitation program to provide your care. This means it sets a fixed dollar amount for the services you receive and uses that fund to pay for all your expenses. To this end, the team of PACE health-care providers that cares for you will limit services to only those you really need. It makes negotiations with CMS regarding payment. In order to keep with these principles, you will be asked to work within the PACE network of health-care providers. This could mean you have to leave your former primary care physician when you enroll.

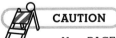

CAUTION

Your PACE prescription coverage may be better than most Part D Plans. You do not have to pay copays for any of the drugs. If you sign up for a Part D plan, you will lose your rights to the PACE drug plan.

PACE programs not only cover the services covered under the Medicaid and/or Medicare umbrellas but may extend care to the following: audiology evaluations, caregiver training, dental care, emergency care, foot care, home health care, hospital care, laboratory studies, meals, nursing home care, nursing services, nutritional counseling, occupational therapy, over-the-counter medications, personal care, physical therapy, prescription drugs, preventive services, primary care, recreational therapy, respite care, social services, social work counseling, specialty care, speech therapy, support groups, transportation to appointments, vision screening, and x-ray services. These services may be offered only if they are considered medically necessary and are approved by the PACE interdisciplinary team taking care of you.

How much you pay for PACE will depend on your participation in Medicaid, Medicare, or both. Medicaid enrollees will not pay a monthly premium for the program, even if they also have Medicare on board. Medicare beneficiaries who do not meet eligibility for Medicaid, however, will have some cost obligations. They will pay monthly premiums for PACE as well as a premium for Part D drugs, even though they are not actively signed up for a Part D plan. Beyond that, members of PACE do not need to pay deductibles, coinsurance, or copays for services approved by your team.

Applications for PACE may take as long as nine months to process, so be patient. It may be time well spent. Should you ever choose to leave the program, you may do so at any time without facing a Part D late penalty because PACE drug coverage is creditable.

Programs for Veterans

Our veterans deserve every respect and that includes offering programs to keep them on their feet, such as assistance with health-care needs as well as resources to aid in other aspects in their lives.

Not all veterans meet eligibility for VHA benefits as discussed in Chapter 9. Some veterans without disabilities may be denied coverage if they do not meet low-income requirements or fit into certain priority groups. That does not mean they will not develop financial hardships in the future. When they do, they may able to gain benefit from the VA Medical Care Hardship Program, even if they have been denied coverage in the past. Situations that may meet criteria for coverage in this program include:

- Decreased income compared to prior year

- Decreased income due to an injury

- Increase in out-of-pocket expenses for personal or family health-care needs

- Job loss

- Reduction in household income

- Reduction in work hours resulting in lower pay

The VA Medical Care Hardship Program provides a means for veterans to pay off bills relating to healthvcare and can also help them to gain access to health-care services through the VA. Veterans in need are encouraged to apply and can reach out through the VA directly or by calling 1–800–273–8255.

Other programs are available to veterans depending on their qualifications:

USA Cares (**usacares.org**) offers services to veterans from the wars in Afghanistan and Iraq. The program has prevented 435 foreclosures and assisted more than 13,000 families with grant dollars.

Disabled American Veterans (**dav.org**) provides benefits to U.S. veterans with disabilities. Services vary from prescription drug discounts to help in finding jobs. With 100 offices nationwide and available in all states as well as D.C. and Puerto Rico, veterans can easily gain access to this valuable resource.

Other agencies that provide financial assistance are open to all veterans regardless of disability. These include The National Association of American Veterans (naavets.org) and The National Resource Directory (nrd.gov).

 ROUND TABLE

George is a disabled veteran who has been having a difficult time due to his low income. He receives VHA benefits for health care purposes but has had difficulty making his mortgage payments. He has applied for assistance from Disabled American Veterans as well as the National Association of American Veterans.

Help with Utilities

Having a roof over your head is an essential first step, but the utilities that allow you to maintain safety within your home are also important to sort out.

Energy Assistance:

The federal government funds a year-round energy assistance program known as the Low Income Home Energy Assistance Program (LIHEAP). The goal is to decrease energy costs for low income households. Preference is given to families with household members with medical needs or for those with high energy usage, especially during extremes of weather in the winter or summer months. Anyone with a low income can apply for the program, whether you own or rent, and even if you do not currently owe money on your utility bills. The program can be used as a preventive measure to keep you out of debt as much as it is to help decrease your debt. You can check out liheap.org for details.

The Citizens Oil Heat Program offers free oil to those in need, as much as 100 gallons of free oil one-time to each family per season. Low-priced oil deliveries may also be offered.

The program is offered in the following states:

Alaska	New Jersey
Connecticut	New York
Delaware	Pennsylvania
Indiana	Rhode Island
Maine	Vermont
Maryland	Virginia
Massachusetts	Washington, D.C.
Michigan	Wisconsin
New Hampshire	

The program is sponsored by Citizens Energy and CITGO who have partnered since 2005 to provide this service. More than 1.8 million people have benefited from the program since its inception.

Apply for the program early in the season before resources run low. Call 1–877–JOE–4–OIL (1–877–563–4645) or visit citgoheatingoil.com.

The federal government also funds a program that helps to make enhancements to help home owners save on energy costs. This Weatherization Assistance Program may include measures such as installing insulation and programmable thermostats. It is available to those with low incomes as well as to the elderly. Weatherization could decrease costs by as much as 35 percent. Visit energy.gov/eere/wipo/weatherization-assistance-program for information on how to apply.

Telephone:

Access to a telephone is important during a crisis to call out for help. The federal government recognizes this need and has developed a telephone assistance program for local calling plans. The program is managed by the state governments and has two components: Lifeline and Link-up. For those meeting low-income criteria, the Lifeline part of the program may decrease local telephone charges by $15 each month. Long distance services or specialty features are not covered by the $15 amount. It may also be given for you to get a cell phone. The Link-up program will pay up to $50 for installation of a new telephone.

Utilities:

Depending on where you live, different utility companies may run the show. Whether it is an electric, gas, or other utility company, each state may have different programs available to help you with expenses if you have low income or if you are elderly. This may help to prevent you from losing power or heat. A helpful resource is available at energynear.org where programs are listed by state.

Water:

Clean water is essential to maintaining proper hygiene and preventing the spread of infection. Inability to pay for water supplies can be a hazard to your health.

Established in 1886, American Water (amwater.com) is the largest water distributor in the nation, providing drinking water and managing waste water across 35 states and parts of Canada. The company does offer a Low Income Payment Program (LIPP) to provide assistance for those having difficulty making payments on their water supplies. Those who meet income requirements may be able to establish an installment plan with the company to spread their payments out over time to decrease how much they have to pay monthly. Criteria may vary from state to state.

For those behind in their payments, American Water further offers its H2O Help to Others Program™ to prevent discontinuation of water service. Grants as high as $500 may be given to families in need but may not always be sufficient to cover the full cost of any overdue bills.

State Health Insurance and Assistance Programs

You always have someone on your side. Every state has a resource available to offer you counseling and advice regarding CMS's different programs. These programs are known as State Health Insurance and Assistance Programs (SHIPs).

SHIPs are manned by volunteers to give you advice on Medicare, Medigap, and Medicaid based on your individual circumstances. They are not a resource for applying to any of these programs, and they do not provide you direct care. The advice they offer, however, may be invaluable, and it is free. They may be able to direct you to resources available in your state to help you cut costs.

Some states do not call their programs SHIPs. The states below use the following acronyms or program names:

Health Insurance Counseling and Advocacy Programs (HICAP): California HICAP, New York HICAP, and Texas HICAP

Senior Health Insurance Benefits Advisors (SHIBA): Idaho SHIBA, Oregon SHIBA, and Washington SHIBA

Serving Health Insurance Needs of Elders (SHINE): Florida SHINE, Massachusetts SHINE, and South Dakota SHINE

Miscellaneous: Connecticut Program for Health Insurance Assistance, Outreach, Information, and Referral Counseling and Eligibility Screening (CHOICES); Delaware Insurance Department ELDERinfo; District of Columbia Health Insurance Counseling Project (HICP); GeorgiaCares Resources; Hawaii SAGE Plus; Michigan MMAP; Missouri CLAIM; New Mexico Benefits Counseling Program; North Dakota Senior Health Insurance Counseling (SHIC); Oklahoma Senior Health Insurance Counseling Program (SHICP); Pennsylvania APPRISE; Senior Health Insurance Counseling for Kansas (SHICK); South Carolina Insurance Counseling Assistance and Referrals for Elders (I-CARE); and Virginia Insurance Counseling and Assistance Program (VICAP)

You may find a list of toll-free telephone numbers for each state's program at shiptalk.org.

The Least You Need to Know

- Medicare does not provide health-care coverage for your dependents.
- Temporary Assistance to Needy Families (TANF) is a short-term welfare program that helps parents develop job skills and reenter the work force.
- Medicaid helps to pay for long-term nursing home care whereas Medicare limits nursing home care to a limited stay after a hospitalization.
- The PACE program expands health-care coverage at low cost for those at least 55 years old and with medical needs.
- Each state makes available financial assistance programs to save on utility costs for the elderly or those with low incomes.

5

Safeguarding Your Future

Retirement should be a time for celebration, not one of financial strain. With life's unpredictable twists and turns, not to mention inflation, it takes some planning to make your retirement years everything they deserve to be.

Health-care expenses can pack an unexpected wallop. Medicare can help with that to an extent, but sometimes you may need assistance in paying for what Medicare leaves behind. Premiums can quickly add up before you even start to receive medical care, and deductibles, coinsurance, and copays pile on top of that.

Medicare, too, may need to adapt. Coverage may change and costs may rise. The truth is that Medicare is expected to run out of funds by 2030. How will changes to Medicare affect your bottom dollar?

This part outlines savings programs for Medicare as well as cost reduction approaches that you can use in other areas of your life. These basic financial planning strategies aim to make your later years as rich as possible.

Getting Finances in Order

The number of years we live may or may not be in our control, but at the very least, we can make those years count. To improve our chances for enjoying a quality life, we need to not only take care of our health but also develop an understanding of our financial situation. After all, if we cannot afford health care and other basic needs, how will we be able to move forward?

This chapter will teach you strategies on how to look at your finances and prepare for your future. By no means is this meant to be an all-inclusive approach to financial planning. Instead it is a way to introduce you to key concepts and common strategies.

In This Chapter

- Breaking down your current spending patterns
- Planning a retirement budget for the future
- How much money you need to save to retire comfortably
- Strategies to cut costs

Time to Do the Math

Not everyone has the courage to sit down and evaluate their finances. The idea can be more than a little intimidating if you do not already have savings in the bank or if you do not have an aptitude for math. Some seniors are not capable of managing their checkbooks as dementia and cognitive decline set in. There are so many personal reasons to delay financial planning, but those reasons are not enough to justify putting off these important considerations.

If you have not already looked at your finances, you have to stop making excuses and get started. You may need a helping hand to guide you on your way, but the time has come for you, a loved one, or a designated financial planner to do the math. The truth is that not doing so is foolhardy and could cost you more than dollars in the future. It could cost you your physical, mental, and social well-being as well.

Cost of Living

Before you can build a plan for the future, you need to take a good hard look at your existing foundation. Until you know what building blocks you have, you cannot erect the walls that will stabilize your retirement years. You do not want that roof to cave in on you.

Basic Needs

Ask anyone what they need in life and you could be surprised by the answers. I am sure you know of more than a few people who would reply that they "need a vacation." You may also hear calls for love, friendship, and partnerships. Some may wish for grandchildren and extended families. These things offer hope and happiness to so many. They are the things that make life worth living.

Every individual has lived through situations you will never experience in the same way. Our priorities are colored by those encounters. When asked what you need in life, how will you answer?

While the answers vary far and wide, the truth is there are a small number of basic items we truly need in order to survive in this world. As much as we may want other things, as much as those things may affect the quality of our lives, they are not essential to live from a physical point of view. They are valuable wants but not needs.

Our basic needs fall into the following five categories:

Groceries. You need nutrition to fuel your body. Without the proper inclusion of protein, carbohydrates, fat, and vitamins in your diet, you could succumb to disease. Not only this, but your personal hygiene can also affect your health, leading to infections as well as social consequences. Access to food and toiletries is a basic necessity.

Health care. If you are one of the lucky ones, you will have no major health issues to cope with as you grow older. The large majority of us, however, will develop medical conditions as our senior years take hold, even if by the simple process of wear and tear. These conditions may require medications and treatments to reduce pain, suffering, and health complications. Access to appropriate health care improves outcomes, quality of life, and longevity.

Housing. You need a roof over your head to protect your body from temperature extremes. Prolonged exposure to excess moisture can also increase risk for developing certain medical conditions and infections, fungal infections and pneumonia for example. Safety issues also become a concern when you do not have a place to stay; crime, theft, and abuse increase broadly in these situations. Not having adequate housing places you at risk for health and social consequences.

Transportation. You may or may not have the faculties to drive in your later years, but you do need a means of transportation to fulfill your basic needs, i.e., access to medical appointments and grocery stores. Social interactions may also be impacted for those who do not have access to a means of transportation. Not all seniors have access to free transportation and have to pay out-of-pocket to get the help they need.

Utilities. If you do not have heat to warm your home during a New England winter or a means to cool the air during a Texan heat wave, your health could be at stake. Some people require electricity to run medical equipment such as CPAP machines for breathing at nighttime or to perform dialysis in their homes. Poor lighting can increase risk for falls and injury. Certain utilities, heat and electricity, are essential to achieve a safe and healthy living environment.

This list of basic needs is subject to debate. Arguments can be made against each of these categories, comparing the United States to third-world countries that have far fewer resources. In our country, these criteria meet our standards of living. Could you do without any of these things?

Current Spending

Unless you are Daddy Warbucks, there is only so much money to go around. You need to carefully calculate your current income, from employment, Social Security, pensions, annuities, and other sources if they are available to you.

What percentage of your income do you spend every month? It is important to note whether you spend more than you bring in, you break even, or you are able to put some of that income toward your savings.

Now consider the big five basic needs discussed earlier in this chapter. How much do you spend in each of those categories? Beyond this, you may also owe debts that require repayment. Debt becomes your sixth category of expenses.

Any money that you spend on something outside of one of these basic needs, you can place in a seventh category. This will be your discretionary fund. Your discretionary fund refers to dollars spent on nonessential needs that you choose at your discretion. This category is where a lot of cost savings can be found, if needed.

Calculating Your Current Expenses

Budget	Monthly Costs	Annual Costs
Debts		
Discretionary		
Groceries		
Health care		
Housing		
Utilities		
Transportation		
Total		

Existing Debt

How much you owe plays a major part in how much you dish out each month. Missing payments will increase your debt burden because of late penalties and added interest. You could easily fall into a financial spiral. Managing your debt will be key in establishing and maintaining good credit, when and if you need it in the future.

 DID YOU KNOW?

The average American cardholder had two credit cards in 2012, though the number increases to four or more credit cards for those over 50 years old. In the same year, 7 percent of credit card applications were rejected.

Credit card debt. Avoid signing up for too many credit cards, if you can help it. More cards only increase your temptation to spend. Most people can get by with one card, two if absolutely necessary. More credit cards than this are likely to cause you more harm than good. Try to find a card that offers the lowest possible interest rate and if possible, waives the annual fee. Whenever you can, pay off the entire bill, or at least more than the requested payment. Each month you make partial payments increases your debt further. Crawl out of that hole and save those dollars otherwise wasted on interest. Use them for the things you really need.

Loan payments. You may owe debt on loans for education, business, car, or home improvement expenses. You name it; there is probably a loan for it. You need to negotiate the best terms of the loan to get the lowest possible interest rates. You may even consider *loan consolidation* through a credit agency, if the option is available to you, to reduce your monthly payments and decrease interest rates. The sooner you pay off a loan, the less you pay in the long-run. Interest rates, unless they are 0 percent, are not our friend.

> **DEFINITION**
>
> **Loan consolidation** is the process of combining two or more loans into a single loan to simplify payments and reduce overall costs.

Mortgage. This is a big one. If you have paid off your mortgage before retirement, congratulations! Retirement will likely be a whole lot easier for you, though you are still on the hook for estate taxes. If you are paying off a mortgage, this can be a tremendous drain on your finances, especially if you are no longer working. Refinancing may be an option to reduce interest rates. When you plan for retirement, you need to take into consideration when your mortgage will be paid off so you can arrange for adequate funds to get you through those years.

Managing debt is not easy. Many people struggle to make ends meet and mount a large debt in the process. Watch your spending, find the best deals on interest rates, and seek help when you need it.

There are many reputable agencies out there that can help you get back on track, but be careful. There are also scams out there that will try to pocket your cash when you are most vulnerable. Do your research before working with any so-called credit company.

You want to be sure any company you work with has established a good reputation. More likely than not, a reliable company will have been in business for several years. You will want to check with the Better Business Bureau (bbb.org) to see if any complaints have been previously filed against that company. The BBB also provides an accredited business directory for you to search for companies. Get help; do not become a victim.

Future Spending

Depending on where you are in the retirement process, your future income may differ from what you have now. The majority of Americans will see their income decrease when they retire. Are you prepared to deal with lower income? How will it impact your budget?

Before you can calculate a retirement budget, you need to know how much income you will have after you stop working. The number of options available to you is based on your work history and contribution to FICA taxes. See Chapter 4 for a discussion on Social Security taxes.

Social Security

The average monthly Social Security benefit is $1,262 if you are 65 years or older. Would you be able to stretch these dollars to meet your basic needs? Few people could, though it has been done.

With Medicare Part B costing at least $104 in monthly premiums, excluding the cost of coin-surance for any care received or even medications, little is left to fend for groceries, housing, utilities, and transportation. What can you do to make ends meet?

> **TIP**
> You can visit ssa.gov to use their calculator to estimate your Social Security benefits based on your expected age of retirement.

A lot depends on when you choose to take your Social Security benefits. If you collect benefits before your designated retirement age, you will collect only a portion of your potential benefits, and these reduced payments will continue as long as you receive Social Security checks. You must assess whether or not you would be able to afford the lower payments. Everyone will have different circumstances depending on their savings and work history.

If possible, it is encouraged that you work until retirement age or beyond to maximize your Social Security income. Anyone working beyond retirement age will earn increased delayed retirement credits as discussed in Chapter 6. These credits could earn you as much as 8 percent more for each year you work beyond your retirement age up to 70 years old. You would continue to earn those higher benefits throughout the life of your Social Security disbursements. This could make a significant impact on your income over the years.

Other Sources of Income

You will also need to take into account other sources of income as you establish your retirement budget.

If you have a pension plan through your former employer, you will want to contact them to get an estimate of monthly benefits that will be paid to you. You will also want to consider whether these benefits will continue for your spouse in the unfortunate event that you pass away.

> **TIP**
> Some people manage investments in stocks and bonds on their own, but a financial advisor may be better suited to deal with the finer intricacies of these transactions to earn you more dollars.

Of course, your savings come into the picture. Investing dollars into your future can sometimes mean the difference between surviving and living well. This is what you have been waiting for! That 401k or IRA? It's time to cash in.

A 401k is an investment you make where money is taken directly from your paycheck and put into a retirement savings account. Those dollars, up to $17,500 per year allowed as of 2014, are invested in money market accounts, mutual funds, and bonds to increase the overall value of your nest egg. Better yet, you pay no taxes on that money while it sits in the 401k. As you take money out during retirement, taxes will be charged. If you withdraw money before you turn 59.5 years old, not only will you pay taxes on the withdrawal, but you will likely also pay a hefty 10 percent fine to the IRS. Talk about an incentive to save your money until after retirement!

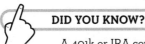

DID YOU KNOW?

A 401k or IRA could mean free money. Some employers will match how much money you put into your 401K every year up to a certain percentage.

Individual Retirement Accounts (IRAs) work in a similar manner but limit your contributions to $5,500 per year as of 2014, though this value may increase to $6,500 once you turn 50 years old. These limit amounts are set by the IRS every year and are subject to change.

A traditional IRA does not tax the money when it first enters the account, whereas funds entered into a Roth IRA have already been taxed. The difference is you pay taxes when you take the money out of a traditional IRA but do not pay taxes when you take them out of a Roth IRA. Withdrawals prior to 59.5 years old have limitations similar to a 401k. A traditional IRA will require you pay taxes and likely a 10 percent penalty to the IRS. Though a Roth IRA does not result in a 10 percent penalty, you will be taxed on any proceeds you made on your investments. It is in your best interest to hold out on using the funds until you reach 59.5 years of age to capitalize on your earnings.

These are only a sampling of the types of retirement accounts. For information on other available programs, please speak with your local bank or financial advisor.

Add 'Em Up

What do you have to work with? Add up your expected monthly Social Security benefits with any other monthly income from pensions, annuities, etc.

Now consider your savings. You will have to decide how much of your savings you will need to use each month to cover any necessary costs.

Financial planners frequently refer to the "4 percent" rule. This rule estimates that you can remove 4 to 4.5 percent of your savings each year without outliving your money. The goal is to make your money last for as many years as possible, especially if you have a long life expectancy, while allowing you to use as much of that money as you can. Who wants to leave money on the table? You earned it, so use it. This means if you saved $100,000, this would give you $4,000-$4,500 per year to play with or roughly $333–$375 per month.

Expected Annual Retirement Funds Based on the 4% Rule

Total Savings	Annual Income Based on 4% Rule	Monthly Income Based on 4% Rule
$250,000	$10,000–$11,250	$833–$938
$500,000	$20,000–$22,500	$1,667–$1,875
$750,000	$30,000–$33,750	$2,500–$2,813
$1,000,000	$40,000–$45,000	$3,333–$3,750

This does not mean that you have to follow the 4 percent rule. You can choose to utilize your funds in any way you see fit. However, the 4 percent rule may allow you to extend your funds further into the future than if you withdraw a larger sum upfront.

Will these dollars, all tallied up, be enough for you to retire comfortably?

How Much Money Do You Need to Retire?

The million-dollar listing in the preceding table is not meant to scare you. A simple internet search will show you that many people say you will need a million dollars to retire! Is this really true?

Get your calculator ready. You outlined your current expenses earlier in the chapter. Taking a look to the future, you have also listed your expected retirement income.

Financial experts estimate that you will need 75 to 85 percent of your prior income in order to maintain the same standard of living. That means if you live on $100,000 annually at the present time, you will need to have $75,000–$85,000 per year to live the same lifestyle you do now. That would equate to $6,250–$7,083 per month. That is pretty far from the Social Security benefits available. The following table provides estimates for different income brackets.

Estimates of Retirement Income Needed to Maintain Standard of Living

Annual Pre-Retirement Income	Goal Annual Retirement Income	Goal Monthly Retirement Income
$30,000	$22,500–$25,500	$1,875–$2,125
$40,000	$30,000–$34,000	$2,500–$2,833
$50,000	$37,500–$42,500	$3,125–$3,542
$60,000	$45,000–$51,000	$3,750–$4,250
$70,000	$52,500–$59,500	$4,375–$4,958

Annual Pre-Retirement Income	Goal Annual Retirement Income	Goal Monthly Retirement Income
$80,000	$60,000–$68,000	$5,000–$5,667
$90,000	$67,500–$76,500	$5,625–$6,375

If you are still paying for a mortgage as you enter retirement, you may well need to plan to have 100 percent of your pre-retirement income on hand until you have paid off your mortgage in full.

What Can You Do?

We have already discussed ways to decrease your existing debts by reducing interest rates, consolidating loans, and utilizing credit reduction agencies. We now need to discuss ways to decrease your actual spending in the other six budgeting categories.

This book as a whole addresses health-care issues. Beyond couponing, purchasing generic instead of brand name products, shopping at less expensive stores, and in appropriate cases, buying in bulk, saving on your grocery shopping is rather straight-forward. We will discuss how you can cut costs in the other budget areas.

Where You Live

Some people live in the town they were born and raised. Others have traveled the country and even the world, living in different places. Whatever the case may be, where you live will impact on your retirement in more ways than one. It could even be advantageous to consider moving. Here are some things to consider when you retire:

Cost of living. Some states are more expensive to live in than others. For example, housing prices may be higher in California than in the Midwest. If you live in a more expensive state, your savings will not last as long.

Crime rates. Safety first. As you age, you may be more vulnerable to crime, whether that be violent crime or financial crimes perpetrated by scam artists. Living where crime rates are low will decrease your risk for harm.

Health-care access. Some areas in the country are at higher risk for physician shortages than others. You want to live in area where you have choice when it comes to health care.

Tax burden. Certain states offer financial benefits when it comes to taxation. Several states do not require you to pay state income taxes, for example. Others may have lower tax rates. Some may even levy taxes on your investments.

Weather. There is a reason California and Florida are popular with seniors. Warmer weather is not only comfortable, especially for arthritic joints, but it may be less dangerous for seniors than areas where winter storms and ice increase risk for falls and injury.

Bank Rate Inc., a financial analysis company, released a top 10 list in 2014 naming the best states to retire. It took each of the factors above into consideration, though the final results didn't necessarily point to warmer weather. The results are listed as follows:

1. South Dakota
2. Colorado
3. Utah
4. North Dakota
5. Wyoming
6. Nebraska
7. Montana
8. Idaho
9. Iowa
10. Virginia

Of course, the results of this list could change in the future, and these results may or may not correlate best to your personal needs.

It only goes to show that where you live could help to save you dollars and offer a higher quality of life. This does not mean it is easy or even feasible for you to move. You may need to be near loved ones who provide care to you. If you find that your finances are overburdened, moving remains an option to be considered.

On the House

Mortgages can pose a high financial burden, and even if the mortgage is paid, upkeep of a house can sometimes be costly. You have a variety of options to consider.

You could sell your house and either rent a house or apartment. You could also downsize to a smaller home or even move into a retirement community with people in your age group. The burden of apartment and ground upkeep could then fall to your landlord or home owner's organization. You could even move in with loved ones, a consideration for those who require extra care.

 **ROUND TABLE**

George was having trouble making ends meet and applied for a reverse mortgage. He was 65 years old and owned his home but it was in a state of disrepair. He needed the money to make home improvements as well as to pay off his credit card debts. He was otherwise limited by his fixed income, going deeper and deeper into debt. To his benefit, the money he received from the mortgage lender was not taxed, and he did not have to pay back the funds as long as he lived in his home.

Reverse mortgages remain an option for some individuals as a means to generate needed funds. The idea is that instead of you paying a mortgage company, the mortgage company pays you. The money you receive is a tax-free loan that you do not have to pay back as long as you live in the home. The borrowed dollars will have to be paid back after you die, if you permanently move out of the residence, or if you sell the home, even if you still live there. Reverse mortgages will impact any inheritance you leave behind for your loved ones as the loan will need to be repaid from your estate.

In order to qualify for a reverse mortgage, you need to be at least 62 years old and own your home or have a low outstanding balance on your mortgage. You are still responsible to pay mortgage insurance and to maintain upkeep of your home. The mortgage lender wants the value of your home to remain as high as possible to make it a worthy investment for them.

There are three different types of reverse mortgages available—single-purpose reverse mortgages, federally insured reverse mortgages, and proprietary reverse mortgages. Which one you choose will require you to look closely at the associated costs and requirements for that particular mortgage.

Financial Hardships

Available programs that address financial hardships are discussed in Chapter 19. Programs range from accessing affordable health care to providing discounts on your utility payments. Also, take advantage of local services that provide free transportation. Your town hall may be able to provide a list of carriers.

Online Programs

There are multiple online tools available to help you manage your finances—calculators, organizers, and more. To make the most of these you need to have information readily available. Do your best to keep track of all your expenditures. Save receipts and keep them filed into the budget categories discussed above. Armed with information, you can keep tabs on your income, watch your spending, and cut costs when possible.

A list of online tools can be found in Appendix B.

The Least You Need to Know

- You need to look at your current spending patterns and determine the costs that are necessary versus those that are discretionary.
- You can maximize your Social Security benefits by working past your designated retirement age.
- 401k and IRA plans can help you save for retirement but may penalize you if you try to access funds before you turn 59.5 years old.
- Reverse mortgages may be an option to bring in extra tax-free income if you meet eligibility criteria.
- Financial planning is hard work; take the time or find the professional help to budget for your future.

The Future of Medicare

There is no denying that the older we get, the more health problems we have. With millions of baby boomers approaching eligibility age, the Medicare Trust Fund is struggling to stay afloat. With more money spent than put into the system, the health-care deficit is already a problem.

The Medicare Trust Fund

The Medicare Trust Fund helps to pay for Part A and is based primarily on tax dollars. Medicare payroll taxes are deducted from your paycheck with the promise that you will have access to a health-care program in the future. Those tax dollars add up over time, but how far can they go? At this time, the Medicare Trust Fund is only expected to last until 2030.

The problem is two-fold. First, health-care costs continue to rise. Money put into the system years ago may not be sufficient to meet the costs of today's health market. Inflation also contributes to increasing health-care expenditures.

Second, the amount of dollars entering the system will drop off as baby boomers come of age. As more people approach 65 years of age and eventual retirement, there will be less

In This Chapter

* Medicare eligibility age and the Medicare Trust Fund
* Increasing Medicare revenue through taxes and premiums
* Defensive medicine and tort reform
* Medicare cuts to hospitals and physicians

income to tax. When you retire, you are no longer actively employed, and you will no longer pay into the Medicare Trust Fund through FICA taxes. This means more people will use Medicare while less people are paying into it through taxes.

DID YOU KNOW?
Medicare accounted for 14 percent of the federal budget in 2013.

Depending on an individual's income, Medicare premiums may cost less than paying taxes. While this may be better for the beneficiary, it increases the burden on the Medicare Trust Fund.

Increasing Medicare Eligibility Age

One way to extend the Medicare Trust Fund is to find ways to have people pay FICA taxes for a longer period of time while delaying their access to Medicare. Social Security has already extended the retirement age from 65 to 67 years old. Controversy has risen on whether or not to increase the Medicare eligibility age to match it.

With millions approaching 65 years of age, such a change could delay expenditures from the Medicare Trust Fund. A government study estimates that increasing eligibility age by two years would save $19 billion between 2016 and 2023. Extending the Medicare Trust Fund could allow more beneficiaries access to care in the long term.

DID YOU KNOW?
More than 87.9 percent of Americans 65 years and older have at least one chronic condition. Nearly 50 percent of them have two or more chronic conditions, and 15 percent have five or more chronic conditions.

That being said, delaying health-care access to those who are getting older could be fraught with ethical dilemmas. Many people may not be physically or mentally able to extend their retirement age due to chronic medical conditions. With increasing chronic conditions come increased health-care expenditures for medications and office visits. The risk for hospitalization likewise increases.

Delaying the Medicare eligibility age may require that the ACA Health Insurance Marketplace be opened to this age group. Currently, access to these plans is limited to those 64 years of age and younger. These supposedly more affordable plans may provide a stop-gap measure for seniors who hypothetically would need to wait until age 67 for Medicare eligibility. The high deductibles of many of these plans, however, may put a strain on many elderly Americans' finances, especially with their increased medical needs.

It's also important to note that while Social Security recommends a retirement age of 67 years of age, it still offers payments to those who retire as early as 62 years old. These payments are lower than if someone works until the preferred retirement age. Changing the Medicare eligibility age would likely be an all-or-none formula. There has been no recommendation to offer partial benefits to those younger than eligibility age, even if they are retired or receive Social Security benefits. The long-term consequences of changing Medicare eligibility are more complicated than what Social Security achieved by raising its retirement age.

Is it fair to delay health-care access to American seniors with low incomes or facing unemployment? Many believe that the amount of dollars saved by the federal government by enacting such a change would be offset by the added amount of dollars needed to subsidize the Medicaid program. The debate wages on.

ROUND TABLE

Eileen is a widowed 65-year-old homemaker. Her husband had not been a federal employee or a veteran so she does not have access to those benefits. If the eligibility age were increased to 67 years of age, she would have to wait two more years to access Medicare. Her options in the meantime would be limited to Medicaid, if her income met criteria, or a plan through the ACA Health Insurance Marketplace if this were offered to her age group.

Increasing Medicare Taxes

Another way to extend the life of the Medicare Trust Fund would be to increase the percentage of FICA taxes paid. Bringing in more dollars would increase how much money is available for spending.

At the current time, Medicare payroll taxes cost 2.9 percent of your total income. If you are hired by an employer, you will pay half of those taxes, 1.45 percent, and your employer will pay the other half. If you are self-employed, you will pay the full 2.9 percent of your income and may be able to deduct half of those taxes on your annual tax return.

In 2013, the Additional Medicare Tax was added to individuals earning $200,000 or more per year or married couples earning more than $250,000 per year. An additional 0.9 percent tax is added after the threshold dollar amount is reached. For example, if a married couple earns $300,000, they would be taxed 2.9 percent on the first $250,000 and 3.8 percent (2.9 percent + 0.9 percent) on the remaining $50,000. The employer does not contribute a share toward the Additional Medicare Tax, though they continue to pay their 1.45 percent share toward the traditional 2.9 percent FICA costs. See Chapter 4 for more details on how this tax works.

DID YOU KNOW?

Medicare Part A is funded 88 percent by payroll taxes and 1 percent by premiums. Additional funds earned via interest and other revenue comprise the remainder.

The Additional Medicare Tax was thought to be a means to increase funds without burdening low-income individuals. Some high earners may be clever and place their extra earnings into tax-free accounts to avoid the additional tax and hence the additional contribution to the Medicare Trust Fund. For this reason, there remains discussion on whether FICA taxes should be raised for everyone.

Increasing the Medicare payroll tax by 1 percent would add an additional 0.5 percent cost to employees and employers respectively. Over ten years, it is estimated this would increase contributions to the Medicare Trust Fund by $651 billion. When you learn that Medicare spent $583 billion in total benefits in 2013, it is easy to see how this change could make a significant impact on the system.

This does not mean that everyone could afford such a change. Would low-income individuals be able to make ends meet with fewer dollars in their paychecks? Would employers hire fewer employees because of the additional tax burden? How much taxation is too much? The answers are unclear and continue to be controversial.

Increasing Medicare Costs to Beneficiaries

One way for Medicare to reduce costs would be to have someone other than the federal government shell out the dollars. Medicare beneficiaries pay monthly premiums and deductibles for their health-care coverage. Adjustments to how much beneficiaries pay out of pocket would reduce government costs. Equally effective in cutting costs would be to decrease access to certain services.

Increasing Premiums

The Medicare Trust Fund helps to pay for Part A insurance. The majority of Americans do not pay for Part A coverage because they have paid their expected share of payroll taxes, so increasing Part A premiums may not have a significant impact on the system at large.

DID YOU KNOW?

Medicare as a whole is paid for by payroll taxes (38 percent), premiums (13 percent), and other revenues (41 percent).

Part B premiums, however, are another matter entirely. Premiums pay for 25 percent of Part B expenses. Raising the cost of these premiums may be a way for Medicare to decrease costs. The question remains as to who should be subjected to higher premiums.

As it stands, Medicare increases monthly premiums for beneficiaries who enroll in Part B if they earn above a certain income. Those earning less than $85,000 per year as an individual or less than $170,000 as a married couple make up 95 percent of all Medicare beneficiaries. They pay the lowest premiums. There are four income brackets above this threshold with increasing premiums charged as you move up the brackets.

The initial 2015 Medicare budget proposal aimed to increase premiums for the upper income brackets. This would have increased payments for 5 percent of all Medicare beneficiaries (2.9 million beneficiaries). Ultimately, the decision was made to keep premiums the same as in 2014. This issue is likely to be raised again with future budget proposals.

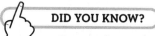 **DID YOU KNOW?**

In 2010, the average income for men over age 65 was $25,704, whereas it was $15,072 for women.

However, proposals also exist to shift these Part B income brackets altogether so that higher premiums may also cover those with incomes less than $85,000 or $170,000 for individual or married couples, respectively. This is again where moral concerns come into question.

Fifty percent of Medicare beneficiaries earned incomes less than $23,500 in 2014. Can Medicare beneficiaries with lower incomes afford increases in their monthly premiums? This could be a considerable percentage of your income. What about your other essential needs? Any changes in premiums or income brackets would need to take into consideration expected costs of living to protect American seniors.

Prescription drug coverage follows a similar approach to Part B premiums, using similar income brackets. The added costs are referred to as Part D income-related monthly adjustment amount (IRMAA). In 2013, 4 percent of beneficiaries (1.5 million) who were enrolled in Part D had to pay toward IRMAA. The 2015 budget proposal also aimed to increase Part D costs via IRMAA.

Increasing Deductibles, Coinsurance, and Copays

Increasing out-of-pocket expenses for beneficiaries would decrease the dependence on federal dollars. One way to do this would be to increase the cost of deductibles, coinsurance, and copays.

If a beneficiary does not have a hospitalization in a given year, he will not pay a Part A deductible. However, if he has multiple stays in a year that span multiple benefit periods, deductibles may cost thousands of dollars. Part B deductibles, on the other hand, are paid by all beneficiaries. There are no limits on out-of-pocket expenses at this time for either Parts A or B.

Increasing Part A deductibles would increase the burden on those needing emergent hospital care, hospice care, or skilled nursing services. That has to raise eyebrows. Those needing hospital services or end-of-life care would be charged more in out-of-pocket costs. That said, those who did not use Part A would not be unfairly subjected to added costs for health-care services they did not utilize. Increasing deductibles for those enrolled in Part B would affect everyone equally.

One proposal is to combine Parts A and B to streamline costs and to make one larger-sized deductible for everyone to pay. Again, those not using Part A services in a given year would be paying more than they would have otherwise been expected to.

Coinsurance and copayment costs, similar to deductibles, could also be raised, increasing how much you would pay for any given service. The question becomes how much can the federal government expect someone on a limited income to pay out of pocket?

The challenge with increasing out-of-pocket costs is that those who have limited finances may be more apt to refrain from getting the care they need. When they finally do access care, their condition may be more complicated than it would have otherwise been.

Advanced-stage diseases cost more to treat, tend to require more medications, and may lead to more costly hospitalizations than those that could have been modified by earlier care. Preventive medicine and routine health care can help to identify medical conditions early and treat them in a manner to slow their progression. This reduces costs to the system but most importantly, it can improve the quality of life of the beneficiaries.

Decreasing Access

Medicare would cost less for the government if it did not cover as many services. As it stands, Medicare does not cover many services that are considered appropriate for an aging population, such as dental, hearing, and vision screenings. Medicare is also heavily criticized for not covering long-term nursing care. See Chapter 3 for a detailed list of services Medicare does not provide.

Decreasing Medicare benefits seems to be contrary to the goals of the health-care program. The ACA actually increased access to preventive screening services for seniors.

In 2014, the Center for Healthcare Decisions (CHCD) led focus groups and panel discussions with nonprofit leaders in California to discuss ways to reduce Medicare spending, taking their own health-care needs out of the equation. The consensus was not to reduce overall benefits.

There was a recommendation, however, to curtail use of expensive treatments that had a low opportunity for benefit in those who were critically ill or at the end of their life. Medications that may extend life for only two months but cost as much as $100,000 may not be reasonable for

Medicare to cover, at least not when you consider that Medicare is meant to service the country at large and not just an individual.

More controversial, however, may be the recommendation to eliminate intensive care unit services for those who are dying. Without expected extension of life, these services can be costly. This may be a little hard to stomach as an idea for most people. Denying coverage to someone in such a vulnerable situation seems quite insensitive, adding a financial burden to families and estates.

Again, these are only some recommendations from this CHCD initiative and not formal legislative measures.

Changing the Practice of Medicine

Changing how medicine is practiced could greatly impact how much Medicare costs. There are a lot of things we do in modern medicine that have improved the health of beneficiaries. There are also many things we are accustomed to doing that may or may not actually provide benefits. Our expectations may not always align with what works best. If we took a different approach to health care, we could save money and increase quality of care.

Defensive Medicine

Medicine currently works on a fee-for service system, in which a health-care provider charges for each service, procedure, or test performed. One could imagine that there could be financial incentives to order more tests. Ordering more tests leads to more payments to those health-care providers. To be honest, some of the extra testing is demanded by patients based on their personal preferences or research.

Extra testing does not mean that your provider is trying to make a buck off of you. Sometimes it means that your provider orders more tests because he feels it is sincerely needed to evaluate your condition or it could be a consequence of *defensive medicine*.

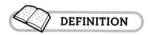 **DEFINITION**

Defensive medicine is the practice of medicine whereby excess tests are ordered to help prevent litigation.

Law suits for medical malpractice can be devastating for beneficiaries and health-care providers alike. Beneficiaries suffer from what they consider to be injuries from malpractice and must wade through a long judicial process before they can be compensated for any damages. Providers may suffer from harm to their reputations and may lose patients in their practices during court proceedings, costing them in professional earnings as well as legal fees.

Like any lawsuit, sometimes the claims have merit and sometimes they do not. We cannot always assume from the media that a case will swing one way or the other. This is why we rely on our judicial system. Here are the statistics:

- 26 percent of medical malpractice cases are dismissed

- 45 percent of cases go to deposition

- 21 percent of cases go to trial

- 80 percent of cases that go to trial are won by the provider

- 5 percent of cases are settled out of court

Ordering additional tests, even if they are expected to be of low yield in diagnosing or treating a condition, may give providers more ammunition in the event they are sued down the road. It stands as evidence that everything that could have been done to evaluate a patient had been taken into account.

The problem is that these extra tests are costing the health-care system in a big way. Most of them are unnecessary. If health-care providers ordered only those tests that they truly believed were medically necessary (note I did not say what Medicare deemed medically necessary), medical expenditures could be considerably reduced.

That may be easier said than done when a career is on the line. Malpractice suits can cost hundreds of thousands to millions of dollars against the defendant when noneconomic damages are considered. After all, how can you really quantify the emotional loss of a loved one? Tort reform laws aim to limit how much can be awarded in noneconomic or "emotional" damages.

Medical malpractice insurance premiums remain high for health-care providers, and the lack of successful tort reform may contribute to this. A surgeon may pay up to $15,000 per year on malpractice coverage; an obstetrician may pay as much as $20,000 per year. These costs may indirectly trickle down to the patient when providers charge a certain amount for their services to recuperate overhead costs in their offices.

Shifting from Fee-for-Service to Quality

There has been a shift in thinking to promote reimbursements based on health-care quality rather than on the specific services rendered. This is a change from the fee-for-service model. We want our providers to deliver quality care at all times, and we want that care to be cost-effective and appropriate. This sounds like the ideal situation, but it may be difficult to implement in practice.

One way to do this has been to pay providers based on whether or not their patients achieve certain health-care measures. For example, quality care could be measured by having sugar levels within a certain goal range for a patient with diabetes. Similar expectations could be set for blood pressures in a patient who has hypertension. Achievement of these goal ranges are a reflection of the care quality offered by that provider. By reducing complications that could arise from these medical conditions, the provider is optimizing care for the patient as an individual as well as decreasing costs to the system at large.

This may not always be a fair approach for health-care providers. It may happen that a patient does not follow the recommendations of the provider. For example, the patient may not take his medications as prescribed or does not follow dietary recommendations. It could be that the office services a low-income community with more financial limitations that cannot easily be rectified by free samples or vouchers. A provider may be offering quality care, but the quantitative outcome measures may not reflect that. He could be reimbursed less for working as hard and as appropriately as a provider who works in another area of the country.

Changing Medicare Reimbursements

Medicare may save money by shifting some of the costs onto beneficiaries, but it can, and does, shift costs to health-care providers and hospital networks just the same. How Medicare changes reimbursements may have long-term impact on who will care for you when you most need it.

Decreasing Payments to Hospitals

Hospitals will see lower reimbursements from Medicare if they do not provide quality care. This is good news for you as a beneficiary. You want to rely on a facility that has demonstrated its reputation for quality care.

One way to measure this is by looking to see how often a hospital has readmissions for different medical conditions. If a patient comes back to the hospital within 30 days for the same medical condition, it implies that the patient did not receive adequate care and follow-up instructions. The Hospital Readmissions Reduction Program reduces payment to hospitals that have readmissions for heart attack, heart failure, or pneumonia. This incentivizes hospitals to improve their care quality.

 DID YOU KNOW?

In 2014, Medicare reduced payments to 2,610 hospitals for having too many readmissions. These fines will save $428 million for Medicare from October 1, 2014 to October 30, 2015.

Unfortunately for hospitals, cuts will also occur regardless of the quality of care they provide. Sequester cuts were put in place with the Budget Control Act of 2011. This resulted in a 2 percent cut to hospital payments through 2021. These cuts have since been extended to 2024.

Hospitals rely on Medicare payments since a large proportion of hospital admissions are for patients older than 65 years of age. With Medicare reimbursements down, some hospitals have turned to layoffs to make up for the lost revenue. Hopefully, this trend will end, and hospitals can find alternative approaches to stay afloat during this time of health-care reform.

Decreasing Payments to Doctors

The Balanced Budget Act of 1997 has not been a friend to health-care providers. The act developed the Sustainable Growth Rate (SGR) as a way to keep Medicare costs down by adjusting how much it pays for physician services each year. The SGR uses data from the prior year's health-care expenditures as well as changes to the gross domestic product (GDP) to calculate how much providers should be paid. The result is an updated physician fee schedule that is announced every year in March. However, due to delays in enforcing SGR, Medicare rates to providers remained unchanged between 2001 and 2014.

Because SGR would have decreased physician payments every year since 2001 if it were enforced, the American Medical Association has lobbied strongly against it. Congress has passed stop-gap measures each year to prevent the cost cuts so that if the cuts finally took place in 2014, physicians would have faced a 25 percent cut in payments.

Failure to implement SGR fee schedules has added to our national deficit. It is estimated that repealing the SGR as it stands would cost $138 billion. A long-term solution to our nation's health-care spending is needed, but cutting costs this drastically to providers could have significant unwanted consequences.

If SGR were to be enforced as it stands, it would cut Medicare payments to such a degree that it is feared that many providers would choose to no longer participate in Medicare. With baby boomers approaching eligibility age and a spike in Medicare beneficiaries expected, losing providers at this stage will decrease health-care access when our country needs it most.

We need to find a way to manage physician payments without making it difficult for medical offices to stay open and remain viable.

The Least You Need to Know

- Increasing Medicare eligibility age to 67 would extend the Medicare Trust Fund.
- Medicare could increase revenues by increasing payroll taxes, premiums, deductibles, coinsurance, and/or copayments.
- Defensive medicine results in higher Medicare costs.
- Accountable care organizations (ACO) receive bonuses from Medicare to keep costs down while improving coordination of care between different health-care providers.
- The Sustainable Growth Rate (SGR) was intended to prevent the national deficit from rising but instead has been an ineffectual and controversial approach to reducing physician payments.

ost of Medicare

Medicare outlined throughout this book, you are now ready to take charge of your Medicare experience. The goal should be not only to make the most of the services the government program offers, but also to save as much money as possible in the process. As you approach retirement, balancing your health-care costs with a fixed income is essential to making the most of your later years.

To Your Health

You didn't think you could get through a book about Medicare written by a family physician without a lecture on how to stay healthy, did you? If you want to minimize medical costs, the best thing you can do is lead a healthy lifestyle to decrease your risk for disease and illness in the first place.

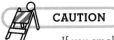

CAUTION

If you smoke, quit. Now. More than 480,000 people die each year from complications of tobacco use. Your life expectancy is decreased by 10 years if you smoke.

Rising Rates of Obesity

What you put into your body is one of the key aspects of healthy living. The American diet is not always the best. Fast food chains and processed foods are inexpensive and readily available. The convenience of those options and the busyness of the American way of life have literally led to an epidemic of large proportions—an obesity crisis.

DID YOU KNOW?

In 2012, more than 34.9 percent of American adults were obese. Due to complications from the condition, health-care costs are increased on average by $1,429 per year for obese Americans as compared to those who are at their goal weight.

In 2013, the American Medical Association officially labeled obesity as a disease. Complications from obesity are myriad and may include any of the following:

- Arthritis
- Cancer (see below)
- Cholesterol and lipid disorders
- Diabetes and prediabetes
- Erectile dysfunction
- Fatty liver disease
- Gallbladder disease
- Heart disease
- High blood pressure

- Infertility
- Irregular menstrual cycles
- Kidney disease
- Metabolic syndrome
- Poor wound healing
- Reflux disease
- Sleep apnea
- Stroke

The previous list is not all-inclusive. Cancers have also been associated with obesity. These include cancers of the cervix, ovaries, and uterus in women, as well as cancers in the breast, colon, esophagus, gallbladder, kidney, liver, pancreas, prostate, and rectum.

Eating Right

Why has America's weight been on the rise? Some people point their finger to lack of exercise, but diet ought to take more of the blame. It may surprise you to learn how much exercise it takes to burn off small amounts of food. A medium-size order of French fries may take 55 minutes on a stair climber machine, a large slice of pepperoni pizza 70 minutes of shoveling snow, a 3-ounce bag of potato chips 50 minutes of rock climbing, a cup of granola 90 minutes of boxing.

Clearly there has to be a balance between what we eat and how much activity we undertake. We need to choose healthier calories to reduce the risk for obesity and to keep our organs functioning properly.

Several studies have shown that low-fat diets have not decreased heart disease as we thought they would. In promoting low-fat options over the years, the food industry has instead added sugar to the vast majority of products to improve taste for competitive advantage. The added sugar in processed foods has in time corresponded to rising obesity rates.

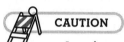

CAUTION

A single 12-ounce can of soda has 35 grams of sugar, which just about meets the American Heart Association's daily recommended allowance for added sugar for men and exceeds that for women.

Try to minimize eating foods, including beverages, with too much added sugar. This means looking at nutrition labels. The American Heart Association recommends no more than 6 teaspoons (24 grams) of added sugar per day for women and 9 teaspoons (36 grams) for men. Sugar that is naturally present in food does not factor into these numbers. For example, the natural sugar in an apple does not count toward your daily limit.

Whenever possible, you should try to purchase fresh produce so you know exactly what is being put into your body. Cooking your own food is the best way to control what you eat. While it takes time to prepare food for cooking instead of popping processed food into the microwave, it can be much healthier for you.

DID YOU KNOW?

Worldwide sodium use averages 4 grams per day. The World Health Organization recommends only 2 grams per day. The American Heart Association is stricter and advises for no more than 1.5 grams per day.

Be careful with your salt intake since extra sodium can increase your risk for heart disease and stroke. Again, reading your nutrition labels can be a guide.

You also want to be sure you get adequate fruits and vegetables to provide the needed vitamins and minerals your body needs. Protein is required to keep your muscles strong, so find ways to include sufficient protein in your diet whether you are a meat eater, vegetarian, or vegan.

Get Moving

Physical activity is important, not only to achieve fitness but also for your mental well-being. Exercise burns off calories, but as described previously, it is insufficient as a means of weight control if your diet choices are not healthy in the first place. Still, the benefits of exercise cannot be beat.

Benefits of Regular Exercise

Exercise Improves	Exercise Reduces
Balance and coordination	Breast cancer risk
Bone strength	Depression
Diabetes control	Heart disease risk
Endurance and stamina	High blood pressure
Female arousal	Erectile dysfunction
Focus and concentration	Fatigue
HDL ("good") cholesterol	Stress
Muscle tone	Stroke risk
Self-esteem	
Sleep quality and duration	

Studies have shown that exercise can decrease depressive symptoms. Walking 35 minutes a day five days a week or 60 minutes three days a week showed significant improvements in a 2005 study. Any degree of activity will be beneficial for your overall health.

Keeping your muscles toned will allow you to maintain better posture and increases your mobility as you age. The old adage "if you don't use it, you lose it" holds true. Several studies have shown increasing activity, even just by walking, can also help to decrease arthritis pain.

The CDC recommends regular activity for all ages, including both aerobic activity and muscle-strengthening activity. For those older than age 65, 150 minutes of moderate-intensity (walking) or 75 minutes of vigorous (jogging, running) aerobic exercise every week is recommended in addition to two or more days of muscle-strengthening activities. The latter may include gardening, push-ups, sit-ups, weight lifting, yoga, or any activity that requires you to apply your muscles against resistance. Exercise in intervals of at least 10 minutes is sufficient to give you the health benefits you deserve.

Get Your Shut Eye

Sleep is important because it allows your body to regenerate after your many hours of wakefulness. During sleep, growth hormones are released that help repair your tissues and muscles. Neurologically, your brains are actively firing, rejuvenating, and laying down memories from the day.

It is recommended that adults average seven to nine hours of sleep daily. People who slept more or less than this amount were found in an American Cancer Society study to have earlier deaths than those who slept the recommended amount. Still, everybody will have different needs. You should aim to get at least six hours of sleep nightly but aim for seven to nine whenever possible.

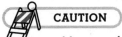

CAUTION

Many people falsely believe that alcohol will help get them to sleep. While alcohol may act as a sedative to help some people fall asleep initially, it also results in rebound awakening several hours later. This leads to fragmented sleep and poor overall sleep quality.

Try to get into a regular sleep schedule, even on weekends. Make sure your sleeping area is dark, quiet, and cool to best promote quality sleep. Your mattress should be comfortable, a worthy investment for your health. Regular daily exercise can also improve sleep quality. Avoidance of caffeine, alcohol, and food within a few hours of bedtime can also help you to more easily fall asleep.

Do Not Fall Victim to Limitations

Too often I hear arguments that people cannot find the time to exercise. Their schedules are simply too busy to fit it into their day. In response I must ask you to reconsider your priorities.

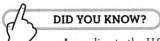

DID YOU KNOW?

According to the U.S. Bureau of Labor Statistics, the average American watched 2.8 hours of television per day in 2013.

Make no mistake. Your health is your most important asset. Without your health, you cannot complete all those things you are so busy doing. You will not be able to care for your loved ones. You may even be harming your longevity by not remaining active. Even a 15-minute walk each day can reap benefits. If you watch television on a regular basis, will missing one program really make that much difference to your quality of life?

Some people have physical limitations that truly limit their ability to exercise in certain ways. That should not stop you from getting out there and exploring what activities you can do.

Visit Your Health-Care Provider

Too much of modern medicine focuses on treating disease rather than preventing it. A pill cannot be the answer for everything. This is where your primary care provider can make a big difference in your life. Preventive medicine is key to not only decreasing your risk for disease in the first place but also catching conditions early so they have a smaller impact on your life.

Establishing care with a primary care provider for routine evaluations is more important than you realize. Face-to-face counseling with your provider may help tailor lifestyle advice to your specific needs. A simple exam could uncover something suspicious. Make the most of Medicare's preventive screening tests to catch diseases early. Not all medical conditions have symptoms at first. Catch them before they do.

Medicare and Your Health

Now that you are making healthy lifestyle choices, you can tie that in with your medical needs. Let's go back to our Round Table to visit with our friends Loraine, Eileen, Thomas, and George. Together we can get the most out of Medicare.

Round Table Summary

Name	Age	Marital Status	SSDI	Veteran
Loraine	65 years old	Married	No	No
Eileen	68 years old	Widowed	No	No
Thomas	48 years old	Divorced	Yes (End-Stage Renal Disease [ESRD])	No
George	65 years old	Single	Yes	Yes

Enrolling in Medicare

Loraine, Eileen, and George all qualify for Medicare based on age. Loraine became eligible for Medicare three months before the month she turned 65 and her Initial Enrollment Period extended over the three months after her birthday. If she applies during this window of time, she avoids paying any late penalties for Parts A and B. If Loraine applies within the first three months of her IEP, her coverage will begin on the first day of her birth month. If she applies in the latter months of her IEP, her coverage may begin anywhere from one month to three months after her birth month depending on when she applies.

George's situation is more complicated in that he also has a disability and has been on Social Security Disability Insurance (SSDI). If he had been on SSDI for longer than 24 months, he may have been eligible for Medicare before turning 65 years old. He would have been automatically enrolled in Medicare with benefits beginning on the twenty-fifth month of his SSDI. Unless he specifically opts out of Medicare, he will not be subjected to late penalties.

Eileen does not have it so easy. Now that she is 68 years old, she missed her Initial Enrollment Period by three years. She must wait to apply for Medicare until the General Enrollment Period that occurs annually from January 1 through March 31. Her Medicare benefits would not kick in until July 1. She will be faced with Medicare late penalties.

Thomas will be eligible for Medicare based on his newly diagnosed ESRD. Rather than waiting 25 months for Medicare benefits to kick in based on his disability, he is immediately eligible based on his qualifying medical condition if 1) he is eligible for SSDI, and 2) he or his spouse has contributed sufficient quarters in Medicare payroll taxes. Medicare enrollment for those who have ESRD is not automatic, and he needs to actively apply for coverage. His benefits will kick in the first day of the first month of his dialysis training program. If he had already been on dialysis, his benefits would begin on the first day of the fourth month he received dialysis. Medicare coverage based on ESRD can be retroactive up to one year.

Part A Late Penalties

Eileen is the only round table member who applied for Medicare after eligibility age. She may be subjected to late penalties.

Eileen is a homemaker. She has not personally contributed to Medicare payroll taxes, and Part A penalties could cost her considerably, 10 percent of her premium over twice the number of years she had not enrolled. Because she contributed less than 30 quarters in taxes, her base monthly Part A premium would cost $426 per month. The late penalty would increase this monthly amount to $468, and she would be required to pay this higher premium for 6 years.

She, however, has been recently widowed, and her spouse had contributed more than 40 quarters in payroll taxes. She may be eligible to use her spouse's record to allow for free Part A premiums and therefore would not be subjected to late penalties. Because she was married to him for more than nine months, she qualifies for premium-free Part A. If her marriage had been shorter in duration, she would not have qualified and would have been required to pay monthly premiums for the duration of her use of Medicare, as well Part A late penalties over the next 6 years.

Thomas would face a similar situation had he not contributed 40 quarters of FICA taxes. As noted in Chapter 2, he was employed for 12 years as a truck driver. Let us look at what would have happened had he not contributed sufficient taxes. He is divorced. He could only potentially qualify on his spouse's employment record if they had been married for 10 years or more. Also, exclusions may exist if he remarried. If his former spouse is alive, he can no longer rely on her record. If his former spouse passed away, he may use the employment record of either spouse to claim premium-free Part A benefits.

Part B Late Penalties

Everyone, regardless of their employment record, must pay for Part B. The cost of monthly premiums will be based on how much someone had earned on their income taxes two years prior to applying for Medicare. At the present time, there are five income brackets for Part B coverage.

Two years ago, Eileen and her husband filed a joint income tax return with income less than $170,000, putting them in the lowest Medicare income bracket for Part B. This means the 2014 premium of $104.90 would be increased by $31.47 (30 percent) for a total amount of $136.37 for the three years she did not enroll but was eligible for Medicare. The late penalty would continue as long as she had Medicare. This increases her annual Part B costs by an extra $377.64 every year.

It is important to note that if George, who is on Medicare based on disability, had declined Part B coverage at the time of his initial enrollment, he could have been subjected to late penalties if he later changed his mind. The same goes for Thomas if he chooses to defer Part B and wants to sign up before he is 65 years old. Thankfully, any late penalties for Part B coverage incurred before age 65 will be waived once you become eligible for Medicare based on age.

Part D Drug Coverage

Similar to Part B, Part D expenses are based on your past income. Your income tax return from two years prior is used for this purpose. The extra amount you pay above your premium is known as the Part D income-related monthly adjustment amount (IRMAA). The income brackets are the same five categories as those used for Part B. Those who earn less than $85,000 as an individual or less than $170,000 jointly do not have to pay a Part D IRMAA. Part D IRMAA costs were set at $0, $12.10, $31.10, $50.20, and $69.30 per month, respectively, for 2014. Eileen earns less than $170,000 on her joint filing and will not have to pay any IRMAA.

However, Eileen will face a Part D penalty for delayed enrollment but only if the drug coverage from her health-care plan was not creditable, meaning it was not as extensive as the standard Part D benefit plan. The late penalty could also come into play even if she did have creditable coverage but waited more than 63 days before she signed up for a Part D plan after losing that creditable coverage.

The Part D late penalty is equal to 1 percent of the national base beneficiary premium (NBBP) for every month of missed eligibility. The NBBP changes every year. In 2014, the NBBP was $32.42. She will pay an extra $11.70, which is equal to 36 percent of $32.42 rounded to the nearest 10 cents. Similar to Part B, the Part D late penalty extends as long as she has Medicare unless the penalty began prior to age 65, at which time it may be waived.

George had access to VA benefits due to his disability. VA drug coverage is creditable and generally less expensive than many Part D plans. He deferred, but if he chose to join one in the future, he will not have to pay late fees if he signs up within 63 days of that creditable coverage.

Employer-Sponsored Health Insurance

You may be wondering why Eileen has to pay late penalties at all. If her husband who recently passed away had been working in Medicare taxed employment, he may have had employer-sponsored health insurance. Indeed he did, and this was why she delayed signing up for Medicare. She already had health-care coverage that met her needs under his plan. Unfortunately, because the company he worked for employed less than 20 full-time employees, he was not eligible for a Special Enrollment Period, and therefore, neither was she. Medicare will only defer late penalties for those who have health-care plans through employers with more than 20 full-time equivalent employees.

DID YOU KNOW?

Special Enrollment Periods extend for eight months after you leave a qualifying employer-sponsored health plan. To be eligible for Medicare without late penalties, the employer must have at least 20 full-time equivalent employees working for at least 20 weeks the preceding year.

This leaves Eileen to wait for her Medicare coverage to kick in the July after she applies for Medicare during the General Enrollment Period. She may be without health-care benefits in the interim. She may need to elect for COBRA coverage through her husband's former employer, if the company offers it. The company is not mandated to provide COBRA based on its small size. She is older than the age limit set on ACA Health Insurance Marketplace plans.

Thomas, who is going to enroll in Medicare based on his ESRD disability, is younger in age than the rest of the Round Table. He has multiple school-aged children to care for and must base his insurance decisions with this in mind. Medicare will not provide benefits for his dependents.

His options are to continue working, but Department of Transportation regulations will not allow him to continue truck driving as a job based on his need for ongoing dialysis. He would need to find other employment with access to an employer-sponsored plan that he could extend to his children. Alternatively, his dependents may be able to gain coverage by going on an ACA Health Insurance Marketplace plan.

How to Pick a Plan

Picking a plan can be a challenge. It is hard to predict your health-care needs from one year to the next. You must make an educated decision based on your medical history and discussions with your primary care provider, including your prognosis in the coming year.

TIP

Visit medicare.gov/find-a-plan to review information about available Medicare Advantage and Part D plans in your area.

Loraine elected for a Medicare Advantage Plan because she had few health problems but anticipated the need for costly hearing aids that would not be covered under Original Medicare. Eileen elected for Original Medicare because she did not anticipate the need for additional services.

Thomas elected for Original Medicare and opted to purchase a Medigap policy to help him pay for his Medicare deductibles and copays. He knew that he could not have a Medicare Advantage Plan at the same time as a Medigap plan.

George had VA coverage and knew he would receive excellent care at his local VA health-care facility. However, if he required care outside of the VA for any reason, he may need to rely on Medicare for coverage. Because of this, he elected for Original Medicare. He did not need extra coverage through a Medicare Advantage Plan because he had additional benefits through the VA.

Changing Plans

You cannot change your Medicare plans whenever you want. Loraine, who had initially selected a Medicare Advantage Plan, wished to change to Original Medicare to reduce her monthly costs after she had purchased her costly hearing aids. Eileen, who had signed up for Original Medicare, developed a lung condition based on her past history for smoking, and she now required increased care. She now felt she would benefit more from a Medicare Advantage Plan.

Loraine and Eileen can change their plans during the annual Open Enrollment period that happens October 15 to December 7 every year. Benefits begin for the new plan selection on January 1. Alternatively, Eileen could sign up for a Medicare Advantage Plan at any time if it is rated as a five-star plan and had been rated this way since the preceding November.

Going to the Hospital

Thomas developed chest pain and went to the hospital for evaluation. The emergency room physician ordered an EKG and blood work to assess for a possible heart attack. He was also placed on a monitor that watched his heart continuously. Thankfully, his chest pain stopped and his laboratory studies did not show any obvious findings. He was placed under observation. Medicare Part B, not Part A, would cover for the services on this first day.

On the second day of his stay, the cardiologist performed a stress test to check the heart further, and the study showed an abnormality. It was suspected that Thomas did in fact have a heart attack. He then underwent cardiac catheterization and had a coronary stent put in to prevent further injury to the heart. His status was changed to inpatient since his health-care provider now expected his total hospital stay to exceed two midnights. The provider clearly documented this on Thomas' medical record. Because orders cannot be changed for preceding days, his first day remains covered by Part B as an observation stay and the second day is covered by Part A as a hospital inpatient because this is the day the order changed.

His total stay ended up being only three days long so he did not qualify for a stay at a skilled nursing facility. That would require three days as an inpatient, which he did not fulfill. He went home with home health-care services to help him rehabilitate over the next two weeks.

Going to the Office

Loraine, Eileen, and Thomas went to their respective health-care providers to have their Welcome to Medicare Exams within their first 12 months of Medicare Part B enrollment. The next year they had their Initial Wellness Visit and subsequently their Annual Wellness Visits.

Loraine and Eileen deferred Pap smear evaluation based on recommendations by ACS, ACOG, and USPSTF. Both women arranged for annual mammograms and pursued colonoscopy screenings. They both signed Advanced Beneficiary Notices of Noncoverage. A colon polyp was detected on Eileen's screening colonoscopy. What she anticipated to be a free screening test was now considered to be a diagnostic colonoscopy and would cost her 20 percent of the cost of the test.

Thomas pursued prostate cancer screenings with a digital rectal exam and a PSA blood test. He also had a low-dose CT scan of the chest performed as screening for lung cancer given his past history for smoking. Medicare declined to cover this latter study. Because he was not asked to sign an ABN before the CT scan to inform him of the possibility that Medicare may not cover the test, he was not responsible to pay for any charges incurred for the procedure.

George received the majority of his care at the VA, where he also had his preventive screening tests done. He did not participate in the Annual Wellness Visits since he already had those services provided at the VA.

Decision Time

There are many intricacies with the Medicare program that are sure to evolve over time. Understanding where the most common financial pitfalls occur and how to take advantage of the services offered will help to keep you ahead of the curve.

The Least You Need to Know

- Complications of obesity have significantly increased costs for individuals as well as to the health-care system at large.
- Added sugar has contributed to the obesity epidemic.
- High salt intake contributes to increased risk for heart disease and stroke.
- The CDC recommends 150 minutes of moderate-intensity aerobic exercise every week, or 75 minutes of vigorous aerobic exercise for those who can tolerate the increased level of activity.
- Studies recommend that the optimal sleep duration is between seven and nine hours nightly.
- Your Medicare choices will depend on your specific situation and health-care needs. To make the most of Medicare, be sure to understand the fundamentals of how the program works.

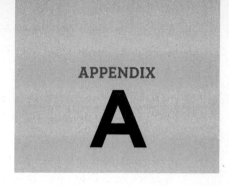

Glossary

30-month coordination period for end-stage renal disease   The period of time Medicare will act as a Secondary Payer after a beneficiary becomes eligible for Medicare based on end-stage renal disease. See *Medicare Secondary Payer.*

AAFP   American Academy of Family Physicians

AAMC   Association of American Medical Colleges

AANP   American Association of Nurse Practitioners

ABN   See *Advanced Beneficiary Notice.*

accepting provider   A health-care provider who signs an agreement with Medicare to accept their policies in order to receive payment.

ACOG   American College of Obstetricians and Gynecologists

ACS   American Cancer Society

additional Medicare tax   A 0.9 percent Medicare tax paid by individuals earning more than $200,000 or married couples earning more than $250,000. The additional taxes only apply to dollar amounts earned above these income thresholds. Unlike other Medicare payroll taxes, the employer does not contribute to these taxes.

Advanced Beneficiary Notice   A form given to a Medicare beneficiary to notify that Medicare may not pay for a particular service. The ABN must be signed before a test or procedure is completed. If not signed in advance, the beneficiary is not liable to pay for those charges.

advanced directives   Written documentation stating an individual's medical wishes if he becomes unable to communicate to his health-care provider at the time of a medical emergency.

Affordable Care Act   A 2010 law that enacted health-care reform under the administration of President Barack Obama. It is often referred to as Obamacare.

AFL-CIO   American Federation of Labor and Congress of Industrial Organizations

ALS   See *amyotrophic lateral sclerosis.*

AMA   See *American Medical Association.*

American Medical Association (AMA)   A professional physician organization that was founded in 1847 to protect the interests of doctors, public health, and medical advancement.

amyotrophic lateral sclerosis (ALS)   A neuromuscular disease that is progressive and debilitating, resulting in death. Medicare allows for immediate eligibility to the program for anyone who has this condition regardless of age.

ANCC   American Nurses Credentialing Center

appeal   A financial complaint filed against Medicare or another insurer. Appeals may focus on failure to cover a service or disagreement about how much should be paid for a service.

attained age-related insurance policy   An insurance policy that charges based on one's age when one signs up. Premiums increase with age.

BBB   Better Business Bureau

BCRC   Benefits Coordination and Recovery Center

beneficiary   The person who is covered by an insurance policy, whether Medicare or a private insurance plan.

benefit period   A fixed period of time where an insurer, Medicare or otherwise, provides coverage based on their program guidelines.

BFCC-QIO   Beneficiary and family-centered care quality improvement organizations

BMI   See *body mass index.*

board-certified provider   A health-care provider who has met certification requirements, including passage of a board examination, in his specialty. Medicare only allows coverage for board certified providers.

board-eligible provider   A health-care provider who has not yet completed certification requirements for board eligibility but who has completed his medical training program.

body mass index (BMI)   An indicator of obesity based on weight and height. BMI is calculated by the following equation: (weight in kilograms)/(height in meters)^2.

bundled payments   Payments made by an insurer, Medicare or otherwise, to a health-care provider or health network based on total expected costs needed to treat a certain medical condition.

CAO   Competitive acquisition ombudsman

catastrophic drug coverage   Part D prescription drug coverage that begins after the donut hole has closed. Costs decrease considerably for beneficiaries who now pay low copayments and coinsurance for their medications See *donut hole.*

CDC   Centers for Disease Control and Prevention

CHAMPUS   Civilian Health and Medical Program of the Uniformed Services

CHCD   Center for Healthcare Decisions

CHIP   Children's Health Insurance Program

CHS   Contract health services for the Indian Health Service

claim   A bill to Medicare or other insurance provider requesting payment for services provided.

CLIA   Clinical Laboratory Improvement Amendments

CMS   Centers for Medicare and Medicaid Services

COBRA   See *Consolidated Omnibus Budget Reconciliation Act.*

collective bargaining   Negotiation between employers and unions to improve wages, benefits, and work conditions.

community-related insurance policy   An insurance policy that charges the same rate to all enrollees regardless of age.

concurrent case   Medical care that is ongoing and occurring at the present time.

conditional payments   Payments made by Medicare when it is uncertain whether another insurer will pay first. Once the second insurer makes its final determination, Medicare may need to be reimbursed accordingly. This may be the case for workers' compensation cases.

Consolidated Omnibus Budget Reconciliation Act (COBRA)   A 1986 law that mandated employers with more than 20 full-time equivalent employees to offer extended coverage of their employer-sponsored health insurance plans to their former employees for a designated period of time.

creditable prescription drug coverage   A prescription drug plan that is as extensive as a standard benefit Part D prescription drug plan.

custodial care   Care that is provided for every day needs, such as for hygiene and food preparation, that does not require skilled medical care.

DEA   See *Drug Enforcement Administration.*

deductible   A set fee agreed upon when signing up for insurance coverage that is paid out-of-pocket before insurance pays for services.

Defense of Marriage Act (DOMA)   A 1996 law that defined marriage as only being between a man and a woman, excluding same-sex marriages from benefits that could be received through federal and state programs. The law was ruled unconstitutional by the Supreme Court in 2013.

defensive medicine   A practice of medicine whereby excessive tests are ordered to help prevent litigation.

diagnosis-related groups   Clustering of medical services by diagnostic categories for the purposes of hospital billing.

diagnostic test   A test that is performed to evaluate for a disease state in the setting of ongoing symptoms.

DMGP   Direct medical graduate payments

DO   Doctor of osteopathy

DOL   Department of Labor

DOMA   See *Defense of Marriage Act.*

donut hole   A coverage gap in Part D prescription drug plans with increases in out-of-pocket expenses after Medicare and the beneficiary has spent a certain amount of dollars. The donut hole came into being in 2006 and is expected to be discontinued by 2020.

DRG   Diagnosis-related groups

Drug Enforcement Administration (DEA)   A federal agency that regulates and monitors controlled substances and narcotic medications.

dually eligible   Someone who is eligible for both Medicare and Medicaid.

dumpster diving   A method by which identity thieves scavenge personal information, including social security numbers and financial data, from discarded materials.

EHR   Electronic health record

employment duration   The period of time one has worked in Medicare taxed employment and contributed payroll taxes to the Medicare Trust Fund. The duration is measured in quarters, which are three-month intervals. Working 40 quarters or more entitles one to Part A hospital insurance without the need to pay monthly premiums.

employment networks for the Ticket to Work Program   Employment agencies approved by the Social Security Administration to provide vocational training and work opportunities for participants of the Ticket to Work Program. See *Ticket to Work Program.*

EN   Employment network for Social Security

end-stage renal disease (ESRD)   Advanced stage kidney disease that requires dialysis or a kidney transplant for treatment.

EPE   Extended period of eligibility for the Ticket to Work Program

EPSDT   Early, Periodic Screening, Diagnosis, and Treatment Medicaid benefits

ESRD   See *end-stage renal disease*.

Family Medical Leave Act (FMLA)   A 1993 law that mandated employers with more than 50 employees to provide unpaid leave for its workers up to 12 weeks per year as needed for medical reasons. This provides job security to the employee, including maintenance of health-care benefits. Employees must have worked at least one year and at least 1,250 hours over the past 12 months with the company to be eligible for FMLA.

FDA   Food and Drug Administration

fee-for-service   A payment model where an insurer, Medicare or otherwise, pays a health-care provider for each separate service performed.

FEHB   Federal employee health benefits

FICA tax   Taxes deducted from one's paycheck to fund both Social Security and Medicare. Both employers and employees contribute to FICA taxes.

five-star plan   Medicare Advantage and Part D prescription drug plans that have the highest ratings for customer service and value. Medicare beneficiaries who wish to change to a five-star plan qualify for a special enrollment period.

FMLA   See *Family Medical Leave Act*.

formulary   A preferred list of medications offered to beneficiaries by a Part D prescription drug plan or other insurer. Medications not included on a formulary may not be paid for by the insurer.

FWA   Fraud, Waste, and Abuse compliance training

GAO   See *Government Accountability Office*.

GAP   Guardianship assistance programs

GDP   Gross domestic product

General enrollment period (GEP)   An annual period of time when one can sign up for Original Medicare. This period is between January 1 and March 31 every year. Coverage does not begin until July 1.

GEP   See *General enrollment period*.

Government Accountability Office (GAO)   A federal organization that investigates and reports how the government is spending tax dollars. The GAO reports to Congress.

grand family   A family where one or more children are raised by their grandparent(s).

grandfathered plan   Health plans that existed before new legislation came into effect. A grandfathered plan does not have to follow the new regulations but also cannot make changes to their original plan policy. Examples of grandfathered plans are found in the Health Insurance Marketplace and with older Medigap plans.

grievance   A nonfinancial complaint filed against Medicare or another insurer.

Health Insurance Portability and Accountability Act (HIPAA)   A 1996 law that aimed to improve protection of health information and to improve efficiencies in administrative health-care management.

Heartbleed   A security bug found in an internet cryptographic software library called OpenSSL. This vulnerability allowed computer hackers to access users' passwords and track their key strokes on the internet.

HIPAA   See *Health Insurance Portability and Accountability Act.*

HMO   Health maintenance organization

HMO-POS   Health maintenance organization with point of service plan

home-bound   Used to describe someone who has difficulty leaving home without considerable effort or without supervision, transportation assistance, or use of special equipment such as a wheelchair.

HPV   Human papillomavirus

ICD-9   The ninth edition of the World Health Organization's International Statistical Classification of Disease used for medical coding in the United States through 2015. The coding system uses five digits to classify disease.

ICD-10   The tenth edition of the World Health Organization's International Statistical Classification of Disease used for medical coding in the United States through 2015. The coding system uses seven digits to classify disease.

IEP   See *initial enrollment period.*

IEQ   Initial Enrollment Questionnaire

IHS   See *Indian Health Service.*

IME   See *independent medical examination.*

independent medical examination (IME)   A physical examination performed by a workers' compensation approved health-care provider to determine whether or not an injury is related to the employee's job and determines how best to manage that injury.

Indian Health Service (IHS)   A program under the Department of Health and Human Services that provides health-care access and employment opportunities for American and Alaskan Indians.

initial enrollment period (IEP)   The window of time one has to apply for Medicare when he first becomes eligible for Medicare based on age or disability. If one does not enroll for Medicare during the IEP, he may be subjected to late penalties.

inpatient hospitalization   An overnight stay in a hospital with an inpatient admission order that meets Medicare's medical necessity requirements and is also expected to span more than two midnights. The majority of services are paid for under Part A though physician fees are paid for under Part B.

International Statistical Classification of Diseases and Related Health Problems   A system for medical coding used worldwide to standardize how diagnoses are categorized. ICD-9 was in place in the United States in 2014 with plans to advance to ICD-10 in 2015.

IRA   Individual retirement account

IRE   Independent review entity

IRS   Internal Revenue Service

issue age-related insurance policy   An insurance policy that charges based on how old one was when he first signed up for the policy. Premiums stay the same over the course of the policy.

IT   Information technology

ITRC   Identity Theft Resource Center

late penalties   Charges incurred to Medicare beneficiaries who enroll for Parts A and/or B after their initial enrollment period has ended and who did not qualify for a special enrollment period.

lifetime reserve days   The maximum number of days over one's lifetime, currently set at 60, that Medicare will cover after a beneficiary stays more than 90 consecutive days in the hospital. Lifetime days start to be used on day 91. Hospital stays less than 90 days long do not use up lifetime reserve days.

LIHEAP   Low Income Home Energy Assistance Program

limiting charge   The 15 percent increase a nonparticipating provider can charge above the Medicare fee schedule. Limiting charges do not apply to nonparticipating suppliers of medical equipment who can charge whatever they want.

LIPP   Low-Income Payment Program for American Water

LIS   Low-Income Subsidy for Part D assistance

Low-Income Subsidy   A Medicare savings program that provides financial assistance for those with low incomes who have difficulty paying for their Part D prescription drug plans.

MAC   See *Medicare administrative contractor.*

MAC   See *Medicare Appeals Council.*

MAPD   Medicare Advantage Prescription Drug plan

MD   Medical doctor

Medicaid   A federal- and state-run health-care program offered to anyone with qualifying low income. Medicaid provides coverage to beneficiaries regardless of age or existing health conditions.

medical necessity   Criteria that must be met for Medicare or another insurance provider to cover the cost of services used for medical evaluation and treatment.

Medicare   A federally funded health insurance program offered to aged and disabled Americans.

Medicare administrative contractor (MAC)   A private organization that signs a contractual agreement with Medicare to process claims for a certain jurisdiction.

Medicare Advantage Plan   Also known as a Medicare Part C plan, an alternative to Original Medicare offered through private insurance companies that includes standard coverage for Parts A and B services as well as additional coverage options.

Medicare Appeals Council (MAC)   The division of the Department of Health and Human Services that oversees Level 4 Medicare appeal cases.

Medicare employment/payroll taxes   See *FICA tax.*

Medicare Part A   Inpatient hospital insurance offered through Medicare. Part A does not include coverage for physician fees. Part A, when combined with Part B, is known as Original Medicare.

Medicare Part B   Outpatient medical insurance offered through Medicare. Physician fees, whether inpatient or outpatient, are covered under Part B. Part B, when combined with Part A, is known as Original Medicare.

Medicare Part C   See *Medicare Advantage Plan.*

Medicare Part D   An optional Medicare prescription drug plan that is offered through private insurance companies. The plan may be purchased separately or as part of certain Medicare Advantage Plans.

Medicare Secondary Payer (MSP)   The condition by which Medicare pays second on any claims when one has another source of health insurance in effect.

Medicare Supplemental Insurance   See *Medigap.*

Medicare Trust Fund   A designated fund used to finance Medicare Part A based on Medicare payroll taxes.

Medigap   A supplemental insurance plan purchased from a private company to help pay towards Medicare costs. Medigap is also known as Medicare Supplemental Insurance.

MMA   Medicare Modernization Act, also known as the Medicare Prescription Drug, Improvement, and Modernization Act

MOH   Medal of Honor

MQGE   Medicare Qualified Government Employment

MSP   See *Medicare Secondary Payer.*

NADP   National Association of Dental Plans

national base beneficiary premium   The minimum premium amount set annually for Part D prescription drug plans. Late penalties are calculated off the NBBP and will therefore change annually.

NATO   North Atlantic Treaty Organization

NBBP   National base beneficiary premium

NCLEX-RN   National Council Licensure Examination for Registered Nurses

nonparticipating provider   An accepting provider who agrees to accept only some of the fee schedule or none at all.

NP   Nurse practitioner

Office of the Inspector General (OIG)   A division of the Department of Health and Human Services that investigates fraud and abuse that may occur in different federal programs.

OIG   See *Office of the Inspector General.*

old age   According to the United Nations, anyone over 60 years of age. The United States uses 65 years of age to establish criteria for the medical need for federally funded health insurance.

OMM   Osteopathic manipulative medicine

Original Medicare   Combined enrollment in Parts A and B.

OT   Occupational therapy

outpatient care   Medical care that is provided outside of the hospital as well as care that is provided when someone is under observation at the hospital.

PA   Physician assistant

PACE   Program of All-inclusive Care for the Elderly

participating provider   An accepting provider who agrees to Medicare's physician fee schedule. See *physician fee schedule.*

PC3   Patient Centered Community Care

PCP   See *primary care provider.*

PFFS   Private Fee-for-Service plan

PFP   Partners for Peace

PHI   Protected health information

physician fee schedule   The pricing list Medicare prepares annually for different services that it covers. Providers who accept assignment cannot charge more than what is recommended on this list.

Physician Payments Sunshine Act   Legislation enacted under the Affordable Care Act that requires pharmaceutical companies to report how much they gave in gifts to physicians. CMS made the list of pharmaceutical gifts public on a website known as the Open Payments portal in 2014.

PPO   Preferred Provider Organizations

practice management   A strategic approach to running a medical office or other business enterprise.

pre-existing conditions   Medical conditions that were known prior to applying for an insurance plan.

premium   A fixed dollar amount paid on a schedule, usually monthly, to an insurer for health-care coverage.

primary care provider (PCP)   A health-care provider who practices the broad scope of medicine and is often the first to diagnose or evaluate a medical condition. A PCP may be considered a gatekeeper to health-care.

priority groups   Categories used in the VA health system to delineate which veterans are in greater need of health-care benefits.

PSA   Prostate specific antigen

PT   Physical therapy

QDWI   See *Qualified Disabled and Working Individuals Program.*

QI   See *Qualifying Individual program.*

QIC   Qualified Independent Contractor

QIO   Quality Improvement Organizations

QMB   Qualified Medicare Beneficiary program

Qualified Disabled and Working Individuals Program (QDWI)   A Medicare savings program that offers financial assistance to low income beneficiaries to help them pay for Part A premiums.

Qualified Medicare Beneficiary Program   A Medicare savings program that offers financial assistance to low income beneficiaries to help them pay for Part A premiums, Part B premiums, deductibles, coinsurance, and copays.

Qualifying Individual program (QI)   A Medicare savings program that offers financial assistance to low income beneficiaries to help them pay for Part B premiums.

RRB   Railroad Retirement Board

Retrospective case   Medical care that occurred in the past.

Screening test   A test that is performed for an at-risk population, even if there are no symptoms present, in the hopes of early detection of possible disease.

Senior citizen   In America, there is no standardized definition. Colloquially, a senior citizen may be someone who is retired or someone over the age of 65 based on Medicare eligibility criteria. That said, some senior citizen discounts are offered by companies starting at age 50.

SEP   See *special enrollment period.*

SGA   Substantial gainful activity for disability determinations

SGR   Sustainable growth rate

SHIP   State Health Insurance Assistance Program

SHOP   Small Business Health Options Program

SIPP   Survey of Income and Program Participation

SLMB   See *Specified Low-Income Medicare Beneficiary Program.*

SLP   Speech-language pathology

SNF   Skilled nursing facility

SNP   Special Needs Plans

socialized medicine   Health insurance provided to a population by its government and paid for by taxes.

SPAP   State Pharmaceutical Assistance Program

special enrollment period (SEP)   A window of time to apply for Medicare without incurring late penalties after one's initial enrollment period has passed. An SEP is reserved for individuals that meet certain criteria. There are many different situations that can trigger an SEP.

Specified Low-Income Medicare Beneficiary Program (SLMB)   A Medicare savings program that offers financial assistance to low income beneficiaries to help them pay for Part B premiums.

SSA   Social Security Administration

SSDI   Social Security Disability Insurance

standard of care   A legal term used to define care that is provided in a given medical situation that meets the general consensus of appropriateness by medical professionals in that field.

TAA   Trade Adjustment Assistance Reform Act

TANF   See *Temporary Assistance to Needy Families.*

Tax Equity and Fiscal Responsibility Act (TEFRA)   A 1982 law that established regulations for employer-sponsored health care and Medicare special enrollment periods. TEFRA included several other tax provisions, but for the purposes of this book, this is the part of the legislation that impacts directly on Medicare.

TEFRA   See *Tax Equity and Fiscal Responsibility Act.*

Temporary Assistance to Needy Families Program (TANF)   A short-term federal welfare program offered to low income families with children under 18 years old that encourages parents and/or guardians to return to work.

Ticket to Work Program   A program offered through the Social Security Administration since 1999 that allows people with disabilities to trial a return to work without losing their Medicare coverage. Training and employment opportunities are offered through the program to improve the odds of successful reentry into the work force.

tort reform   A proposal that recommends setting limits on how much can be awarded for damages in a lawsuit.

Two-Midnight Rule   Legislation that was enacted in 2013 that added a timeline requirement to inpatient hospital admissions. Not only do hospital stays require medical necessity for coverage, but due to this legislation also require an expected length of stay spanning more than two midnights.

TWP   Trial work period for Ticket to Work Program

TWWIIA   Ticket to Work and Work Incentives Improvements Act

under observation   Outpatient care offered to someone who is being evaluated in a hospital setting. Services are covered under Part B.

under the table   Work performed for an employer who does not report those wages to the government, thereby avoiding payroll taxes.

USMLE   United States Medical Licensing Examination

USPSTF   United States Preventive Screening Task Force

VA   United States Department of Veterans Affairs

WCMSA   Workers' Compensation Medicare Set-aside Arrangement

WHO   See *World Health Organization.*

World Health Organization (WHO)   A specialized agency of the United Nations founded in 1948 to address public health issues.

Resources

There are many resources available to help you understand not only Medicare but how to work your way through the American health system and your retirement planning.

For Medicare

Frequently accessed links related to Medicare are included here, ranging from links to quality improvement organizations where you can report your grievances to links for money-saving programs.

medicare.gov

Centers for Medicare & Medicaid Services
7500 Security Boulevard
Baltimore, Maryland 21244
1–800–MEDICARE
TTY 1–877–486–2048

Quality Improvement Organizations

Two private organizations, KePro and Livanta, review all grievances pertaining to Medicare. You may contact Medicare directly, as well as these organizations, with your concerns.

KePro: keproqio.com

Livanta: livanta.com/#!bfcc-qio/c1qro

Open Payments Portal

The Centers for Medicare and Medicaid Services publishes a list of physicians who have received gifts from pharmaceutical companies. Did your doctor make the list?

portal.cms.gov/wps/portal

Medicare Advantage and Part D Prescription Drug Plans

Get help finding a Medicare plan that works for you.

medicare.gov/find-a-plan

Hospital Readmissions Reduction Program

When patients are readmitted to a hospital within a short time period, it raises a question of the quality of care. To this end, the federal government has established this program to penalize hospitals that do not meet their standards to encourage improvement in care. Are there local hospitals near you that have been fined?

medicare.gov/hospitalcompare/readmission-reduction-program.html

Medicare Part D Low Income Subsidy

If you need assistance in paying for your Part D prescription drug plan, you may be able to apply for this low-income subsidy to help make ends meet.

socialsecurity.gov/extrahelp

Medicare Savings Programs

If you need assistance in paying your Parts A and/or B premiums and deductibles, there are multiple programs available that can decrease your costs if you meet certain income criteria.

medicare.gov/your-medicare-costs/help-paying-costs/medicare-savings-program/medicare-savings-programs.html

Other Health Programs

For those who are not eligible for Medicare or for those who need additional sources of health-care in addition to Medicare, the following resources may provide you benefits if you qualify.

Children's Health Insurance Program (CHIP)

If you have a low income and need to access care for your dependents under age 19, you may be able to get them health care under this program.

insurekidsnow.gov

COBRA Continued Health Coverage

COBRA health insurance may be available for a limited amount of time for those who leave their employer-sponsored health plans. Learn about COBRA coverage through the U.S. Department of Labor.

dol.gov/dol/topic/health-plans/cobra.htm

Health Insurance Marketplace

If you are under 65 years old, you may be able to access a health-care plan through the Health Insurance Marketplace that was formed under the Affordable Care Act.

healthcare.gov

Medicaid

Low-income individuals and families may be able to apply for health-care coverage through this federally funded state-run program.

medicaid.gov

The Partnership for Prescription Assistance

This organization offers assistance to those having difficulty paying for prescription medications. Find out if you qualify for one of their programs.

pparx.org

Program for All-Inclusive Care for the Elderly (PACE)

If you are over 55 years old and require medical care, you may qualify for this low-cost health-care program.

npaonline.org

For Social Security

Enrollment for Medicare takes place not with the Centers for Medicare and Medicaid Services but with the Social Security Administration. Key links to Social Security and its programs are listed for you here.

ssa.gov

Social Security Administration
1100 West High Rise
6401 Security Blvd.
Baltimore, MD 21235
1–800–772–1213
TTY 1–800–325–0778

Compassionate Allowances Program

Applications for Social Security disability can take considerable time to process. Medical conditions listed on the Compassionate Allowances list may help to expedite the process.

ssa.gov/compassionateallowances/conditions.htm

Medicare Enrollment

If you are not receiving Social Security benefits when you become eligible for Medicare, you will not be automatically enrolled in the program. You will need to apply for Medicare at your local Social Security office or at the following website.

socialsecurity.gov/medicare/apply.html

Social Security Benefits Calculator

If you want to find out how much money you can expect from Social Security when you retire, this calculator will give you an estimate.

ssa.gov/oact/quickcalc

Social Security Insurance

The ins and outs of Social Security Insurance can be as tricky as Medicare to navigate. This summary page will give you a rundown and a link for an application.

ssa.gov/ssi

Social Security Office Locator

If you are unsure where the closest Social Security office is to your home, this link will lead the way.

secure.ssa.gov/ICON/main.jsp

Ticket to Work Program

This program enables people on Social Security Disability Insurance to have a trial period of going back to work without losing their health-care benefits.

ssa.gov/work

For State Support

Your state health insurance assistance programs (SHIPs) may be able to give you free advice regarding Medicare and Medicaid. Some of the state programs run under different program titles such as Health Insurance Counseling and Advocacy Programs (HICAP), Senior Health Insurance Benefits Advisors (SHIBA), and Serving Health Insurance Needs of Elders (SHINE). (Refer back to Chapter 19.) Following are up-to-date program listings for each state:

State	Website	Telephone
Alabama	adss.alabama.gov	800–243–5463
Alaska	dhss.alaska.gov/dsds/Pages/medicare/default.aspx	800–478–6065
Arizona	azdes.gov/daas/ship	800–432–4040
Arkansas	insurance.arkansas.gov/Seniors/divpage.htm	800–224–6330
California	aging.ca.gov/hicap/default.aspx	800–434–0222
Colorado	dora.colorado.gov/insurance	888–696–7213
Connecticut	ct.gov/agingservices/cwp/view.asp?a=2511&q=313032	800–994–9422
Delaware	delawareinsurance.gov/services/elderinfo.shtml	800–336–9500
Florida	floridashine.org	800–963–5337
Georgia	mygeorgiacares.org	800–669–8387
Hawaii	hawaiiship.org	808–586–7299
Idaho	doi.idaho.gov/shiba/shwelcome.aspx	800–247–4422
Illinois	insurance.illinois.gov	800–548–9034
Indiana	in.gov/idoi/2500.htm	800–452–4800
Iowa	shiip.state.ia.us/FindACounselor.aspx	800–351–4664
Kansas	kdads.ks.gov/shick/shick_index.html	800–860–5260
Kentucky	chfs.ky.gov/dail/ship.htm	877–293–7447
Louisiana	ldi.louisiana.gov/Health/SHIIP/index.html	800–454–9573
Maine	maine.gov/dhhs/oes/resource/health_insurance.htm	877–353–3771
Maryland	dhmh.maryland.gov/ship/SitePages/Home.aspx	800–243–3425
Massachusetts	massresources.org/health-care.html	800–243–4636
Michigan	mmapinc.org	800–803–7174
Minnesota	health.state.mn.us/ship	800–333–2433
Mississippi	mdhs.state.ms.us/aas_ship.html	800–948–3090
Missouri	missouriclaim.org	800–390–3330
Montana	dphhs.mt.gov/sltc/services/aging/SHIP/ship.shtml	800–551–3191
Nebraska	doi.nebraska.gov/shiip	800–234–7119
Nevada	nvaging.net/ship/ship_main.htm	800–307–4444

continues

continued

State	Website	Telephone
New Hampshire	nh.gov/servicelink/medicareinfo.html	866–634–9412
New Jersey	state.nj.us/humanservices/doas/services/ship	800–792–8820
New Mexico	nmaging.state.nm.us/State_Health_Insurance_Assistance_Program.aspx	800–432–2080
New York	aging.ny.gov/HealthBenefits/Index.cfm	800–701–0501
North Carolina	ncdoi.com/SHIIP/Default.aspx	800–443–9354
North Dakota	nd.gov/ndins/shic	800–575–6611
Ohio	insurance.ohio.gov/aboutodi/odidiv/pages/oshiip.aspx	800–686–1578
Oklahoma	ok.gov/oid/Consumers/Information_for_Seniors/SHIP.html	800–763–2828
Oregon	oregon.gov/DCBS/SHIBA	800–722–4134
Pennsylvania	portal.state.pa.us/portal/server.pt/community/state_health_improvement_plan_(ship)/14132	800–783–7067
Rhode Island	dea.ri.gov/insurance/	401–462–4000
South Carolina	aging.sc.gov/contact/Pages/SHIPContactInformation.aspx	Phone numbers vary by region—please refer to website.
South Dakota	shiine.net	800–536–8197
Tennessee	tn.gov/comaging/ship.html	877–801–0044
Texas	tdi.texas.gov/consumer/hicap/hicaphme.html	800–252–3439
Utah	daas.utah.gov/senior-services	801–538–3800
Vermont	medicarehelpvt.net	800–642–5119
Virginia	vda.virginia.gov/vicap.asp	800–552–3402
Washington	insurance.wa.gov/about-oic/what-we-do/advocate-for-consumers/shiba	800–562–6900
Washington, D.C.	law.gwu.edu/Academics/EL/clinics/insurance/Pages/About.aspx	202–739–0668
West Virginia	wvship.org/AboutWVSHIP/tabid/132/Default.aspx	877–987–4463
Wisconsin	dhs.wisconsin.gov/benefit-specialists/ship.htm	800–242–1060
Wyoming	wyomingseniors.com/services/wyoming-state-health-insurance-information-program	800–856–4398

For Your Health

Staying well is the best way to keep your health-care costs down. Be wary of random internet searches. A great deal of the information out there can be misleading, false, or even unsafe. Each of the following sites offers reliable medical information and resources to help you make educated decisions about your health. The names of the organizations speak for themselves.

Administration on Aging

aoa.gov

American Academy of Family Physicians

familydoctor.org

American Cancer Society

cancer.org

American Diabetes Association

diabetes.org

American Heart Association

heart.org

Centers for Disease Control and Prevention

cdc.gov

Diagnosis Life

diagnosislife.com

Eldercare Locator

eldercare.gov/Eldercare.NET/Public/Index.aspx

The National Council on Aging

ncoa.org

The National Federation for the Blind

nfb.org/free-cane-program

United States Preventive Services Task Force

uspreventiveservicestaskforce.org/Page/BasicOneColumn/28

World Health Organization

who.int/en

For Your Credit

You need to know what resources are available to protect your credit. First and foremost, you should check your credit reports with at least one of the leading credit agencies annually to assure there are no discrepancies. Errors in your credit report can affect your ability to borrow money and can have a lasting financial impact on your future.

Equifax

equifax.com
1–800–525–6285

Experian

experian.com
1–888–397–3742

TransUnion

transunion.com
1–800–680–7289

You may also consider using a credit counseling service if you have problems with outstanding debt. A reputable agency is typically a nonprofit entity, though that does not necessarily mean their services will be free. Unfortunately, there may be agencies that prey on your financial vulnerabilities. Find one that has a good reputation and that has the support of federal agencies.

Federal Trade Commission—Choosing a Credit Counselor

consumer.ftc.gov/articles/0153-choosing-credit-counselor

National Foundation for Credit Counseling

nfcc.org
1–800–388–2227

U.S. Department of Justice—List of Approved Credit Agencies

justice.gov/ust/eo/bapcpa/ccde/cc_approved.htm

It is also crucial to report identity theft as soon as possible so you can stop it in its tracks. You should place a report with each of the following organizations with any suspicious activity on your accounts.

Federal Trade Commission

consumer.ftc.gov/features/feature-0014-identity-theft
1–877–ID–THEFT

Internal Revenue Service

irs.gov/uac/Identity-Protection
1–800–908–4490

Internet Crime Complaint Center

ic3.gov

Index

Numbers

C

I

J–K

L

M

S

There's a lot of crummy "how-to" content out there on the internet. A LOT. We want to fix that, and YOU can help!

idiotsguides.com

READ

Quick Guides on most any topic imaginable!

CONTRIBUTE

Edit quick guides, request guides, or write your own!

EARN

Badges reflect your expertise and influence.

You are an expert! Your expertise may be knitting, bowling, fishing, jumping jacks, Super Mario Kart®, photography, grammar nitpickery, or anything else!

Let's band together and put an end to junky how-to articles written to get page views instead of actually teaching you how to do anything. It's easy as 1, 2, 3!

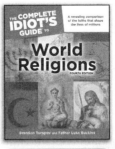

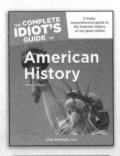

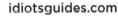